ANTISEMITISM IN ONLINE COMMUNICATION

Antisemitism in Online Communication

Transdisciplinary Approaches to Hate Speech for the Twenty-first Century

Edited by Matthias J. Becker, Laura Ascone,
Karolina Placzynta and Chloé Vincent

https://www.openbookpublishers.com

We acknowledge support by the Open Access Publication Fund of Technische Universität Berlin

ISBN Paperback: 978-1-80511-260-0
ISBN Hardback: 978-1-80511-261-7
ISBN Digital (PDF): 978-1-80511-262-4
ISBN Digital eBook (EPUB): 978-1-80511-263-1
ISBN HTML: 978-1-80511-265-5

DOI: 10.11647/OBP.0396

Cover image: Photo by Marc Bloch, 2023, CC-BY. Cover design: Jeevanjot Kaur Nagpal.

Contents

Acknowledgements

This volume was produced in the context of the research project Decoding Antisemitism: An AI-Driven Study on Hate Speech and Imagery Online, the pilot phase of which was generously funded by the Alfred Landecker Foundation.

Furthermore, this open access volume was made possible by the support of the TU Berlin Publication Fund.

We express our profound appreciation to Open Book Publishers for their indispensable support throughout the entire publication journey.

Our heartfelt thanks go out to the authors of this compendium, consisting of the committed members of the Decoding Antisemitism research team.

Introduction

This book showcases key findings and analyses of an innovative research project in the field of web-related antisemitism studies. Established at the Centre for Research on Antisemitism (ZfA) at the Technische Universität Berlin in 2020, Decoding Antisemitism: An AI-Driven Study on Hate Speech and Imagery Online[1] brings together researchers from different disciplines with the aim of exploring the patterns of antisemitic communication on social media. Each researcher has brought their particular experiences, insights and interests from the fields of semiotics—including linguistics (semantics and pragmatics) and image analysis—(social) media studies, history, as well as political and social sciences. Such collaboration ensures that the analyses of the online datasets collected as part of the project have been detailed, nuanced and comprehensive.

At the same time, each of the researchers has been making additional observations, in part thanks to the scope and richness of the dataset: the multitude of topics it contains, the varied angles they can be viewed from, and the multiple overlaps and differences between antisemitic hate speech and many other pertinent phenomena. So far, the joint project-related publications have not been able to completely reflect this diversity of both research interests and discourse phenomena. In this volume, we finally provide a space for broader conclusions from the analysis of current expressions of online antisemitism within the political mainstreams of the UK, Germany and France, but also in exploratory studies in relation to the US as well as to other, more extremist online discourse, carried out within this research project from 2020 to 2024.

---

1   For further information on the project, see https://decoding-antisemitism.eu. The pilot phase was conducted in collaboration with HTW Berlin, University of Michigan's School of Information, Cardiff's HateLab and King's College London.

   https://doi.org/10.11647/OBP.0406.00

The eight studies in this volume are therefore not just an extension of the work within the project, but a product of the interdisciplinary format of Decoding Antisemitism—a format designed to explore a complex object of study (antisemitism), produced in varied patterns (user statements in online threads) in a highly dynamic sphere of communication (the interactive web) that in many ways remains a black box, notoriously difficult to illuminate. Intensifying the efforts in describing, raising awareness of, preventing and regulating online antisemitism, and online hate more generally, is an urgent task not only because of its kaleidoscopic multiplicity and evolving nature, but also because its various expressions seem to be increasing in both number and strength (Zannettou et al. 2018). This became particularly evident after the attacks perpetrated by Hamas on 7 October 2023 (CST 2023, RIAS 2023, SPCJ 2023). However, even such a noticeable trend is difficult to capture fully with the analytical methods available so far, due to this complexity present at the different levels.

The *first level* is the communication space of the interactive web, which "has dramatically changed the very time/space axes of the subject's existence" (Kramsch 2009: 159). Comment sections are the core dialogical spaces, where web users address each other as well as an imaginary audience, similar to that of mass media (Virtanen and Kääntä 2018). They can interact with people from across the globe in a spontaneous and immediate manner, reproducing oral interactions (Ko 1996, Herring 2010). As a result, their language can differ markedly from traditional written text. The online comment genre is also characterised by a certain fluidity, which can come across as "less correct, complex and coherent than standard written language" (Herring 2008: 616). At the same time, online communication has gained a new type of complexity, enriched, influenced and modified by hashtags, memes and other multimodal elements. It is also affected by various more general conditions online that have a long-term effect on our communication behaviour (Troschke and Becker 2019, see also Schwarz-Friesel 2013). Web users have the possibility to remain anonymous: this identity distance contrasts with accelerated, intensified, and sometimes even escalated communication processes. Everything can be said, at any time; the outlook of being sanctioned or even prosecuted for online statements has existed for only a short time. The fact that explosive sources and radicalising content are accessible at all times and locations further reinforces this escalation. All these aspects or conditions of communication have a lasting effect on the way we behave on the internet, but also on how we think and feel, and thus perceive the world in its entirety. The internet now functions as an amplifier, which "increases our potential for good and productive work as well as for inappropriate and immoral endeavors" (Banschick and Banschick 2003: 161).

On social media, web users may be exposed to various and sometimes conflicting viewpoints (Bakshy et al. 2015). However, this exposure does not necessarily result in bridging the divides; instead, web users tend to perceive these divergencies as a threat to their own identities and outlooks. This can lead them to either avoid the confrontation (John and Dvir-Gvirsman 2015) or attack the differing points of view (Mor et al. 2016). They also tend to seek out sources confirming their existing opinions (Stroud 2011, Monnier and Seoane 2019, Wolleback et al. 2019), and to join virtual communities which already share their interests and points of view. Even though the notion of such *echo chambers* is starting to come under critique (Arguedas et al. 2022), several researchers nevertheless propose their existence (Matuszewski and Szabó 2019, Wolleback et al. 2019). Echo chambers strengthen both the bonds among the web users and the ideologies they express (Pariser 2011), a polarisation which may become particularly dangerous when the ideologies circulating within these communities are hate ideologies, as they may lead to an increased dehumanisation of *the Other* through the language they employ (Pacilli et al. 2016, Cassese 2019). The spread of hate speech is facilitated, again, by the sense of anonymity such online milieus create (Mondal et al. 2017), which in turn escalates the expression of hateful and exclusionary ideas which web users may not have articulated in offline interactions (Schwarz-Friesel 2013).

Normalisation of hate speech informs the *second level* of the intricate phenomenon at hand. As hate speech spreads from extremist milieus (Ebner 2023) into mainstream communication, the boundaries of what can be said without fear of condemnation from one's peers, or banishment from publicly shared spaces are pushed ever further. This emboldens individuals to express hatred in online spaces more frequently and more freely; through repetition, hate-speech fallacies and stereotypes, they create new discourse norms, often mirrored by official or legal regulations. Statements by public figures and internet celebrities explicitly or implicitly encouraging hate can boost and accelerate this process, even as online discourse can equally quickly turn against them. Despite the efforts invested in moderating online communications, the amount of data is so vast that it is difficult for the various platforms to track all the hate speech content. Furthermore, to avoid detection by human or automated moderators, but also to convey messages in an attractive manner, web users resort to regularly updated discursive strategies, such as wordplay, allusions and coded memes.

The effect of normalised verbal violence can perhaps be felt in the rise in physical violence (Saha, Chandrasekharan and De Choudhury 2019, Müller and Schwarz 2020). In recent years, its increased presence has at the very least correlated with the radicalisation of social and political movements and counter movements, as well as political groups (Tappin and McKay 2019) or segregating tendencies through extreme polarisation. It also coincides with the trend of dehumanisation of out-groups and invisibilisation of suffering. When analysing hate speech online, it is difficult, if not impossible, to determine whether the speaker intended to hurt the target. Therefore, in both the project and this volume we adopted the INACH definition of cyber hate, which includes both intentional and unintentional discriminatory statements.[2]

Antisemitism, the *third level* of the object of our study, is a chameleon-like hate ideology which has kept morphing and adapting throughout its existence over two millennia (Wistrich 1992, Bergmann 2016; for the distinction between anti-Judaism and antisemitism see Julius 2010, Williams and Wald 2023). From anti-Judaism in times of Christianity to the racially charged antisemitism of modernity, two further forms were added in the twentieth century: secondary (post-1945) and Israel-related antisemitism, which prove how highly complex and adaptable this hate ideology can be, embedding itself in various social and political milieus, and now also thriving online (for secondary antisemitism, see Becker et al. 2024). On the one hand, the conceptual (i.e. content-related) repertoire of antisemitism has become broader; on the other, classical

---

2   INACH (International Network Against Cyber Hate) is a network of 34 member organisations from 27 EU countries, jointly working to combat the spread of online hate, https://www.inach.net/cyber-hate-definitions/

stereotypes such as DEICIDE, GREED, EVIL or MENDACITY[3] have been partly or entirely modernised. The antisemitic notion of Jewish GREED (and partly also immorality) has been updated to the idea that Jews or Israel exploit the Holocaust in order to achieve pecuniary or symbolic gains. This new framing has been achieved via the concept of instrumentalisation, of either antisemitism or the Holocaust, centrally anchored in secondary antisemitism. Similarly, the classical concept of innate Jewish evil is now being applied to Israel, in particular in the form of the Nazi analogy. These two instances demonstrate how versatile antisemitism is, and how highly compatible it seems to be with a wide spectrum of political positioning and social environments.

Antisemitism is not only a threat to Jewish communities but is also one of the greatest challenges to social cohesion and the future of democracy, as hatred of Jews often correlates with a resentful attitude and a simplistic binary worldview pitting a supposedly homogenous 'us' against a destructive and malign 'them' in the arena of politics, the media, as well as in academia and science.[4] Moreover, and in stark contrast to other forms of hate, the continuing impact of contemporary antisemitism seems to be dismissed and misunderstood—as shown, for example, by the long gestating but broadly unnoticed antisemitism within the UK left, which finally emerged onto the public domain during Jeremy Corbyn's leadership of the Labour Party (see the various studies on Labour antisemitism and Jeremy Corbyn; for David Miller, the academic in Bristol accused of spreading conspiracy theories regarding Israel, see Becker et al. 2021). This culture of debate is all too attached to the political positioning or educational background of the person, group or party in question, and loses sight of antisemitism in the process. A similar pattern occurred in the *Documenta 15* art exhibition in the German city of Kassel in the summer of 2022, when multimodally conveyed hostility towards Jews was trivialised or indirectly justified through the idea of cultural relativism; the art sector displayed a gross lack of understanding of the subject and simplified, dichotomous world views (see Ascone et al. 2022, Burack 2023).

---

3   With regard to the usage of small caps, see explanation at the end of this introduction.

4   See also the rise of antisemitism in the context of dismissive attitudes towards science and educational elites in the context of Covid-19.

A sudden awakening in the political and media context could then be observed when fears of a rise in antisemitism (and other hate ideologies) online arose as a result of Elon Musk's takeover of *Twitter* (now *X*), as he announced a reduction in content moderation and a significant cutback in collaborations with the political and academic sectors (Miller et al. 2023; see also Jikeli and Soemer 2023). The antisemitic death wishes and overt conspiracy theories voiced by Kanye West, a successful musician and influencer with a gigantic following, proved that antisemitism has found its place in the mainstream and cultural sector of the West (Chapelan et al. 2023). Repercussions of these events are of international proportions and will not fuel various fires in the US discourse alone; they have an enormous impact on the presence and openness of antisemitism on social media worldwide, which makes hatred of Jews permissible and brings it back to the streets. It is precisely this mainstream antisemitism that—partly camouflaged in its communicative guise, partly legitimised by the speaker's social position—has the potential to spread throughout society, and is therefore far more dangerous than that hostility towards Jews by radicalised fringe groups, which is rejected from the outset and (in certain cases) sanctioned.

In addition to the complexity of the virtual, dialogue-based communication space and of language, the object of study itself thus poses major hurdles for research-based examination and counter-strategies within the realms of politics and civil society.

Political and legal answers: Measures adopted to counter antisemitism and hate speech

At a global level, numerous countries and institutions have taken steps to counter hate speech and antisemitism. The past few years saw the implementation of the *Loi Avia* and *NetzDG*, in France and Germany respectively. According to the latest report by the European Union Agency for Fundamental Rights (FRA),[5] 14 European countries have already implemented *NetzDG* measures in order to tackle antisemitism, while eight countries are currently developing new strategies to adopt.

---

5   FRA 2022. "Antisemitism online far outweighs official records", https://fra.europa. eu/en/news/2022/antisemitism-online-far-outweighs-official-records

Likewise, the Institute for Strategic Dialogue (ISD), together with B'nai B'rith International and the United Nations Educational, Scientific and Cultural Organization (UNESCO), has provided a toolkit to help civil society tackle antisemitism online.[6] The Digital Services Act (DSA) is a legislative proposal put forth by the European Commission in December 2020. The aim of the DSA is to regulate digital services and online platforms within the European Union (EU) to ensure a safe and accountable digital environment for web users.[7] Furthermore, the Inter-Parliamentary Task Force to Combat Online Antisemitism has recently organised two summits, in Washington, DC (September 2022) and Brussels (June 2023), in order to promote an ongoing dialogue between lawmakers and social media platforms.

Despite the national and international efforts to understand and tackle antisemitism online, various gaps are becoming visible. It is imperative to reflect more deeply on how antisemitic discourse comes about and is circulated in the first place, as language is the most important vehicle of any ideology (Althusser 1970 [2011], Pêcheux 1975). Particular attention needs to be paid to the seemingly acceptable, usually unsanctioned dog whistles or implicit and coded forms that are difficult to detect and can therefore spread into politically moderate (online) milieus. This approach will help to understand the impact of online antisemitism on contemporary social, political and cultural contexts and practices in different language communities and to develop counter-strategies against corresponding trends.

State of the art: Current research on antisemitic communication

The political and legal actors are not the only ones dealing with antisemitism online. Academic researchers and organisations using digital methods are also committed to shedding more light on the issue. Among others, the Anti-Defamation League (ADL) and the Institute for Strategic Dialogue (ISD) monitor and analyse antisemitism in the United

---

6   ISD and B'Nai B'rith Internation 2022. "Online antisemitism: a toolkit for civil society", https://unesdoc.unesco.org/ark:/48223/pf0000381856
7   See European Commission 2024. "Questions and answers on the Digital Services Act", https://ec.europa.eu/commission/presscorner/detail/en/QANDA_20_2348

States and Europe respectively, aiming at providing tools to counter this hate ideology both online and offline. Coming from different disciplines, researchers investigate this phenomenon from very discrete angles: from studies on Hungarian Jewish Displaced Persons (Barna 2016) to research on anti-Jewish conspiracy theories (Finkelstein et al. 2020).

The interactive web has generated an incredibly large amount of data. Due to the relatively large presence of hateful content, various new techniques have been developed to track antisemitism and other hate ideologies. The institute CyberWell collects antisemitic statements posted online and offers the possibility to report them to the different social media platforms; ADL and Zannettou et al. (2020) use vector analyses to investigate antisemitism on platforms such as *4chan* and *Gab*. Meanwhile, the London-based Community Security Trust, in collaboration with Signify, has been analysing antisemitic hate speech on *Twitter* with the use of machine learning.

Qualitative approach to the study of antisemitic web comments has received little attention so far. The goal of these analyses is to examine the way antisemitism is expressed explicitly and/or implicitly, as well as to identify linguistic patterns that might have gone unnoticed when adopting a quantitative approach only (see Schwarz-Friesel 2019, Becker 2021). Furthermore, some of these qualitative studies have been conducted to develop and improve algorithms that would better detect antisemitic content online. In this context, corpus linguistics (Gries 2009, Leech 2014) proves to be a good methodology for investigating the different forms of antisemitic expressions. By collecting a large amount of original data from the web, it is possible to identify the linguistic characteristics specific to online antisemitic discourse as well as to determine its statistically significant features.

In order to achieve more solid results, some researchers have adopted mixed-method approaches. Jikeli and Soemer (2023) highlight the importance of combining quantitative and qualitative analyses when studying phenomena as complex as online hate speech. Similar approaches have been employed to closely examine antisemitic content in popular social media, such as X (formerly *Twitter*) (Jikeli et al. 2014), *Facebook* and *YouTube* (Allington and Joshi 2020). In the context of the Decoding Antisemitism project, Mihaljević et al. (2023) have tested Google's tool Perspective API, which uses machine-learning models to identify abusive web comments and provide a score of toxicity, with the goal of assisting readers and moderators in tackling hate content. These tests, conducted on large corpora of data collected from mainstream media, provide new and additional insights to the analysis of online antisemitism in extreme milieus (Hübscher and von Mering 2022).

Decoding antisemitism: An AI-driven study on hate speech and imagery online

The pilot project Decoding Antisemitism is based at the Centre for Research on Antisemitism at the Technische Universität Berlin, carrying out research in close collaboration with the HTW (University of Applied Sciences) in Berlin, and with the support of HateLab at Cardiff University and King's College London. The project seeks to find new, technologically enhanced ways to identify and analyse antisemitism online, in both its explicit and disguised forms. As mentioned at the start of this introduction, it has brought together an international, interdisciplinary team of expert researchers with the goal of investigating the frequency, content and structure of antisemitic hate speech posted on mainstream news websites and social media platforms in the UK, France and Germany.

At the core of the analyses presented in the chapters of this anthology is the project's research design and the data collected in its course (more than 130,000 comments from the three language communities). Contrary to the approach adopted in many of the existing studies into hate speech, here the collection of the data is not based on a list of keywords such as 'Israel' or 'Jews,' but rather on news events that are likely to trigger antisemitic reactions. Such events include—to name but a few—the escalation phase in the Arab-Israeli conflict in May 2021, the war in Ukraine and Kanye West's antisemitic remarks, which have strongly influenced the online debate culture in Europe as well. The threads—i.e. comment sections of news websites and their official social media platforms—were fed into the analysis while retaining their chronological and dialogue structure. The analysis is based on a mixed-method approach: first, the data is examined within the framework of Mayring's qualitative content analysis (2015). Here, the experts' annotation follows a classification system developed for the purposes of this research project, which comprises both deductive and inductive categories (Meibauer 2008), depending on the patterns that emerge in the data studied. The categories in the classification system comprise both classic and new forms of antisemitic concepts (Schoeps and Schlör 1996, Julius 2010), as well as the linguistic and multimodal phenomena employed by web users in the analysed comment sections. For the context-sensitive analysis of a comment within a thread, this means that each statement is examined in terms of content (above-mentioned concepts) as well as form (explicitly vs. implicitly communicated), and care is also taken to consider any references to the article topic as well as other user comments.

The results of these qualitative analyses then form the basis of algorithms that replicate the experts' decisions and are intended to enhance the detection of antisemitic content on the internet to a completely new level. The iterative process between experts from the fields of humanities and social sciences on the one hand and data science experts on the other will shift the in-depth qualitative analysis to a much broader scale, so that disparately larger amounts of data can be categorised in a reliable way. The findings obtained in the previous steps also form the basis of quantitative analyses in order to identify statistically significant patterns, completing the picture of trends in contemporary antisemitism.

The chapters collected in this anthology reflect the project's research design. While the research is based on a solid foundation of traditional antisemitism studies, as well as seminal works from the fields of linguistics, semiotics, history and philosophy, it is innovative in terms of both the data used for analysis, and the approach applied to it. The studies presented here employ empirical analysis of content published in the comment sections of online news outlets and different social media platforms in the past few years. This is crucial for a body of work that emphasises the characteristics of *current* hate speech expressions, and of online hate speech in particular. The fact that it has been sourced from platforms within the political mainstream makes it highly relevant as well: while there is, naturally, a great value to the study of extremist milieus (Barna and Knap 2019, CST 2019, Zannettou et al. 2020, ADL 2021, Hübscher and von Mering 2022), our focus is on the discourse that can directly impact the majority of web users in the language communities we explore. Moreover, so-called mainstream antisemitism poses an enormous challenge not only for academic analysis, but also for Jewish communities and society as a whole. While recent antisemitic shootings in Pittsburgh, Halle and Poway are clearly rejected across society, antisemitism in politically moderate contexts—in art, culture and academia—is all too often minimised, as the position of the discourse absolves it of antisemitism. The results presented in this publication make it clear that this is a misguided judgement. In this respect, the chapters are to be understood as a plea to take a closer look at this desideratum in the context of web-related antisemitism studies and hate studies in general.

Owing to the integrative nature of the Decoding Antisemitism project, the authors of the work presented in this collection have also been able to incorporate a similarly interdisciplinary approach into their individual research. In doing so, they offer a comprehensive view of the issues they focus on, which enriches their findings and creates interest for a wider audience. It is also mindful of the frameworks of examination, where the subject matter is treated in a holistic and intersectional manner and operationalised within its methodologically rigorous analysis. In terms of content analysis, it focuses on conceptual units as well as the linguistic and visual patterns carrying these units. Finally, the data is analysed both qualitatively and quantitatively—the former still being underrepresented in the field of internet studies. By reflecting the current reality of contemporary antisemitic hate speech online in mainstream discourses, and by analysing its ability to remain hidden in plain sight by continuously adapting to the current context, this anthology aims to give a full picture of contemporary antisemitism on every level: in terms of its mixed-methods approach, the cross-disciplinary outlook, and the wide range of themes encompassing media, society and culture.

The volume begins with the development of selected conceptual questions in the context of antisemitism studies, which are presented on the foundation of our empirical analysis of language data. **Karolina Placzynta** explores the intersections of antisemitism and misogyny in online debates around public figures (Chapter 1). Next, we present linguistic and discourse analytical case studies centred on the reproduction, support and rejection of antisemitic tropes: **Matthias**

J. Becker examines the dividing line between conservative and far-right antisemitism by analysing projections onto Jordan Peterson, a conservative intellectual, after interviewing the Israeli PM (Chapter 2); **Alexis Chapelan's** study shows the way web users express their support to contested media personalities such as Dieudonné and Kanye West (Chapter 3). **Matthew Bolton** investigates the concept of GENOCIDE and its use in the context of the discourse around the Arab-Israeli conflict, a topic that has been of intense interest in the wake of the 7 October attacks and Israeli retaliation in Gaza (Chapter 4), while **Laura Ascone** assesses the links between the web comments conveying antisemitism and those countering it, and how counter-narratives can sometimes fuel antisemitism and other forms of hate speech (Chapter 5). We also include the emergence of new forms of hate speech: this aspect is examined by **Marcus Scheiber** in his qualitative analysis of antisemitic memes and the potential of verbal and visual elements to mutually integrate antisemitism into online communication (Chapter 6).

The qualitative analyses are complemented and enriched by quantitative assessments prepared by **Chloé Vincent**, who looks at the structure of the comment trees in online discussions in relation to the occurrence of antisemitic comments, using the dataset accumulated in the project so far (Chapter 7). Finally, to integrate research questions from the field of data science, **Elisabeth Steffen**, **Milena Pustet** and **Helena Mihaljević** elaborate on recent work regarding the capabilities of content-moderation tools in recognising antisemitic posts as toxic, and report on current achievements in training deep-learning-based models for automated detection of such content (Chapter 8).

Practical considerations

Across all the chapters, the authors use numerous examples from the project dataset; they have been taken from the comment sections of mainstream news outlets of the UK, France and Germany. The examples have been anonymised; however, in order to present the data as faithfully as possible, they retain their original spelling, punctuation and grammar, including any errors, inconsistencies or offensive terms. Whenever French or German comments are used to illustrate the text, they have been translated into standard British English, with the original provided in footnotes. The list of specific sources of the examples can be found at the end of each chapter.

The frequent mentions of antisemitic concepts, such as stereotypes and analogies, are presented in small caps, in accordance with the conventions of cognitive linguistics, which uses this format to highlight phenomena that exist on the mental level and can be reproduced through language. Linguistic phenomena, such as irony, puns or death wishes are not distinguished in such a way.

Finally, the chapters will make reference to *Decoding Antisemitism—A Guide to Identifying Antisemitism Online* (Becker et al. 2024)—a publication also linked to the Decoding Antisemitism project. It is a comprehensive guide to both the explicit and coded forms of contemporary antisemitism, including traditional and modern concepts which have been clearly organised, defined and illustrated with a diverse audience in mind. It is an extension of the classification system used in the project, and therefore a useful framework of reference for the studies in this volume.

References

ADL (Anti-Defamation League). 2021. *Gab and 8chan: Home to Terrorist Plots Hiding in Plain Sight*, https://www.adl.org/resources/reports/gab-and-8chan-home-to-terrorist-plots-hiding-in-plain-sight

Allington, Daniel and Tanvi Joshi. 2020. "What others dare not say": An antisemitic conspiracy fantasy and its YouTube audience. In: *Journal of Contemporary Antisemitism 3* (1): 35–54

Arguedas, Amy Ross, Craig T. Robertson, Richard Fletcher and Rasmus Kleis Nielsen. 2022. *Echo Chambers, Filter Bubbles, and Polarisation: A Literature Review*, https://reutersinstitute.politics.ox.ac.uk/echo-chambers-filter-bubbles-and-polarisation-literature-review#header—0

Ascone, Laura, Matthias J. Becker, Matthew Bolton, Alexis Chapelan, Jan Krasni, Karolina Placzynta, Marcus Scheiber, Hagen Troschke and Chloé Vincent. 2022. *Decoding Antisemitism: An AI-Driven Study on Hate Speech and Imagery Online. Discourse Report 4.* Technische Universität Berlin. Centre for Research on Antisemitism, https://doi.org/10.14279/depositonce-16292

Bakshy, Eytan, Solomon Messing and Lada A. Adamic. 2015. "Exposure to ideologically diverse news and opinion on Facebook". In: *Science 348* (6239): 1130–1132

Banschick, Mark R. and Josepha Silman Banschick. 2003. "Children in cyberspace". In: Shyles, Leonard (ed.). *Deciphering Cyberspace: Making the Most of Digital Communication Technology*: 159–199

Barna, Ildikó and Árpád Knap. 2019. "Antisemitism in contemporary Hungary: Exploring topics of antisemitism in the far-right media using natural language processing." In: *Theo-Web 18* (1): 75–92

Becker, Matthias J. 2021. *Antisemitism in Reader Comments: Analogies for Reckoning with the Past*. London: Palgrave Macmillan

Becker, Matthias J., Daniel Allington, Laura Ascone, Matthew Bolton, Alexis Chapelan, Jan Krasni, Karolina Placzynta, Marcus Scheiber, Hagen Troschke and Chloé Vincent. 2022. *Decoding Antisemitism: An AI-Driven Study on Hate Speech and Imagery Online*. Discourse Report 2. Technische Universität Berlin. Centre for Research on Antisemitism, https://doi.org/10.14279/depositonce-15310

Becker, Matthias J., Hagen Troschke, Matthew Bolton and Alexis Chapelan (eds). 2024. *Decoding Antisemitism: A Guide to Identifying Antisemitism Online*. London: Palgrave Macmillan, https://link.springer.com/book/9783031492372

Bergmann, Werner. 2016. *Geschichte des Antisemitismus*. Munich: Beck

Bergmann, Werner and Rainer Erb. 1986. "Kommunikationslatenz, Moral und öffentliche Meinung. Theoretische Überlegungen zum Antisemitismus in der Bundesrepublik Deutschland". In: *Kölner Zeitschrift für Soziologie und Sozialpsychologie 38* (2): 223–246

Burack, Cristina. 2023. "Documenta 15 trivialized antisemitism, report finds". *Deutsche Welle* (10 February 2023), https://www.dw.com/en/documenta-15-trivialized-antisemitism-report-finds/a-64663005

Cassese, Erin C. 2021. "Partisan dehumanization in American politics". In: *Political Behavior 43*: 29–50

Chapelan, Alexis, Laura Ascone, Matthias J. Becker, Matthew Bolton, Jan Krasni, Karolina Placzynta, Marcus Scheiber, Hagen Troschke and Chloé Vincent. 2022. *Decoding Antisemitism: An AI-Driven Study on Hate Speech and Imagery Online*. Discourse Report 5. Technische Universität Berlin. Centre for Research on Antisemitism, https://doi.org/10.14279/depositonce-17105

CST (Community Security Trust). 2019. "Engine of hate: The online networks behind the Labour Party's antisemitism crisis". *CST Blog*, https://cst.org.uk/news/blog/2019/08/04/engine-of-hate-the-online-networks-behind-the-labour-partys-antisemitism-crisis

CST (Community Security Trust). 2023. *Antisemitic Incidents Report 2023*, https://cst.org.uk/news/blog/2024/02/15/antisemitic-incidents-report-2023

Ebner, Julia. 2023. *Going Mainstream: How Extremists Are Taking Over.* London: Bonnier Books.

Gadet, Françoise. 2010. "Enjeux de la langue dans l'analyse du discours". In: *Semen 29*: 111–123

Herring, Susan C. 2010. "Computer-mediated conversation Part I: Introduction and overview". In: *Language@ Internet 7* (2)

Jikeli, Günther, Damir Cavar and Daniel Miehling. 2019. *Annotating Antisemitic Online Content. Towards an Applicable Definition of Antisemitism,* https:// arxiv.org/abs/1910.01214

Jikeli, Günther and Katharina Soemer. 2023. "The value of manual annotation in assessing trends of hate speech on social media: Was antisemitism on the rise during the tumultuous weeks of Elon Musk's Twitter takeover?" In: *Journal of Computational Social Science,* https://doi.org/10.1007/ s42001-023-00219-6

John, Nicholas A. and Shira Dvir-Gvirsman. 2015. "'I don't like you any more': Facebook unfriending by Israelis during the Israel–Gaza conflict of 2014." In: *Journal of Communication 65* (6): 953–974

Julius, Anthony. 2010. *Trials of the Diaspora. A History of Anti-Semitism in England.* Oxford: Oxford University Press

Ko, Kwang-Kyu. 1996. "Structural characteristics of computer-mediated language: A comparative analysis of InterChange discourse". In: *Electronic Journal of Communication/La revue électronique de communication 6* (3)

Kramsch, Claire J. 2009. *The Multilingual Subject: What Foreign Language Learners Say About Their Experience and Why It Matters.* Oxford: Oxford University Press

Matuszewski, Paweł and Gabriella Szabó. 2019. "Are echo chambers based on partisanship? Twitter and political polarity in Poland and Hungary". In: *Social Media + Society 5* (2), https://doi.org/10.1177/2056305119837671

Mondal, Mainack, Leandro Araújo Silva and Fabrício Benevenuto. 2017. "A measurement study of hate speech in social media". In: *Proceedings of the 28th ACM Conference on Hypertext and Social Media,* http://people. cs.uchicago.edu/~mainack/publications/hatespeech-ht-2017.pdf

Miller, Carl and David Weir, Shaun Ring, Oliver Marsh, Chris Inskip, Nestor Prieto Chavana. 2023. "Antisemitism on Twitter before and after Elon Musk's acquisition". *ISD,* https://www.isdglobal.org/isd-publications/ antisemitism-on-twitter-before-and-after-elon-musks-acquisition

Monnier, A. and A. Seoane. 2019. "Discours de haine sur l'internet". In: *Publictionnaire. Dictionnaire encyclopédique et critique des publics,* http:// publictionnaire.huma-num.fr/notice/discours-de-haine-sur-linternet/

Mor, Yifat, Neta Kligler-Vilenchik and Ifat /Maoz. 2015. "Political expression on Facebook in a context of conflict: Dilemmas and coping strategies of Jewish-Israeli youth". In: *Social Media + Society* 1 (2), https://doi.org/10.1177/2056305115606750

Müller, Karsten and Carlo Schwarz. 2020. *Fanning the Flames of Hate: Social Media and Hate Crime* (5 June 2020), https://ssrn.com/abstract=3082972 or http://dx.doi.org/10.2139/ssrn.3082972

Nirenberg, David. 2013. *Anti-Judaism*. London: Head of Zeus

Pacilli, Maria Giuseppina, Michele Roccato, Stefano /Pagliaro and Silvia Russo. 2016. "From political opponents to enemies? The role of perceived moral distance in the animalistic dehumanization of the political outgroup". In: *Group Processes & Intergroup Relations* 19 (3): 360–373

Pariser, Eli. 2011. *The Filter Bubble: What the Internet Is Hiding from You*. London: Penguin

RIAS (Bundesverband RIAS e.V. Bundesverband der Recherche- und Informationsstellen Antisemitismus). 2023. *Antisemitische Reaktionen auf den 07. Oktober. Antisemitische Vorfälle in Deutschland im Kontext der Massaker und des Krieges in Israel und Gaza zwischen dem 07. Oktober und 09. November 2023*, https://report-antisemitism.de/publications

Saha, Koustuv, Eshwar Chandrasekharan and Munmun De Choudhury. 2019. "Prevalence and psychological effects of hateful speech in online college communities". In: *Proceedings of the 11th ACM Conference on Web Science 2019:* 255–264

Schwarz-Friesel, Monika. 2013. "'Juden sind zum Töten da' (studivz.net, 2008). Hass via Internet—Zugänglichkeit und Verbreitung von Antisemitismen im World Wide Web". In: Marx, Konstanze and Monika Schwarz-Friesel (eds). *Sprache und Kommunikation im technischen Zeitalter. Wieviel Internet (v) erträgt unsere Gesellschaft?* Berlin: De Gruyter: 213–236

Schwarz-Friesel, Monika and Jehuda Reinharz. 2017. *Inside the Antisemitic Mind: The Language of Jew-Hatred in Contemporary Germany*. Waltham, MA: Brandeis University Press

SPCJ. 2023. *Les chiffres de l'antisémitisme en France en 2023*, https://www.spcj.org/antis%C3%A9mitisme/chiffres-antis%C3%A9mitisme-france-2023-b

Stroud, Natalie J. 2011. *Niche News: The Politics of News Choice*. Oxford University Press

Troschke, Hagen and Matthias J. Becker. 2019. "Antisemitismus im Internet. Erscheinungsformen, Spezifika, Bekämpfung". In: Jikeli, Günther and Olaf Glöckner (eds). *Das neue Unbehagen. Antisemitismus in Deutschland und Europa heute*. Hildesheim: Olms: 151–172

Virtanen, Mikko T. and Liisa Kääntä. 2018. "At the intersection of text and conversation analysis: Analysing asynchronous online written interaction. In: *AFinLA-e: Soveltavan Kielitieteen Tutkimuksia 11:* 137–55

Weitzman, Mark, Robert J. Williams and James Wald (eds). 2023. *The Routledge History of Antisemitism*. Abingdon: Routledge

Wistrich, Robert. 1992. *Antisemitism: The Longest Hatred*. New York: Pantheon

Wollebæk, Dag, Rune Karlsen, Kari Steen-Johnsen and Bernard /Enjorlas. 2019. "Anger, fear, and echo chambers: The emotional basis for online behavior". In: *Social Media + Society* 5 (2), https://doi.org/10.1177/2056305119829859

Zannettou, Savvas, Joel Finkelstein, Barry /Bradlyn and Jeremy /Blackburn. 2020. "A quantitative approach to understanding online antisemitism". In: *Proceedings of the International AAAI Conference on Web and Social Media* 14 (1): 786–97, https://ojs.aaai.org/index.php/ICWSM/article/view/7343

1. The Cases of Riley and Rooney

Intersections of Misogyny with Antisemitism and Counter Speech in British Online Discourse

Karolina Placzynta

Despite the benefits of the intersectional approach to antisemitism studies, it seems to have been given little attention so far. This chapter compares the online reactions to two UK news stories, both centred around the common theme of cultural boycott of Israel in support of the BDS movement, both with a well-known female figure at the centre of media coverage, only one of which identifies as Jewish. In the case of British television presenter Rachel Riley, a person is attacked for being female as well as Jewish, with misogyny compounding the antisemitic commentary. In the case of the Irish writer Sally Rooney, misogynistic discourse is used to strengthen the message countering antisemitism. The contrastive analysis of the two datasets, with references to similar analyses of media stories centred around well-known men, illuminates the relationships between the two forms of hate, revealing that—even where the antisemitic attitudes overlap—misogynistic insults and disempowering or undermining language are being weaponised on both sides of the debate, with additional characterisation of Riley as a "grifter" and Rooney as "naive".

More research comparing discourses around Jewish and non-Jewish women is needed to ascertain whether this pattern is consistent; meanwhile, the many analogies in the abuse suffered by both groups can perhaps serve a useful purpose: shared struggles can foster understanding needed to then notice the particularised prejudice. By including more than one hate ideology in the research design, intersectionality offers exciting new approaches to studies of antisemitism and, more broadly, of hate speech or discrimination.

1. Introduction

Close and systematic monitoring of reactions to news items in the context of antisemitic discourse can over time reveal certain regularities: it can highlight which antisemitic concepts are most widespread within a language community, or point to the most common triggers for the increase in antisemitism levels (Hübscher and Von Mering 2022). In terms of the online comment sections of UK mainstream media, such triggers tend to be news stories focusing on the State of Israel, which spark web-user debates on Israeli politics; genuine and legitimate critique of Israeli government or its policies will then sometimes cross the line into antisemitism (Schwarz-Friesel 2020). Another such type of trigger seems to be media coverage centred around a well-known figure and a statement they have made in relation to Jews or Israel, at times open to interpretation, or otherwise directly and unequivocally antisemitic. Whether they have made their name in the political arena, the arts or the world of show business, the controversy will inevitably attract the attention of both new and existing supporters as well as critics, resulting in a flurry of media reports about their statements and a lively discussion in the comment sections regarding the impact, seriousness and truthfulness of their words.

The framing of the public figure's pronouncement is likely to affect web-user reactions as well. An accusation of antisemitism in the press articles themselves seems to fuel the debate further, on the one hand prompting affirmation and agreement, on the other a proliferation of counter speech (see Ascone in this volume). This chapter focuses on two case studies in which well-known figures with similar visibility, television presenter Rachel Riley and novelist Sally Rooney, publicly voiced their opinions on issues regarding the cultural boycott of Israel, in both cases triggering a significant amount of coverage by mainstream media in the UK, broadly discussed by web users of the media in the comment sections. The chapter compares the findings in terms of antisemitic hate speech found in the comment sections, but also the misogyny present in both debates. By comparing the two, it hopes to contribute to the conversation on the different hate ideologies co-existing in the same mainstream spaces, and their potential to be weaponised.

Over the past three years, the research team of the Decoding Antisemitism project analysed several discourse events centred around prominent figures and media personalities. These have included the 2021 case of the sociology lecturer Professor David Miller, who had made incendiary statements about the State of Israel,[1] as well as the British left-wing politician Diane Abbott and the US musician Ye (formerly known as Kanye West), both of whom have been accused of antisemitism on separate occasions—based on their comments about Jews in, respectively, her letter to the British weekly *The Observer*, and his social media posts. Outside of the UK, similar news stories in recent years have involved the French comedian Dieudonné M'Bala M'Bala[2] and German politician Hans-Georg Maaßen; all these events have provoked lively debates in the comments under the media posts on the topic in the respective countries. Such focus on a recognisable public figure makes the conversation more appealing to both the media and the public opinion, and the figure's actions provide a specific trigger for the discussions on antisemitism. Antisemitic ideology can then be pinned onto a particular individual rather than discussed in the abstract, allowing the media and the comment boxes to sidestep the difficulty of elucidating the long and rich history of antisemitism, its complexity and illogicality, and its ever-changing guises which often depend on their temporal, geographical or cultural context. It is perhaps easier for the public opinion to focus the discussion instead on one person's biography and the various aspects of their professional or private identity, using them as arguments or counter-arguments. The public figure is thus collectively dissected, and a narrative is built around them.

Studying such events purely from the point of view of the hallmarks of antisemitism and its specific stereotypes, analogies or strategies

---

1 This resulted in Miller's dismissal from his post at the University of Bristol, which was later ruled unfair by Bristol Employment Tribunal on 6 February 2024, https://www.judiciary.uk/wp-content/uploads/2024/02/Miller-judgment-1400780.2022-JDT.pdf.

2 See Chapelan in the same volume for a discussion of French social media reactions to the Dieudonné and West's controversies.

undoubtedly helps construct a good overview of the overarching patterns of antisemitic discourse. However, taking into consideration other hate ideologies as well can provide further insights, particularly into the specific abuse suffered by various groups in connection with not just their Jewish identity, but also with their gender, sexual orientation, skin colour, ethnicity, age, disability. In the recent years, several public figures in the UK have been vocal about the particular type of hate speech they have been targets of as Jewish women, including the politicians Luciana Berger, Ruth Smeeth and Margaret Hodge, or actor and writer Tracy-Ann Oberman. On the other hand, looking at more than one hate ideology in the analysis of antisemitic discourse can also show how one can be instrumentalised in the fight against another: many comments countering antisemitism contain misogyny, racism, or anti-Muslim sentiment, which become an unwelcome feature of counter speech and create more and stronger divides instead of educating or fostering understanding. The many comments denouncing Diane Abbott's letter to *The Observer* in April of 2023, in which she seemed to relativise and downplay the seriousness of contemporary antisemitism (Scheiber 2024), attacked not just the accuracy of her statement or her professional competence as a politician and a Member of Parliament, but also her race, gender and age.[3] Outrage against Kanye West's antisemitic social media posts and claims made in an interview was at times expressed through the means of anti-Black discourse in comment sections and deriding his mental health diagnosis (Chapelan et al. 2023). In commentary on the ongoing events of the Arab-Israeli conflict, counter speech comments made by web users regularly rehash Islamophobic narratives. In other words, the specific identity (real or perceived) of a person or people at the receiving end of the criticism, even when the actual criticism is due, is unfairly instrumentalised against them in *ad hominem* attacks. Studying the interactions of the various hate speech ideologies, their

---

3   Based on Decoding Antisemitism team's analysis of 4,000 online comments, posted under media reports about Abbott's letter in late April and early May 2023 on mainstream news websites and on their social media accounts. Examples include: "I also wonder why she straightens her cultural Afro hair ? If white woman are chastised for the Corning of their hair, why does this duplicitous cr.3t1n think nothing of cultural appropriation of a white persons hair ?" (EXPR[20230424]), "Sack the racist bint" (BBC-TW[20230424]), "I'm surprised the old 🐸 was awake long enough to write this 💩" (BBC-FB[20230504]).

possible correlations, and contextual or universal specificities yields a fuller picture of online hate speech.

Despite such clear indications of the benefits of this intersectional approach to the study of antisemitic hate speech, as well as counter speech—an approach which recognises that a person or group can experience discrimination, marginalisation or oppression in a distinct way, depending on the specific aspects of their individual identity (Cho et al. 2013, Thomas et al. 2023)—it seems to have been given little attention so far: "global antisemitism is only rarely included in intersectional theory, and Jews are often excluded from feminist anti-racist social movements that claim to be guided by intersectionality" (Stögner 2020). Its application in the field of antisemitism studies, or more specifically in the study of the structure of antisemitic speech online, could result in new, illuminating and more particularised findings, steering away from dichotomy and towards a more comprehensive and nuanced view of both the antisemitic discourse and counter-antisemitic narratives.

2. Antisemitism and misogyny

One such pairing of hate ideologies that seem to frequently intersect or interact in online discourses are antisemitism and misogyny. Misogyny—a contemptuous view of women—and sexism, an unequal view of the genders, are extremely widespread and hardly need an introduction; sexist and misogynistic discourses have been amply studied (Vickery and Everbach 2018, Cameron 2020), also in contemporary online spaces (Jane 2014, Ging and Siapera 2018, KhosraviNik and Esposito 2018), sometimes including the specific types of abuse encountered by transwomen or queer women (Jane 2016: 70–71). While men are, of course, also targeted by hate speech or 'cancelled' (that is, strongly criticised and ostracised), prominent female figures seem to bear the brunt of more frequent, and more violent, hate speech, including more death or rape threats; increased visibility can arguably increase the amount of hate speech they receive, and a positive public image does not immunise them from public opinion quickly turning on them.[4]

---

4   Recent examples of this pattern in the UK context include e.g. member of the British royal family Meghan, Duchess of Sussex, or US actress Amber Heard, both

There is a considerable amount of literature on the specificities of historical gender-based antisemitic prejudice. Both male and female Jews have been presented at various times throughout history as sexually deviant and therefore reprehensible, depraved and abnormal (Drake 2013), feeding into the more general, classic antisemitic stereotypes of monstrosity and repulsiveness, both moral and physical. However, Jewish men have also been portrayed as emasculated and weak (Pellegrini 1997, Schüler-Springorum 2018), and Jewish women as deceitful and witch-like. These stereotypes find their way into later cultural, literary and cinematic tropes which dilute the message and are therefore not immediately recognisable as negative at their root, such as the nineteenth-century *"la belle juive"*—seductive and tragic (Rindisbacher 2018), the contemporary "nice Jewish boy"—gentle and respectful, the "Jewish American Princess"—somewhat spoilt and materialistic, a play on capitalistic greed (Keiles 2018), and the "Jewish mother"—overbearing and pushy (Ravits 2000, Abrams 2012: 47–48). The latter, present-day tropes often become reflected in pop culture, particularly in the films and television series created in the United States, which sustains them via such acceptable, light-hearted iterations and contributes to spreading them ever further.[5]

Expressions of gender-based antisemitic stereotypes found in the comment sections of UK mainstream media, especially once the content has been moderated by human or automated moderation, are likely to be similarly watered down and therefore deemed innocuous and inoffensive, or at least palatable. Likewise, the moderation will have removed the most extreme forms of anti-feminism and misogyny, such as pro-rape comments found, for instance, in the discourse of the antisemitic far-right; such discourse is expressed more freely in unmoderated spaces, including group chats on the messaging app Telegram, where it "actively promotes sexual violence as a political weapon" against women as well as the LGBT+ community (Lawrence, Simhony-Philpott and Stone 2021). Nevertheless, even casual expressions

---

of whom had initially received favourable mainstream media coverage, which then switched to primarily negative portrayal.

5 Arguably, this dilution could also help the relevant groups reclaim such stereotypes, i.e., re-appropriate them as a positive or neutral aspect of their group identities.

of a hate ideology, as inconsequential as they may seem in isolation, have the potential to harm their targets and normalise the prejudice, for both the targets and anyone who comes across them. While very explicit hate speech can alienate a mainstream media reader, regular exposure to casually expressed antisemitism can lead them to, for example, accept outbreaks of violence against Israeli civilians as understandable. By the same token, institutional sexism and misogyny have been cited as an obstacle to investigating rape accusations made by women against men (Casey 2023). Often, the power of antisemitic or misogynistic statements is not in their individual shock value, but in their sheer repetition, accumulation and acceptability; while one comment or image might not radicalise a reader, their continued and persistent presence could lead to the boundary of what is acceptable to say and do moving ever further (Oboler 2021).

3. The two case studies: Riley and Rooney

In early 2019, mainstream news outlets in the UK reported that the next Eurovision Song Contest would take place in May of that year, in the Israeli city of Tel Aviv. Soon after the announcement, at the end of January, around 50 British artists and celebrities signed an open letter which called on the British Broadcasting Company (BBC) to petition Eurovision organisers (the European Broadcasting Union) to move the event to a different location in order to show their opposition to Israel's policies and actions in relation to Palestine. The letter stated that "Eurovision may be light entertainment, but it is not exempt from human rights considerations—and we cannot ignore Israel's systematic violation of Palestinian human rights", in effect calling for a cultural boycott of Israel (The Guardian 2019); the signatories included fashion designer Vivienne Westwood, actor Maxine Peake and musician Roger Waters. The letter followed on from an earlier, similar campaign organised by the Boycott, Divestment and Sanctions (BDS) movement in September of 2018, which had been supported by numerous artists from across Europe. BDS, a Palestinian-led initiative which aims to put pressure on Israel through encouraging economic, cultural and political measures, is shaped in the image of the anti-apartheid boycott actions aimed at South African policies in the second half of the twentieth century (Barghouti 2011).

The appeal prompted a response from other figures within the UK entertainment, arts and culture industry. In a second open letter, made public in April of 2019, they opposed the boycott arguing that "while we all may have differing opinions on the Israeli-Palestinian conflict and the best path to peace, we all agree that a cultural boycott is not the answer", and calling Eurovision a "unifying event [...] crucial to help bridge our cultural divides and bring people of all backgrounds together" (Creative Community for Peace 2019). Although the second letter was signed by over a hundred members of the industry, most media reports on the topic mentioned only a handful of best-known names in either the article headlines or content. Among these, they frequently included Rachel Riley, a popular television show presenter, who had spoken publicly about antisemitism in the UK, notably in relation to the antisemitism allegations in the Labour party. Riley has also related being a target of antisemitism and misogyny as a Jewish woman on various occasions; taking a stance on the issue of cultural boycott of Israel in the context of a popular entertainment event made her vulnerable to such attacks in the comment sections of mainstream news outlets. Was the discourse used against her different from the attacks on other women? Would a comparison of two case studies—one focusing on Riley, and the other on a non-Jewish woman with similar visibility, who has spoken publicly on a similar topic—reveal parallels or differences?

In an effort to answer these questions, a sample of web-user reactions in the 2019 cultural boycott case have been compared with a similar sample of responses to an event from October 2021, when the best-selling Irish novelist Sally Rooney announced her decision not to grant translation rights to an Israeli-based publishing house for her recently released third novel (BBC News 2021). Rooney explained her decision with her support for the BDS movement; her announcement was widely reported by the mainstream media in the UK across the political spectrum, and it prompted many web users to comment on it under the media posts (Ascone et al. 2022). While multiple comments agreed with Rooney's stance and similarly aligned themselves with the idea of a cultural boycott of Israel or expressed direct approval for BDS, others criticised her decision. Often, the criticism did not stop at her words and extended to the person herself—her supposed political sympathies, for example—and, on occasion, the criticism became a xenophobic attack on her Irish origins, or misogynistic abuse based on her gender.

3.1 The dataset

Despite the fact that the two cases are two and a half years apart, there are significant parallels between them (see Fig. 1.1). Both central figures, Rachel Riley and Sally Rooney, are young white woman that have become famous in the UK by virtue of their professional activity in the British entertainment, arts and culture industry: Rooney as a popular and acclaimed novelist, and Riley as a successful television presenter, and later also an author. At the time of the media reports, they were of a similar age; ageism is often an element of misogynistic or sexist discourses and therefore a potentially relevant factor in this analysis. Both women have used their professional recognition as a platform to make a political statement on a similar issue, albeit on opposing sides. However, out of the two only Riley identifies as Jewish.

The issue on which they have both publicly expressed their views, in the context of this analysis, has been the idea of boycotting the State of Israel through the means of mainstream cultural output, on both occasions in connection with the broader BDS movement. In both instances, the mainstream media coverage of their stance on the issue sparked a lively debate in the comment sections of UK news outlets. In each of the two cases, the basis for analysis was a dataset built of eight online comment threads, taken from the comment sections of a range of UK mainstream media websites and their official social media accounts (Fig. 1.2). Each of these threads was the source of a 200-comment sample, totalling 1,600 user comments per case.[6]

---

6   A larger dataset of 3,750 web user comments on the Rooney announcement has been analysed by the Decoding Antisemitism research team and presented in *Discourse Report 4* (Ascone et al. 2022).

Riley dataset	Rooney dataset
Common themes in dataset: cultural boycott of Israel, the BDS movement, apartheid analogy	Common themes in dataset: cultural boycott of Israel, the BDS movement, apartheid analogy
Central figure: popular British television show presenter in her early 30s, white, female, Jewish Opposing cultural boycott of Israel (as reported in UK media in 2019)	Central figure: popular Irish novelist aged 30, white, female, not Jewish Supporting cultural boycott of Israel (as reported in UK media in 2021)

Figure 1.1: An overview of the case studies.

3.2 Methodological approach

The methodological framework applied to the two datasets comes from the Decoding Antisemitism project, whose aim is to study the contemporary presence of antisemitic hate speech in the (politically moderate) mainstream in all its forms, including its implicit expressions which, due to their hidden or unfixed nature, evade immediate detection and therefore pass through moderation, with time contributing to the normalisation of antisemitic attitudes online. The project analyses three language communities: the UK, Germany and France, looking for both the universals in their antisemitic discourses online, and their specificities in terms of frequency, triggers and linguistic formats and patterns, bringing into focus the discourse and its potential impact rather than the identity of commenters or the intentionality of their statements.

The analysis presented in this chapter uses the project's approach to data collection and the same classification system. The online comment threads used to build the two datasets were first systematically collected using a custom crawling tool, based on selected key words and a specific date range, and downloaded in a text format retaining the comment thread structure. The threads were then organised into a corpus balanced in terms of representation of mainstream news outlets and their political alignment. Each of the longest comment threads in the corpus was sampled by selecting the first 200 comments, and manually analysed with two research tools. The first of these was content analysis software MAXQDA, which allows the researcher to annotate textual and visual content. The second instrument was a classification system developed by the research project team based on classic and modern antisemitic concepts—both deductively and inductively, as the initial project analyses revealed further patterns in the examined data. Apart from a detailed and precisely defined conceptual categories and sub-categories, the classification system also allows for the content to be analysed in terms of linguistic structures and devices present in the comment, with categories such as irony, rhetorical questions, wordplay, and more.

While the classification system used in the project makes it possible to analyse the antisemitic content in minute detail, it does not currently reflect misogynistic ideology in the same fine-grained approach. For the purposes of analysing the two datasets, the above-mentioned inductive approach was therefore applied in order to identify the specifics of the misogynistic discourse they contained, referencing existing literature on such discourse. The Sally Rooney corpus had first been analysed by the research team in a report published in October 2022; this dataset was used in part (preserving the balance of sources) and reanalysed from the point of view of misogynistic hate speech for this chapter. Meanwhile, the Rachel Riley dataset has been collected and analysed in terms of both antisemitic and misogynistic content expressly for the purposes of presenting this comparison.

Riley dataset	Rooney dataset
1,600 comments	1,600 comments
8 comment threads	8 comment threads
Data sources: *Facebook* pages of *The Independent, The Guardian, The Metro, The Spectator, Evening Standard, The Daily Mail.*	Data sources: *Facebook* pages of *The Independent, The Guardian, The Times, The Spectator, The Telegraph* and *The Daily Mail* website.

Figure 1.2: An overview of the datasets.

4. Discussion of findings

4.1 Antisemitic content: Frequency and concepts

The in-depth empirical analysis of the two datasets has uncovered many similarities, not least in the level of antisemitic comments they contain, as well as the types of stereotypes, analogies and strategies used by the commenters to convey antisemitic attitudes. The average share of antisemitic comments, both explicit and implicit, reached just over 11% in both corpora—a finding not dissimilar to the typical percentage revealed in regular analyses of similar datasets in the Decoding Antisemitism project. The antisemitic comments typically revolved around the same themes and triggers; that is, Israeli politics in the context of the Middle East conflict, including frequent comparisons of Israel to an apartheid state, and support for the BDS movement.

4.1.1 "Support the boycott"

Riley dataset	Rooney dataset
(1) Boycott the Fcuking <a></a>Izrahells so that they learn they are not gods chosen. (SPECT-FB[20190506]) (2) [...] WE NEED TO BOYCOTT ISRAELI GOODS, CULTURAL EVENTS ETC PLEASE BOYCOTT TO PUT PRESSURE ON THE RACIST STATE OF ISRAEL (INDEP-FB[20190430])	(3) do your own research. I'm defending her decision to support the boycott. (TIMES-FB[20211012]) (4) She should boycott Hebrew altogether. Modern Hebrew was invented as part of the Zionist project. (TIMES[20211012])

In both datasets, many web users took to comment sections simply to express respect, support or admiration for the cultural boycott of Israel, and often calling for others to do the same, as in (1), (2) and (4). While some comments, such as (3), simply affirmed the antisemitism (in 9% of antisemitic comments in the Riley dataset and 8% in the Rooney dataset), the support was often accompanied by, or argued through, the attribution of further problematic concepts to Israel. In (1), the commenter hinted at two such antisemitic stereotypes: first, the idea of supposedly EVIL Jewish nature is expressed in the pun "Izrahells" (Bolton 2024b); second, the reference to the "chosen one" trope signals the commenter's disapproval for the alleged PRIVILEGE enjoyed by the Jewish state (Placzynta 2024b). In (2), Israel is called a "RACIST STATE", and in (3) the legitimacy of its existence is placed into doubt by alleging that "[m]odern Hebrew was invented as part of the Zionist project". Referring to Israel as a "project" rather than a country or state is a vivid feature of Israel-related antisemitic discourse or, to be more precise, of DENIAL OF ISRAEL'S RIGHT TO EXIST (Vincent and Bolton 2024); all of the above concepts are consistent features of English-language antisemitic discourse online.

4.1.2 "The brutal, racist apartheid state"

Riley dataset	Rooney dataset
(5) Togetherness with an apartheid state—that sounds like a good idea—yeah right. GUARD-FB[20190429]) (6) #BDS ISRAEL is an exterminationist genocidal apartheid colonialist settler state#FreePalestine 🏴 (METRO-FB[20190519])	(7) How is it that when it's Jews having an Apartheid state suddenly opposing it is allegedly 'racist'? (INDEP-FB[20211012]) (8) Well done girl. Expose the brutal, racist apartheid state. (TIMES-FB[20211012])

In the comments supporting the cultural boycott, multiple user comments employed the apartheid analogy as an argument for their attack on Israel, either on its own or in combination with several other accusations. The frequent (23% and 28% of antisemitic comments respectively) use of the analogy in the two datasets is perhaps to be expected in this context, as the BDS movement has modelled itself after the anti-apartheid campaigns in South Africa in the latter half of the last century, contributing to the construction of the analogy in the public imagination. The application of the apartheid analogy also seems to be a common strategy to prepare ground for other, less socially acceptable and more controversial characterisations of Israel as "genocidal"[7] (6),

---

7   It should be acknowledged that at the time of writing the validity of the genocide accusation levelled at Israel due to its military actions in Gaza is a topic of an urgent debate. On 26 January 2024, the International Court of Justice (ICJ)

"brutal" or "racist" (8) (Bolton et al. 2023, Bolton 2024a). However, it is also often used on their own, rendered even more subtle by the use of linguistic structures that obscure the sentiment. One example of this is that the use of irony in (5) gives the comment the appearance of agreement with the letter signed by Riley and other artists, which called for unity between the supporters of Israel and Palestine; this illusion is broken by the contextual, pejorative reference to Israel as "an apartheid state". Similarly, a rhetorical question asked by (7) uses the same label, further suggesting that antisemitism is instrumentalised to allow "Jews [to] hav[e] an Apartheid state" (Becker 2024a).

4.2 Misogynistic content: Parallels and differences

The issue of the validity of a cultural boycott as a measure against the State of Israel, debated in the two datasets, provoked strong responses on both sides of the discussion regarding the topic, as well as the figures named in the media coverage around the issue. The two women were both targeted by misogynistic language which often, if not always, followed similar schemata, despite the fact that the two represented opposing sides of the boycott debate. At times they took the forms of straightforward insults, many of which were gendered, but also of disempowering or undermining language or negative characterisation; it was the latter that revealed especially telling differences. Only 3% and 5% respectively of all the analysed comments in the Riley and Rooney datasets were considered clearly misogynistic; their lower share in comparison to antisemitic comments could perhaps suggest greater sensitivity of either human or automated moderators on the platforms the comments were taken from. However, a more likely reason for this imbalance is the focus of the media trigger on Israel and antisemitism, with the female identity of the figures at the centre purely incidental. The higher amount of misogyny in the Rooney corpus could reflect the fact that she was the only figure involved in the event reported on by the media, rather than one of a few, as in the case of Riley.

---

ordered Israel to "take action to prevent acts of genocide", https://www.reuters.com/world/middle-east/key-takeaways-world-court-decision-israel-genocide-case-2024-01-26/. See also Bolton in this volume.

4.2.1 Insults: "Zionist cow" vs. "ignorant cow"

Riley dataset	Rooney dataset
(9) Rachel Riley signing is is the give away, Zionist cow. (INDEP-FB[20190430])	(11) Make no mistake. This is Jew hate. She is Some whiny 🇮🇪 Harpy (SPECT-FB[20211014])
(10) So Rachel Riley says that we shouldn't boycott it! Quelle surprise that she supports an apartheid state. Nasty piece of work. 🇵🇸🇵🇸 (INDEP-FB[20190430])	(12) Ignorant cow.... actually terrible reviews... maybe she thinks the notoriety will help book sales...oh, I forgot...most BDSers are too dumb to.....read! (TEL-FB[20211012])
	(13) mad old trout (TEL-FB[20211012])
	(14) silly girl (TIMES-FB[20211012])

In the two analysed datasets of web-user comments, misogynistic comments contained insults (present in 16% of all comments categorised as misogynistic in the Riley dataset, and 21% in the Rooney dataset). Some were expressed through gendered words or phrases whose dictionary definition specifies that the referent is only ever a woman or a girl. In (9), Rachel Riley is called a "cow", and in (11) and (13) Rooney is dismissed as "[s]ome whiny 🇮🇪 Harpy" and a "mad old trout". Interestingly, all of these insults dehumanise their targets by comparing them either to animals or, in the case of "Harpy", a mythical half-human, half-bird creature known for her malevolence. Additionally, in two of the examples, the insults were personalised with references to the women's identity, real or perceived—in one, it is Rooney's Irish nationality,[8] in the other, Riley's Jewish identity and possibly her defence of Israel against a cultural boycott; although, in the UK discourse, a "Zionist" label is often simply a stand-in for the attribute of "Jewish" or "Israeli".

Some insults included lexical items which could be applied to any gender but are most commonly used when referring to women. Frequent examples of this in the English language are adjectives like "bossy",

---

8   Throughout the dataset, Rooney's Irishness is a reference point in many more comments, both negative or positive, but not necessarily linked to her gender and therefore not of relevance here. Examples include: "the irish understand and celebrate antisemitism" (INDEP-FB[20211012]) or "A racist irish author is not going to be missed"(SPECT-FB[20211014]).

"abrasive" or "hysterical"; such discrepancies can be addressed through corpus linguistic studies into the discourse about women (Baker 2013). This could also be true of the word "whiny", more often than not used to characterise children or women, and akin to the gender-marked epithet "shrill" (Cameron 2016). One of the comments calls Riley a "[n]asty piece of work"; the epithet of "nasty"—though again applicable to people of any gender—has been highlighted by discourse analytical studies as unproportionally targeting women. One of its most-known connotations in recent years has been the pervasive portrayal of Hillary Clinton in public statements made by Donald Trump as "a nasty woman" (Harp 2019). The ubiquity of such words reinforces the so-called likeability bias—the social expectation towards women which dictates the greater need to be pleasant and approachable; that is to speak, act and present themselves in a non-intimidating way, or even to be less visible (Menegatti and Rubini 2017).[9] The use of the attribute "nasty" towards Riley may also, to some extent, echo the stereotypes of a loud and pushy Jewish woman, or that of EVIL Jewish nature (Bolton 2024b); however, without further study of this specific word in more contexts, it is impossible to say if it indeed conveys any antisemitism-specific overtones here.

Elsewhere, a comment refers to Rooney as a "silly girl". The adjective "silly" is, once again, not applied to female referents exclusively, but much more commonly so. Its use serves to undermine or dismiss the target: not just her intelligence or rationality, but also her stature, especially in combination with the infantilising reference "girl" attributed here to an adult woman, in the context of a debate provoked by a statement she had made publicly, using her professional platform and considerable recognition and following. Instead of countering her words on the same level, the anonymous comment chooses to ridicule and diminish (Krook 2022). Similar intelligence-based insults are a feature of the counter-commentary on Diane Abbott's recent statements comparing discrimination encountered by various groups, including Jews. It did not, however, seem to be part of the characterisation of David Miller during the 2021, likewise accused of antisemitism based

---

9   The bias may be experienced even more strongly by women of colour, who are often burdened with the 'angry Black woman' stereotype and forced to counteract it in social interactions.

on his public statements, where the personal attacks focused mainly on his carelessness of incompetence as a university lecturer, rather than his intelligence or autonomy of views (Becker et al. 2021).[10]

4.2.2 Disempowering language: "Sour, dull, petulant"

Riley dataset	Rooney dataset
(15) Rachel Riley signed it!!! Obviously heavyweights … (GUARD-FB[20190430])	(17) A nobody wanting to be noticed for her inferred virtue signalling (SPECT-FB[20210114])
(16) there is nothing pretty about Rachel Riley, her spite shows in her face (SPECT-FB[20190506])	(18) should worry about fixing those yellow teeth first (INDEP-FB[20211012])
	(19) Photos of Rooney would seem to perfectly capture her personality. Sour, dull, petulant, disapproving, misery guts (TEL[20211012])

Several more examples in both datasets use comparable language which attempts to undermine or disempower the two women in a range of ways. One strategy is to reduce their professional standing. (15) ironically quips "Rachel Riley signed it!!! Obviously heavyweights …", while (17) calls Rooney "[a] nobody wanting to be noticed for her inferred virtue signalling". By objective measures, Sally Rooney is a successful professional, who has published three bestselling and critically acclaimed novels by the age of 30; Rachel Riley is similarly accomplished in her respective field of work. Referencing them as a "nobody" or as a "lightweight" denies their importance and influence, and by extension the potential impact of their statements in the debate around the cultural boycott of Israel.

Another discursive method aiming to disempower the target is to distract from the topic of the discussion and the views or ideologies the person has expressed by commenting on their physical appearance. This

---

10   Based on the analysis of a dataset comprising 1,750 online comments, comparable in size and structure to the two presented in this chapter.

seems less prominent in debates surrounding male figures.[11] In (18), the web user suggests that Rooney "should worry about fixing those yellow teeth first", while (16) and (19) make judgments about Rooney's and Riley's looks and extrapolate these judgments to their character: "[p]hotos of Rooney would seem to perfectly capture her personality"; "[Riley's] spite shows in her face". Both these strategies—that is, not acknowledging the opponent's clout and denigrating them based on their appearance—are commonly used against women, e.g. in political debates.

4.2.3 Divergent narratives: Naïve vs. devious

Riley dataset	Rooney dataset
(20) sadly shows lying grifters do profit (METRO-FB[20190519]) (21) Rachel Riley known for screaming anti-semitism at every opportunity because she uses the Natanyahu definition "the new antisemitism is to be anti Israel". Probably the most famous on that list - internationally - is Gene Simmons, born in Tel Aviv. Hardly surprising he supports his home city. (INDEP-FB[20190430]) (22) Rachel Riley regularly raises money for Israeli soldiers to murder children. of course she signed it (INDEP-FB[20190430])	(23) She isn't a hero though. She is a not very bright anti-Semite (SPECT-FB[20211014]) (24) Rooney's laughably naive gesture politics are amusing enough but also a demonstration of stupidity (TIMES-FB[20211012]) (25) It's not her fault she's a stupid ..... (MAIL[20211013]) (26) Another brainwashed woke c**t (TIMES-FB[20211012])

While most of the derogatory examples presented so far seem to follow a similar pattern, this is not true of all of the analysed comments. The first hint of that was the portrayal of Rachel Riley as a "nasty piece of work" in (10) and of Sally Rooney as a "silly girl" in (14). In subsequent

---

11   It should be said, however, that Jewish figures in general are frequently represented, verbally or visually, as grotesque caricatures, which dehumanises and depersonalises them, de-emphasises their individuality, and insinuates their supposed moral monstrosity. However, this strategy normally aims not to distract from the discussion at hand but to emphasise its premise, e.g. the alleged evil or amorality of all Jews/Israel.

analysis, this characterisation of each woman seems to be confirmed further. Rooney is, on more than one occasion, referred to as limited and unaware, with comments such as (23) and (24) calling her "a not very bright anti-Semite" and her pronouncement "laughably naive gesture politics" and "a demonstration of stupidity". Further comments narrowly avoid using derogatory swear words, but make their contempt for Rooney clear by referring to her as "a stupid ....". in (25) and "[a]nother brainwashed woke c**t" in (26). The narrative which emerges from these and other examples dismisses the idea that she might hold her own, independent views; while interpreting her decision regarding the Hebrew translation of her book as antisemitic and then criticising it, the comments arbitrarily deny her both intelligence and agency.

However, where Rooney is presented as someone who does not realise the weight of her words or actions, Riley is shown as not just aware and intentional, but also taking an opportunity to manipulate and profit. Suggesting that she is dishonest or duplicitous, (20) states resignedly that "lying grifters do profit". The following comment accuses her of exercising the taboo of criticism (Chapelan 2024c), claiming she is "known for screaming anti-semitism at every opportunity because she uses the Natanyahu definition 'the new antisemitism is to be anti Israel'".

Both these comments seem to echo antisemitic stereotypes constructed around the idea of untrustworthiness: one—the alleged LYING, DECEITFUL OR IMMORAL as well as INSTRUMENTALISING and exploitative Jewish nature (Becker 2024a, Becker 2024b, Krasni 2024), and the other—a supposed JEWISH CONSPIRACY (Chapelan 2024a). Meanwhile (22), while referencing the signing of the open letter opposing the boycott of Israel, implicates her in the BLOOD LIBEL trope (Placzynta 2024a), implying that her morally reprehensible behaviour is to be expected. The comment not only suggests that one of the aims of Israeli soldiers is to "murder children", but also apportions at least part of the blame to Riley, since she supposedly makes this crime financially possible. In contrast to the "naive" and "stupid" Rooney, Riley is painted as manipulative and IMMORAL. Such portrayal is not, of course, necessarily gender-based or particular only to Jewish women; similar accusations are present in the narratives around well-known male Jewish figures such as the entrepreneur and philanthropist George Soros (Becker and Troschke 2022), routinely portrayed in online media discourses as EVIL (Bolton

2024b). However, the comments about Riley's alleged dishonest nature are also in line with the historical stereotype of a deceitful Jewish woman. It is therefore possible that the Jewishness of the object of the commenters' allegations could have led to activating the association with the negative character traits central to the historical stereotype, mentioned in an earlier section, in a way that is absent from the case where the target is a non-Jewish woman.

5. Closing remarks

Contrastive analysis of web-user reactions to the two cases has indicated several points of interest, and the directions in which further research can advance. The first of these points is that misogynistic language can be, and is, weaponised on different sides of the debate in antisemitic discourse. The very same notion of a cultural boycott against Israel is debated in the comment sections of the same media, in the same country and therefore the same cultural and social setting, set two years apart. Within the same topic of conversation, two women are targeted by misogynistic language that often follows similar schemata. This illogicality is not necessarily surprising, as the public opinion can very quickly turn against women who were previously admired (cf. Lawrence, Simhony-Philpott and Stone 2021). The many analogies in the prejudice and abuse suffered by both Jewish and non-Jewish women can perhaps serve a useful purpose: that of highlighting the shared struggles and perhaps even building more understanding as a result. This may then become a point of departure for noticing the differences and the particular struggles of people identifying as female and Jewish, both online and in real life.

The presence of both antisemitism and misogyny in the same comment sections of mainstream news outlets, albeit to different degrees, is also a signal that many of the harmful antisemitic and misogynistic stereotypes are similarly normalised or expressed implicitly in everyday discourses, and that both pass unnoticed by the moderation. Some of them are only circumstantial: it is their context or co-text which determines their antisemitic or misogynistic message; a different target—non-Jewish or non-female, respectively—would deprive the comment of this interpretation. This suggests that the research design tools developed in the Decoding Antisemitism project can be extended and adapted to studying the mechanisms of both hate ideologies.

Where the two cases diverge in terms of the content of the attacks on the figures central to each event is the characterisation of each woman. While both are insulted, dismissed and undermined, the Jewish woman is additionally vilified and presented as untrustworthy and devious. This portrayal echoes the negative stereotypes more broadly ascribed to Jews, Israelis or the Jewish state as well as some of the historical representations of Jewish women. These findings could, of course, be unique to these two cases; more research comparing discourses around Jewish and non-Jewish women is required to ascertain whether this pattern is consistent.

Further research is also needed in order to build an understanding of how antisemitism and misogyny relate to and intersect with each other. Further examinations could also focus on the specific experiences of abuse encountered by Jewish transwomen as opposed to Jewish ciswomen, or focus on more than one gender. The analytical framework can be applied to various pairings, in a way that is increasingly popular in the broader field of discrimination and prejudice research. An upcoming project by a group of British scholars aims to examine Jewish and Muslim women's experience of abuse online in order to improve practice in the area of legislation (Bakalis et al. 2023), and a recent report by the Milan-based L'Osservatorio antisemitismo (2023) raises awareness of online insults which blend antisemitism and homophobia. As the intersectionality approach aims to grant all identities express consideration, while still including those already given attention by research or professional practice, it offers exciting new perspectives on approaching and designing studies of hate speech online.

References

Abrams, Nathan. 2012. *The New Jew in Film: Exploring Jewishness and Judaism in Contemporary Cinema*. New Brunswick, NJ: Rutgers University Press, https://doi.org/10.1093/acprof:oso/9780190265427.003.0028

Ascone, Laura, Matthias J. Becker, Matthew Bolton, Alexis Chapelan, Jan Krasni, Karolina Placzynta, Marcus Scheiber, Hagen Troschke and Chloé Vincent. 2022. *Decoding Antisemitism: An AI-driven study on hate speech and imagery online. Discourse Report 4.* Technische Universität Berlin. Centre for Research on Antisemitism, https://doi.org/10.14279/depositonce-16292

Baker, Paul. 2013. *Introduction: Virtual Special Issue of Gender and Language on Corpus Approaches*. Sheffield: Equinox Publishing, https://doi.org/10.1558/8psxqda5wh3d

Barghouti, Omar. 2011. *BDS: Boycott, Divestment, Sanctions: The Global Struggle for Palestinian Rights*. Chicago: Haymarket Books

BBC News. 2021. "Irish author Sally Rooney in Israel boycott row". *BBC News*, https://www.bbc.co.uk/news/entertainment-arts-58886915

Becker, Matthias J. 2024a. "Instrumentalisation of antisemitism and the Holocaust". In: Becker, Matthias J./ Hagen Troschke, Matthew Bolton and Alexis Chapelan (eds). *Decoding Antisemitism: A Guide to Identifying Antisemitism Online*. London: Palgrave Macmillan, https://link.springer.com/book/9783031492372

Becker, Matthias J. 2024b. "Lie and deceit". In: Becker, Matthias J., Hagen Troschke, Matthew Bolton and Alexis Chapelan (eds). *Decoding Antisemitism: A Guide to Identifying Antisemitism Online*. London: Palgrave Macmillan, https://link.springer.com/book/9783031492372

Becker, Matthias J., Daniel Allington, Laura Ascone, Matthew Bolton, Alexis Chapelan, Jan Krasni, Karolina Placzynta, Marcus Scheiber, Hagen Troschke and Chloé Vincent. 2021. *Decoding Antisemitism: An AI-driven study on hate speech and imagery online. Discourse Report 2.* Technische Universität Berlin. Centre for Research on Antisemitism, https://doi.org/10.14279/depositonce-15310

Becker, Matthias J. and Hagen Troschke. 2022. "How users of British media websites make a bogeyman of George Soros". *Journal of Contemporary Antisemitism*, 5 (1): 49–68, https://doi.org/10.26613/jca/5.1.100

Bolton, Matthew. 2024a. "Apartheid analogy". In: Becker, Matthias J., Hagen Troschke, Matthew Bolton and Alexis Chapelan (eds). *Decoding Antisemitism: A Guide to Identifying Antisemitism Online*. London: Palgrave Macmillan, https://link.springer.com/book/9783031492372

Bolton, Matthew. 2024b. "Evil/The devil". In: Becker, Matthias J., Hagen Troschke, Matthew Bolton and Alexis Chapelan (eds). *Decoding*

Antisemitism: A Guide to Identifying Antisemitism Online. London: Palgrave Macmillan, https://link.springer.com/book/9783031492372

Bolton, Matthew, Matthias J. Becker, Laura Ascone and Karolina Placzynta. 2023. "Enabling concepts in hate speech: The case of the apartheid analogy". In Ermida, Isabel (ed.) *Hate Speech in Social Media.* London: Palgrave Macmillan, https://doi.org/10.1007/978-3-031-38248-2_9

Cameron, Deborah. 2016. *The Taming of the Shrill,* https://debuk.wordpress.com/2016/03/12/the-taming-of-the-shrill/

Cameron, Deborah. 2023. *Language, Sexism and Misogyny.* Abingdon: Taylor & Francis, https://doi.org/10.4324/9781003294115

Casey, Baroness Louise. 2023. *An Independent Review into the Standards of Behaviour and Internal Culture of the Metropolitan Police Service,* https://www.met.police.uk/SysSiteAssets/media/downloads/met/about-us/baroness-casey-review/update-march-2023/baroness-casey-review-march-2023a.pdf

Chapelan, Alexis. 2024. "Conspiracy theories". In: Becker, Matthias J., Hagen Troschke, Matthew Bolton and Alexis Chapelan (eds). *Decoding Antisemitism: A Guide to Identifying Antisemitism Online.* London: Palgrave Macmillan, https://link.springer.com/book/9783031492372

Chapelan, Alexis. 2024. "Repulsiveness and dehumanisation". In: Becker, Matthias J., Hagen Troschke, Matthew Bolton and Alexis Chapelan (eds). *Decoding Antisemitism: A Guide to Identifying Antisemitism Online.* London: Palgrave Macmillan, https://link.springer.com/book/9783031492372

Chapelan, Alexis. 2024. "Taboo of criticism". In: Becker, Matthias J., Hagen Troschke, Matthew Bolton and Alexis Chapelan (eds). *Decoding Antisemitism: A Guide to Identifying Antisemitism Online.* London: Palgrave Macmillan, https://link.springer.com/book/9783031492372

Chapelan, Alexis, Laura Ascone, Matthias J. Becker, Matthew Bolton, Pia Haupeltshofer, Jan Krasni, Alexa Krugel, Helena Mihaljević, Karolina Placzynta, Milena Pustet, Marcus Scheiber, Elisabeth Steffen, Hagen Troschke, Victor Tschiskale, Chloé Vincent. 2023. *Decoding Antisemitism: An AI-driven study on hate speech and imagery online. Discourse Report 5.* Technische Universität Berlin. Centre for Research on Antisemitism, https://doi.org/10.14279/depositonce-17105

Cho, Sumi, Kimberlé Williams Crenshaw and Leslie McCall. 2013. "Toward a field of intersectionality studies: Theory, applications, and praxis". *Signs: Journal of Women in Culture and Society,* 38 (4): 785–810, https://doi.org/10.1086/669608

Creative Community for Peace. 2019. *Press Release: Celebrities and Entertainment Industry Leaders Speak out in Favor of Eurovision and Against Cultural Boycott,* https://www.creativecommunityforpeace.com/blog/2019/04/30/celebrities-and-entertainment-industry-leaders-speak-out-against-israel-eurovision-boycott/

Drake, Susanna. 2013. *Slandering the Jew: Sexuality and Difference in Early Christian Texts*. Philadelphia, PA: University of Pennsylvania Press, https://doi.org/10.1017/s0364009414000105

Ging, Debbie and Eugenia Siapera. 2018. "Special issue on online misogyny". *Feminist Media Studies, 18* (4): 515–524, https://doi.org/10.1080/14680777.2018.1447345

Harp, Dustin. 2019. *Gender in the 2016 US Presidential Election: Trump, Clinton, and Media Discourse*. Abingdon: Routledge, https://doi.org/10.4324/9781315167916

Hübscher, Monika and Sabine Von Mering (eds). 2022. *Antisemitism on Social Media*. Abingdon: Routledge, https://doi.org/10.4324/9781003200499

Jane, Emma Alice. 2014. "'Back to the Kitchen, Cunt': Speaking the Unspeakable About Online Misogyny". *Continuum, 28* (4): 558–570, https://doi.org/10.1080/10304312.2014.924479

Jane, Emma Alice. 2016. *Misogyny Online: A Short (and Brutish) History*. London: Sage, https://doi.org/10.4135/9781473916029

Keiles, Jamie Lauren. 2018. "Reconsidering the Jewish American princess". In: *Social Critics and Social Criticism series, Vox*, https://www.vox.com/the-goods/2018/12/5/18119890/jewish-american-princess-jap-stereotype

Krasni, Jan. 2024. "Immorality". In: Becker, Matthias J., Hagen Troschke, Matthew Bolton and Alexis Chapelan (eds). *Decoding Antisemitism: A Guide to Identifying Antisemitism Online*. London: Palgrave Macmillan, https://link.springer.com/book/9783031492372

Krook, Mona Lena. 2022. "Semiotic Violence Against Women: Theorizing Harms Against Female Politicians". *Signs: Journal of Women in Culture and Society, 47* (2), 371–397, https://www.journals.uchicago.edu/doi/10.1086/716642

Lawrence, David, Limor Simhony-Philpott and Danny Stone. 2021. *Antisemitism and Misogyny: Overlap and Interplay*, https://antisemitism.org.uk/wp-content/uploads/2021/09/Antisemitism-and-Misogyny-Overlap-and-Interplay.pdf

Menegatti, Micheal and Monica Rubini. 2017. "Gender bias and sexism in language". *Oxford Research Encyclopedia of Communication*. Oxford: Oxford University Press, https://doi.org/10.1093/acrefore/9780190228613.013.470

Oboler, Andre. 2021. "Solving antisemitic hate speech in social media through a global approach to local action". In: Lange, Armin, Kerstin Mayerhofer, Dina Porat and Lawrence H. Schiffman (eds). *An End to Antisemitism! Confronting Antisemitism in Modern Media, The Legal and Political Worlds*. Berlin: De Gruyter: 343–368, https://doi.org/10.1515/9783110671964-022

Pellegrini, Ann. 1997. "Whiteface performances: Race, gender, and Jewish bodies". In: Jonathan Boyarin and Daniel Boyarin (eds). *Jews and Other Differences: The New Jewish Cultural Studies*. Minneapolis, MN: University of Minnesota Press, 108–149, https://doi.org/10.4324/9781315475615-27

Placzynta, Karolina. 2024a. "Blood libel/child murder". In: Becker, Matthias J., Hagen Troschke, Matthew Bolton and Alexis Chapelan (eds). *Decoding Antisemitism: A Guide to Identifying Antisemitism Online*. London: Palgrave Macmillan, https://link.springer.com/book/9783031492372

Placzynta, Karolina. 2024b. "Jewish privilege and the 'free pass'". In: Becker, Matthias J., Hagen Troschke, Matthew Bolton and Alexis Chapelan (eds). *Decoding Antisemitism: A Guide to Identifying Antisemitism Online*. London: Palgrave Macmillan, https://link.springer.com/book/9783031492372

Ravits, Martha A. 2000. "The Jewish mother: Comedy and controversy in American popular culture". *Melus*, 25 (1): 3–31, https://doi.org/10.2307/468149

Rindisbacher, Hans. 2018. "The dangerous belle juive". *The European Legacy, 23* (6): 692–697, https://doi.org/10.1080/10848770.2018.1461777

Scheiber, Marcus. 2024. "Relativisation and denial of antisemitism". In: Becker, Matthias J., Hagen Troschke, Matthew Bolton and Alexis Chapelan (eds). *Decoding Antisemitism: A Guide to Identifying Antisemitism Online*. London: Palgrave Macmillan, https://link.springer.com/book/9783031492372

Schüler-Springorum, Stefanie 2018. "Gender and the politics of anti-semitism". *The American Historical Review*, 123 (4): 1210–1222

Schwarz-Friesel, Monika. 2020. "'Antisemitism 2.0'—The spreading of Jew-hatred on the World Wide Web". In: Lange, Armin et al. (eds). *Volume 1: Comprehending and Confronting Antisemitism: A Multi-Faceted Approach*. Berlin: De Gruyter: 311–338, https://doi.org/10.1515/9783110618594-026

Stögner, Karin. 2014. *Antisemitismus und Sexismus. Historisch-gesellschaftliche Konstellationen*. Baden-Baden: Nomos, https://doi.org/10.5771/9783845257389

Stögner, Karin. 2020. "Intersectionality and antisemitism—A new approach". *Fathom*, https://fathomjournal.org/intersectionality-and-antisemitism-a-new-approach/

The Guardian. 2019. "The BBC should press for Eurovision to be moved from Israel". *The Guardian*, https://www.theguardian.com/tv-and-radio/2019/jan/29/the-bbc-should-press-for-eurovision-to-be-moved-from-israel

Thomas, Ebony Elizabeth, Autumn A. Griffin and S. R. Toliver. 2023. "Intersectionality and discourse analysis". In: Handford, Michael and James Paul Gee (eds). *The Routledge Handbook of Discourse Analysis*. Abingdon: Routledge: 217–230, https://doi.org/10.4324/9781003035244-18

Vickery, Jacqueline Ryan and Tracy Everbach. 2018. *Mediating Misogyny*. London: Palgrave Macmillan, https://doi.org/10.1007/978-3-319-72917-6

Vincent, Chloé and Matthew Bolton. 2024. "Denial of Israel's right to exist". In: Becker, Matthias J., Hagen Troschke, Matthew Bolton and Alexis Chapelan (eds). *A Guide to Identifying Antisemitism Online*. London: Palgrave Macmillan, https://link.springer.com/book/9783031492372

Sources

Rachel Riley

GUARD-FB[20190430], *The Guardian* (30 April 2019). "An affront to both Palestinians and Israelis", https://www.facebook.com/theguardian/posts/pfbid037GxAG75YHcKWrj1Vp4jhjyMNPL6ohD3s WVRPWyhPkWusvgLEanmWkcgtSxXvQ6Egl

INDEP-FB[20190430] *The Independent* (30 April 2019). "Stephen Fry, Sharon Osbourne, and Marina Abramović are among the celebrities who have signed the open letter", https://www.facebook.com/TheIndependentOnline/posts/pfbid02snu5S34Y5ArfkohiqLLXWn1jEX6KWkrP6q 3b4KRmTkHV6xycVcwYRfR8GGHYsY5Gl

METRO-FB[20190519] *The Metro* (19 May 2019). "As their points were announced during the results, the band were seen on camera holding up the Palestinian flag and banners reading Palestine", https://www.facebook.com/MetroUK/posts/pfbid02Xz1SK yFTdM8CrmUoDyVmksRVogmWoeZK ruwCr8DB4zV9furksHi11TNCa3JU9Zmil

SPECT-FB[20190506] *The Spectator* (6 May 2019). "The fact is this boycott singles out Israelis for collective punishment [...]", https://www.facebook.com/Spectator1828/posts/pfbid02oy6KXBZAiN1puspa8Uz3NVjFMH85jzqCc3E6Mnve Ni48nwRUv11TDyGoEmNoDyjVl

Sally Rooney

INDEP-FB[20211012] *The Independent* (12 October 2021). "Several prominent figures from across the arts world have previously committed to a cultural boycott of Israel, in support of Palestine", https://www.facebook.com/TheIndependentOnline/posts/10159739501741636

MAIL[20211013] *Mail Online* (13 October 2021). "Israel accuses 'narrow-minded' Sally Rooney of 'impeding peace' and backing a campaign 'tainted with anti-Semitism' [...]", https://www.dailymail.co.uk/news/article-10087177/Normal-People-author-Sally-Rooney-accused-impeding-peace-Middle-East-translation-row.html

SPECT-FB[20211014] *The Spectator* (14 October 2021). "Rooney has been lionised by the left, which hates Israel with a venom that is, to most normal human beings, out of all proportion", https://www.facebook.com/Spectator1828/posts/5027556697273893

TEL[20211012] The Telegraph (12 October 2021). "Sally Rooney, the acclaimed Irish author, has reportedly refused to allow her new novel to be published in Hebrew", https://www.facebook.com/TELEGRAPH.CO.UK/ posts/10160351205049749

Diane Abbott

(BBC-TW[20230424]) *BBC News* (24 April 2023). "Diane Abbott's comments were antisemitic, Labour leader Keir Starmer says", https://twitter.com/ BBCNews/status/1650530828923854849

(BBC-FB[20230504]) *BBC News* (23 April 2024). "Her suspension comes pending an investigation into a letter she wrote about racism for the Observer newspaper, the party has said", https://www.facebook.com/ bbcnews/posts/pfbid036msV7GGEtnxMM27UBi7cFgU1bcNvJGgh6y54 PDx5qgxuUv3iqHZ2yTqHd5bit5oZl

(EXPR[20230424]) *Daily Express* (24 April 2023). "The Nazis were clear about racism Diane, maybe you should be too", https://www.express.co.uk/ comment/expresscomment/1761792/Diane-Abbot-letter-racism-observer- jewish-people-antisemitism-holocaust-red-hair

TIMES-FB[20211012] The Times (12 October 2021). "Sally Rooney, the acclaimed author of Normal People, has refused to allow her new novel to be published in Hebrew [...]", https://www.facebook.com/ timesandsundaytimes/posts/ pfbid02M9h8cDCWMNwo8fid1H3q6HVwVKMc5Jgs 17CX8tY6RWTpru7GtSGk8eTZvN4v3sY8L

2. Jordan Peterson and Conservative Antisemitism Online

The Dethroning of an Intellectual Icon Following His Interview with Netanyahu

Matthias J. Becker

You Either Die a Hero, or You Live Long Enough to See Yourself Become the Villain[1]

The age of digitalisation is characterised by an explosion of information as well as opinion exchange, but also by uncertainty and disorientation. In view of the polyphony of speakers and multitude of information, many web users tend to orient themselves to a range of new opinion leaders who could not have established their huge visibility prior to the era of the interactive web. Jordan Peterson, a former psychology professor, embodies perfectly the new 'globalised' public intellectual surrounded by a bevy of followers.

In December 2022, Peterson interviewed Israel's Prime Minister Benjamin Netanyahu. The reactions of web users were numerous and—in stark contrast to the bulk of Peterson's contributions—clearly negative. Peterson's fascination with

---

1   User comment extracted from the analysed YouTube thread.

    https://doi.org/10.11647/OBP.0406.02

political heavyweights or strongmen is nothing new. Here, however, he provided a forum to one of the world's best-known Jewish figures and the representative of the Jewish state.

Peterson and Netanyahu's conversation seems to have triggered various antisemitic ideas among those with a far-right worldview. However, many of the comments seem to come from the conservative online milieu to which Peterson belongs. The online thread discussing the clip thus forms a symbolic arena for proximity and friction between conservative and alt-right milieus in relation to Jew-hatred—a relationship that is not given enough space in the media and in academic analysis, as the focus is too often on the confrontation between the left and the alt-right and white-supremacy milieus.

This paper qualitatively examines the commenters' diverse reactions—of disillusionment and reorientation, but also of their devaluation and exclusion of a former idol—identified in the corresponding *YouTube* comments section and reconstructs the underlying concepts in a pragma-linguistic framework.

1. Introduction

This chapter presents the case study examining *YouTube* comments on Jordan Peterson's interview with Israeli Prime Minister Benjamin Netanyahu. On 5 December 2022, the 1.5-hour conversation was uploaded to Peterson's *YouTube* channel.[2] Within two months, it was viewed at least 1.2 million times; almost 44,700 comments were counted. The assessment of many critics that the conservative public intellectual[3] made a serious strategic mistake with this interview is reflected in the

---

2   "Israel's Right to Exist? | PM-Elect Benjamin Netanyahu | EP 311", *YouTube*, video uploaded by Jordan B. Peterson, 5 December 2022, https://www.youtube.com/ watch?v=4OcaMRLTyGI. By 23 June 2023, the clip had been viewed 1,502,444 times; moreover, *YouTube* showed 44,811 comments, i.e. almost no increase from February, which may be due to intensive content moderation. The dataset for the analysis presented here was secured at the end of February.

3   On the changes in the status of the 'public intellectual' in the digital age, where traditional epistemological gatekeepers (such as universities, publishing houses, etc.) have eroded considerably, see Dahlgren 2012, https://doi.org/10.1007/ s10767-012-9124-5; Miller 2020; Peters 2022, https://doi.org/10.1080/00071005.20 22.2141859, and Basaure, Joignant and Théodore 2023, https://doi.org/10.1007/ s10767-022-09417-y; see also Chapelan in this volume.

ratio of up- to downvotes below the line of the clip, as well as in various irritated statements by viewers highlighting the contrast with previous contributions, such as: "28k upvotes, 67k downvotes [...] interesting to see a negative ratio for the votes on a Jordan Peterson video".

The viewers' negative attitude towards the interview may come as a surprise, as Peterson is a dazzling figure of the conservative milieu in the online sphere. Most of his clips are regularly celebrated in the community, and he is constantly praised for his ability to convey complex ideas with simplicity and persuasiveness (compatible with the conditions of social media discourse). His popularity is explained by the explosion of pop culture and lifestyle influencers—a trend that also affects the status of public intellectuals. New ways of constructing intellectual authority have emerged, sometimes complementary, sometimes in opposition to traditional institutions such as universities, think tanks or major publishing houses. Peterson, a former psychology professor, embodies perfectly this new 'globalised' public intellectual. His no-nonsense self-help content has also been increasingly embraced, in particular, interestingly, by young, white, heterosexual men. In this way, Peterson became a driving force in anchoring conservative ideas throughout mainstream discourse. With this contextual knowledge, the interview should not really have created an uproar, because, all in all, Peterson's position sits quite comfortably with what the hardline conservative position in North America: pro-Israeli, nationalistic (seeing the Israeli right's unabashed embrace of nationalism as a model for the West) and anti-Iran (some might even say suspicious of Islam as a whole). Peterson, because of his conservative leanings,[4] looks favourably on the brand of religious ethnonationalism Netanyahu advances. He has expressed sympathy for Hungary's Viktor Orbán and Poland's PiS [Law and Justice] party on similar grounds before.

Additionally, over the years, Peterson has gradually become a resolutely right-wing media figure, harbouring controversial positions on Islam, rejecting feminism[5] and 'cultural Marxism' and serving as a mouthpiece for anti-progressive thought.

---

4   Jordan Peterson is considered part of the *Intellectual Dark Web*, a broader movement against the perceived political correctness and multiculturalism (Kelsey 2020, https://doi.org/10.1007/978-3-030-55038-7_7, Finlayson 2021, https://doi.org/10.1177/02632764211036731).

5   "Jordan Peterson debate on the gender pay gap, campus protests and postmodernism", *YouTube*, video uploaded by Channel 4 News, 16 January 2018,

Despite these observations, the downvotes mentioned above and the analysis presented on the following pages prove that Peterson's assumption about his audience's generally favourable attitude towards the Israeli prime minister was hasty. Unlike most of the posts, podcasts, interviews and debates with which Peterson has been involved, this event showcases a clear break in his media record and a chasm between the influencer and his followers. Many commenters see this manoeuvre as a turning point in Peterson's career, deploring that all his "good work" has gone "all up in flames" and that his followers now feel "completely lost". In contrast to these empathetic, regretful statements, tendencies of a clear and highly emotional rejection of Peterson set the tone in large parts of the *YouTube* comment section—and these objections are in many cases underpinned by Jew-hatred.

The material here suggests that the reason for this response could be that, while conservatives today tend to point to their support for Israel as evidence of their lack of antisemitism, political affiliation is often perceived as an elite-only affair. Denying antisemitism in that spectrum ignores the fundamental realisation that hostility towards Jews is a phenomenon that affects society as a whole and does not stop at any political milieu.[6] As a hate ideology, antisemitism is persistent and corrosive enough to break the bonds in any particular context (even those between an idolised influencer and his flock). Another cause may be that, in line with Peterson's aforementioned role as a public (and very successful) mouthpiece for anti-progressive worldviews, Peterson has been accused of accelerating the mainstreaming of not only conservative but also alt-right opinions towards the general public.[7]

I see the online debate that followed the publication of the Netanyahu interview as the symbolic arena of a conflict between conservative and alt-right milieus in the US—a conflict that is not given enough space in the media and in academic analysis, as the focus has all too often been on the conflict between left or left-liberal and Trump supporters

---

https://www.youtube.com/watch?v=aMcjxSThD54

6   For this, see also the results of the Decoding Antisemitism project in relation to antisemitism in threads of conservative leaning media outlets in Britain, France and Germany, https://decoding-antisemitism.eu/publications/#discourse-reports.

7   "They think [Peterson] could be the culture war's Weapon X", see Lynskey 2018. On the mainstreaming of antisemitic worldviews in the extreme right see also Nagle 2017, Wendling 2018 and Ebner 2023.

or the alt-right and white-supremacy milieus (and in relation to antisemitism, the latter political milieus have also been discussed much more frequently). Nor are the dissenting commenters exclusively troublemakers coming from an extremist, openly anti-Jewish milieu. Rather, they are supporters of Peterson's earlier positioning, in which no devaluation or exclusion was to be found, at least not in relation to Jews. Despite this ideological basis, the interview provides a strong trigger for the reproduction of antisemitic stereotypes and, especially, conspiracy theories in various forms.

By projecting negative qualities onto Peterson, web users participate in his *desacralisation*. They enact this in the comments section in four main patterns:

a. by expressing their fundamental disappointment about Peterson's alleged lack of background knowledge, but also about his lack of authority in discussing the subject matter;

b. by alleging that Peterson is the victim of 1) a vaguely external influence or 2) a clearly JEWISH POWER;

c. by accusing Peterson of now showing his true colours. He is characterised as demonstrating traits of GREED, HYPOCRISY and, ultimately, EVIL, which in certain contexts may be understood as bringing forth antisemitic projections; and

d. by discursively excluding Peterson from the non-Jewish in-group based on his overt "judaisation".

The disavowal of a former idol, his marginalisation and exclusion by his erstwhile devoted followers, takes place linguistically in a variety of ways. In the following sections, I will present the theoretical framework and the methodological specifics applied to capture these patterns—a qualitative content analysis enriched by deductive and inductive categories drawn from the disciplines of antisemitism studies and pragma-linguistics. I will then mention quantitative specificities in this corpus analysis and, finally, discuss the qualitative results, following the main categories presented above to pre-structure my observations of the complex and lengthy online debate.

2. Dataset, theoretical framework and methodological approaches

Peterson's interview with Netanyahu was uploaded to Peterson's *YouTube* channel on 5 December 2022, with the title "Israel's Right to Exist? | PM-Elect Benjamin Netanyahu | EP 311".[8] The analysis presented here refers to this one thread, which consists of about 44,700 user comments (as of 8 February 2023).

In order to examine the discursive dynamics enabled by the interview, this case study follows the theoretical framework of web-related antisemitism studies, in which the Decoding Antisemitism research project is also embedded. Here, the research fields of applied and pragma-linguistics (as well as multimodal analysis) are combined with antisemitism research and social media studies (see Becker 2019 and 2021, Becker and Bolton 2022; see also Schwarz-Friesel and Reinharz 2017, Schwarz-Friesel 2019, and Troschke and Becker 2019).[9] The aim of this research is to make statements about the form, frequency and trends of Jew-hatred in different online milieus through detailed pattern analyses. Hence, the focus is not on individuals and groups who may be conspicuous through antisemitic communication on the internet but on a precise understanding of the communicated patterns themselves, as these are ultimately the vehicles for the spread and transmission of antisemitic ideas in society.

The Decoding Antisemitism project aims to analyse the presence and normalisation of antisemitic hate speech in socially relevant, politically moderate online milieus in Europe on the basis of large-scale pattern analyses. The case study presented here takes up this research interest and the associated methodological approach but applies it to

---

8   "Israel's Right to Exist? | PM-Elect Benjamin Netanyahu | EP 311", *YouTube*, video uploaded by Jordan B. Peterson, 5 December 2022, https://www.youtube.com/watch?v=4OcaMRLTyGI

9   Due to the limited scope of this contribution, reference is made to Becker and Bolton 2022, https://doi.org/10.26613/jca/5.1.105, and to Becker and Troschke 2022, https://doi.org/10.26613/jca/5.1.100, for questions on the theoretical background, the state of research on web-related antisemitism studies and on the definitional framing and operationalisation in our research. See also the 'About' page of the Decoding Antisemitism project's website (https://decoding-antisemitism.eu/about) and its Discourse Reports linked in footnote 5.

an international discourse event[10] where the conditions (conservative interviewer, well-known Jewish interviewee) allow us to take a closer look at the relationship between conservative and right-wing milieus. To understand how far-right, openly antisemitic ideas can find their way into conservative spheres, the ideological transfer and dynamics of this thread need to be examined through a detailed study of its comments. In this respect, this case study relies almost exclusively on qualitative content analysis, in which both manifest and latent constituents of meaning are categorised and studied using very detailed classification guidelines (Mayring 2015).

Using a custom-designed tool that searches and crawls data from news websites and social media platforms, the content of the *YouTube* thread was downloaded in various data formats while maintaining its chronological and dialogic structure. A randomly-selected sample of 7,996 comments has been retained as the basis for the analysis. Wanting to include all comments that mention the word 'Peterson', I followed a mixed methods approach and started the analysis with a keyword search. The search for 'Peterson' in the corpus yielded a total of 576 hits. The ensuing qualitative content analysis focussed on a total of 791 viewer comments (about 10% of the total sample), taking into account the comments containing 'Peterson', their immediate context and relevant references to other statements. A data analysis programme for qualitative and quantitative analysis, MAXQDA, was used to examine the comments. By implementing the Decoding Antisemitism classification system in the programme, which is composed of (content-related) antisemitic as well as (form-related) linguistic and image-based categories, comments could be annotated in a systematic way, including the application of inductive categories that emerged during the study of this online debate (cf. Becker et al. 2024). The latter was crucial to the process of this case study, as the focus was not on antisemitism *per se* but on the argumentative link between Jordan Peterson and an alleged external, often Jewish factor.

---

10   The term *discourse event* refers to incidents in extra-linguistic reality, e.g., news items that have the potential to trigger antisemitic reactions in politics, conventional media as well as in web communities. In the research described here, these discourse events are used as a starting point for the focussed study of online reactions, whereby—analogous to a stimulus-response scheme—the conditions of antisemitic speech in different milieus and language communities can be reconstructed.

3. Quantitative insights

Presence of antisemitism

- Of the qualitatively analysed 791 comments, 237 comments (30%) contained at least one antisemitic concept;[11]

- In this sub-corpus, the proportion of comments in which antisemitism could be reconstructed context-free (explicit as well as implicit forms) was 38.8% (92 comments);

- The number of comments where the immediate context in the thread was needed to decode the communicated meaning— as the commenters used anaphors, for example—was 145 (61.2%).

Rejection of Peterson

- Among the 791 comments, the proportion of comments disapproving of Peterson was 67.5% (534 comments);[12]

- Here, by far the largest proportion—326 comments or 61%— showed openly verbalised disappointment with Peterson (*Group A*);

- 206 comments (or 38.6%) problematised his externally influenced victim status (*Group B*);

- 151 comments (28.3%) spoke of Peterson's "true colours" and accused him of negative character traits (*Group C*);

- And 12.2% (65 comments) constructed a Jewish identity to explain why Peterson initiated the interview or conducted it as he did (*Group D*).

---

11   As mentioned above, the qualitatively analysed comments have been pre-selected by the keyword search ('Peterson'). In this respect, the 30% are not the result of a consistent analysis of a thread excerpt but, rather, detailed analyses of comments with 'Peterson' hits as well as the immediate context and further references to previous comments.

12   Since several of the patterns described here can occur simultaneously in one comment, the total number of all patterns is higher than 534 hits.

Overlaps of antisemitism and rejection of Peterson

- The overlap with antisemitism in *Group A* was 14%;

- In *Group B*, the number of comments (explicitly or implicitly) conveying antisemitic concepts (such as JEWISH POWER or CONSPIRACY) is 34%; the comments in which no antisemitic notions could be identified were, thus, 66%;

- In *Group C*, antisemitism was (explicitly or implicitly) reproduced in combination with negative character traits projected onto Peterson in 12% of comments;

- *Group D* overlaps completely with antisemitism due to its specificity.

4. Empirical findings

4.1 A disappointing hero (*Group A*)

This section discusses statements in which commenters seem to justify their distancing from Peterson on the grounds that he has undergone a fundamental change in the context of this interview, evidenced by his uncharacteristic lack of competence and/or assertiveness and, ultimately, leading to Peterson losing respect and reputation. It must be emphasised that this first set of comments does not constitute antisemitism; however, comments such as these can often lead to antisemitic conclusions that are presented in the following sub-sections.

1. "I have never seen any of JP's videos getting such scathing reviews/comments. Jordan you have lost a lot of respect in the eyes of many of your admirors. Terrible interview no hard questions absurd theories on right to ownership and absolute free pass to Netanyahu on his corruption record. What a shame!!!"

2. "Peterson caught out, inept and out of his depth".

3. "It's a shame someone so familiar with solzhenitsyn's work could fall so hard".

4. "What do you think of Jordan Peterson after you've watched his interview with this man fully?"

5. "Everyone is noticing. Jordan Peterson has enlightened us enough that his true fans would be a mirror for him to see himself...if he wants to look".

6. (6)"People fall from grace all the time. Peterson would be correct not to give a shit about anonymous comments that boil down to trolling or shit-posting. However, when it's thousands of genuine and heartfelt messages coming from people who quite believably express they've always been a fan now come out to question Peterson's motives, why, yes of course, that should be of Jordan's concern".

In addition to direct expressions of disappointment and rejection (as in (1), (2) and (3)), the alleged fundamental change on Peterson's part becomes clear from change-indicating phrases such as "out of his depth" or "fall so hard", which suggest that Peterson used to be on a much higher intellectual level. Disapproval is also communicated indirectly via rhetorical questions—such as in (4), where the request for an evaluation of Peterson's choice to interview Netanyahu, referred to by the distancing choice of words "with this man", indicates that the commenter considers the latter's presence in this interview to be at least unsatisfactory.

Moreover, what is striking in (5) and (6) is the reversal of the relationship between Peterson and his followers. Their relationship until this point was, apparently, characterised by a hierarchical 'teacher-student dynamic' that was not called into question. As a result of the discourse event discussed here, users now more or less directly call on Peterson to take an example *from them*, to reposition himself by taking the reactions and concerns of his fans to heart. Their "enlightened" status, which was ultimately triggered by Peterson (at least in part), should now serve as a point of reference for an intellectual who seems to be derailed. With the background knowledge of Peterson's earlier public presence, it can be reconstructed that what is at stake here is his restless adherence to principles and an idealistic search for truth that does not stop at authority and oppressive (or at least hindering) centres of power.

In various statements, commenters ironically question this former reputation of Peterson by saying: "Mr. Truth-Seeker Peterson" or "Mr. Speak-Truth-To-Power Peterson". It is precisely this search for truth that, in their opinion, is absent from this interview. With formulations such as "You are the one who has changed. We are just noticing", Peterson's followers seem to have his decaying integrity firmly in view.

The counter-figure who, according to various commenters, captivates and provides support through loyalty, sincerity and rebellion against power is, significantly, the musician and influencer Kanye West. In the preceding months, he had made headlines for his pun-laden antisemitic DEATH WISHES and CONSPIRACY THEORIES (ADL 2022, Wilson 2022, Solomon 2023), provoking antisemitism in all kinds of online contexts (see Chapelan et al. 2023 and Chapelan in this volume). According to the commenters, West—also known as Ye—would provide guidance because he could see behind the scenes and would not shy away from reality. By openly endorsing West and his views, these comments, in contrast to those discussed in the first part of this section, can be classified as clearly antisemitic:

7. "bring back kanye the truth teller"

8. "God bless Ye. The truth is a lonely warrior".

9. "Ye has opened a lot of people's eyes to what is really going on. Peterson fawning all over an Israeli politician isn't going to change that".

10. "Who would have thought a year ago that Kanye had more wisdom, courage and insight than Jordan Peterson? What a crazy world we live in. Respect to you Ye!"

11. "So disappointed to see my intellectual godfather sitting there like statue. No questioning the right or wrong. I would just go and listen to Kanye West speak the truth".

The commenters do not always clearly embed their disappointment with Peterson in a larger framework, as they leave semantic and conceptual gaps concerning what brought about Peterson's change of direction. However, the multiple positive references to West and the knowledge of his explosive statements at the time easily allows for a reconstruction in which public figures such as Peterson and West are understood as being driven by (or at least directing their focus towards) JEWISH CENTRES OF POWER. The commenters consider how differently the two react to these to be very revealing. In the following section, the notion of Peterson bowing to power is more clearly verbalised. The unspecified notion is then followed by antisemitic constructions, as users refer to an external influence compatible with or supported by ideas of a JEWISH LOBBY or STRING-PULLERS in the background.

4.2 The intellectual as a victim of an outside power (*Group B1*)

The questioning of Peterson's authority or intellectual desacralisation discussed in 4.1 becomes more evident in those comments in which users explicate, to a greater or lesser extent, the presumed external cause of his change of direction. According to such comments, it is not a causeless, random re- or disorientation. Peterson is not suffering from a self-inflicted moral or intellectual weakness but, rather, a victim status they assume to be part of the larger, (sometimes) invisible power structures that prompted him to conduct the interview. Such claims can be communicated in an extremely subtle way, for example, by simply expressing irritation, as in "Jordan you really have blinders on for this particular issue. I wonder why?" or "Jordan B Peterson didn't use his full guns on this debate,...strange". Alternatively, commenters speak more clearly of a hierarchical relationship—albeit with an unknown counterpart:

12. "Good job jordi . Even your worst enemies wouldn't have dreamed of seeing you next to this person, and we all know that you can't twist the realty ,It will snap back at any Moment (that's what you taught us)..., Anyway... don't worry, you were the most and only agreeable Pe'te'rson on the show, the talk-show Host kind of JP and not the Professor , did exactly what was supposed to do, and never bit the hand that fed you"

In this statement, the commenter uses irony and malice to effectively express his rejection of Peterson's role in this discourse event. The criticism—apart from the already mentioned point of betrayal of Peterson's behavioural maxims, which occurs increasingly in the thread—is mainly based on the insinuation that the public intellectual would implement this betrayal in submissive accordance with a script or guideline that was imposed on him by an external power. Similar metaphorical phrases, some of them dehumanising, such as "He's simply a dog that refuses to bite the hand that feeds it", are a popular rhetorical device in the thread in order to sloganise Peterson's obedience. This idea is also expressed in the following statements:

13. "this is not shocking as he is just following orders"

14. "JP knows who his master is".

15. "Whoever "forced" you to host this murderer has damaged your image and reputation Dr. Peterson".

16. "My first thought..... JP is compromised"

Here, comments conceptualise Peterson as, on one hand, a simple recipient of orders, someone who was "forced" to act; on the other hand, they portray him as simply compromised. In either case, his behaviour is framed as contrary to what is expected of him. The comments specify the opposition, that is, the centre of power from which this forced reorientation emanates, only vaguely, in the frame of passive constructions or by general, ambiguous terms as in (14)—the site of power will be articulated in the following contributions.

4.3 The intellectual as a victim of JEWISH POWER (Group B2)

Examples in this group name the external power with sufficient specificity that their comments do not remain in the communicative grey area, but can be counted as part of the repertoire of antisemitic constructions.

17. "Peterson went from biblical lectures to being in bed with Satan Now that's a plot twist 😂".

18. "I was very excited and intrigued to see how Jordan Peterson was going to investigate and challenge many of the repulsive ideas but this was a big disappointment. Eventually everyone must bow down to their bosses and we all know who controls media".

19. "we are simply pointing out the idiocy of Peterson. And yes, I do get jumpscared when a mighty nose appears from around the corner".

In (17), Peterson's interviewee is identified as the devil. With this reference, the user means Netanyahu himself (and not, as in 4.2, an ominous lobby operating in the dark). Thus, the driving force behind Peterson's repositioning is the interviewee, who is demonised in a historically charged way. Even if the reference to "Satan" is used here as a characterisation of a politician (which could generally be understood as sharp criticism *ad hominem*), it must be taken into account that references to the DEVIL are a popular characteristic of antisemitism throughout its history (Trachtenberg 2002, Bolton 2024). Its hyperbolic mode of action leaves the ground of justified (neutral, but also harsh) criticism since, firstly, it is directed against a person whose Jewish identity and role as representative of the Jewish state are known worldwide; and secondly, the notion activated by such demonising hyperboles dichotomously divides the world into good and evil, with the figure of the *Devil*, *Satan* or *Shaytan* as the fundamental evil and climax of evil among monotheistic religions. Conceptualising Netanyahu in this sense as a universal EVIL potentially establishes the construction of an antisemitic image in the framing of which Peterson plays the role of a subjugated bedfellow.

In (18), the reference to the centre of power through "bosses" remains similarly vague as in (14), which militates against a hasty classification of the comment as antisemitic. However, the last turn in the comment indirectly reproduces the stereotype of JEWISH POWER (in the form of assumed media control). It insinuates an unspecified bias in the media that can be traced back to one or two corporations, and the reading of an antisemitic stereotype arises from the general context—namely, that Peterson interviews a Jewish person and, according to the comment, "bow[s] down" in the process. In (19), the commenter accuses Peterson of "idiocy", which they contrast, however, with the feeling of fear, whereby this admission almost reads like a justification of the lack on Peterson's side. The originator of this fear felt by the commenter is a danger described synecdochically as a "mighty nose". The physiologically oriented imaginary devaluations of Jews—be it the long nose, the fingers that look like claws (expressing GREED), the feminine body, the stooped gait—have shaped the verbal and visual caricatures of antisemitism ever since the earliest times (see Chapelan 2024, see also Königseder 2022);[13] the deictic-metaphorical turn of phrase thus activates an antisemitic notion that memorably communicates acting in secret and causing fear. The image that sticks in the reader's mind is the idea of a foolish Peterson, but at the same time one guided by a comprehensible fear, acting out of his victim status.

In addition to insinuating a DIABOLICAL nature, POWER and specific physical characteristics, comments do not shy away from using conventions of white supremacists—as in the form of the triple parentheses:

20. A: "This one [interview] should be titled Message to Corporate 😄"
    B: "message to ((((them))))"

21. "the quality and content of Jordan's Peterson's videos sure took a (((strange))) direction after joining Daily Wire"

These brackets, also known as *echoes*, are typically used as semiotic markers to implicitly identify, deride and exclude Jews (Fleishman and Smith 2016). In (20), A claims that Peterson serves certain economic interests—a contextual form of antisemitism, as the implied idea of 'pleasing Israel' (due to the interview) is read as a positive message to "Corporate", which, in turn, corresponds to the classic trope of SERVILITY or close ties of the financial sector to Jews. B, then, breaks the context-depending ambiguity by resorting to the rather unequivocal device of echoes and thus evaluating the interview as Peterson's attempt to align himself with the Jewish out-group. (21) initially only voices criticism of what the commenter sees as the qualitatively questionable orientation of Peterson's most recent contributions. Via the specific use of semiotic markers, the characterisation of the realignment that is imputed to Peterson as "strange" coincides with the imputed triggers (or driving force) for this change. Another implicit reference to the Jewish community is enacted through the mention of the *Daily Wire*, a

---

13   In the analysed thread, this antisemitic concept even goes as far as one comment calling himself a "nose noticer". Not only do racist tropes appear in their comments, but also holocaust denial and instrumentalisation in the form of puns directed at other users: "Your religion Holohoax". Moreover, in response to counter speech from obviously Jewish commenters, remarks such as "No one is reading that nose", "Noseberg" or "hand rubbing and big nose intensifies" appear.

conservative news website headed by Ben Shapiro, a Jewish American vocal supporter of Israel. Snide jokes also express Peterson's alleged subservience to the Jewish community:

22. "Next Peterson book, 'Seven More Rules for Life: How to be a Noahide Goy'"

This, on one hand, is an allusion to Peterson's bestseller *12 Rules for Life: An Antidote to Chaos*, through which, in addition to his online appearances, the author gained fame and popularity. The variation, on the other hand, activates a second allusion: The "seven more rules" refers to the "Seven Noahide Laws", also known as the "Noahide Laws". In Judaism, these represent a set of universal moral laws given by God as a covenant with Noah. This comment thus indirectly presents Peterson as a mouthpiece of Judaism. The recourse to the term "goy" as a pejorative (and sarcastic) designation for a non-Jew, which is also often used in far-right repertoires (for example, by the neo-Nazi *Goyim Defense League* or *Goyim TV*), clearly suggests that Peterson himself is not part of the Jewish in-group but a mere servant. This connects back to the idea of Peterson being a (consenting) victim of JEWISH POWER, an argument that destroys his reputation for intellectual agency and assertiveness.[14]

Another notable response from the thread, in which Peterson's submissiveness is implied, is the reframing and revaluation of a past scene against the backdrop of the clip discussed here. "I can't do it" is used several times to allude to another public event in 2019 in which Peterson was asked during a Q&A whether he believed Jews were taking advantage of their perceived powerful position in US politics and media to retaliate against "Europe and Russia who have a history of expelling Jews".[15] In response to this question, Peterson turned away and signalled to the audience—non-verbally, by means of posture but

---

14   Indirect references to Jews crop up constantly in the thread, including in compounds such as "tinyhatbergs", alluding to the kippah, the cap traditionally worn by Jewish men, and the typically Jewish name ending *-berg*. These reinforce the implied reference to the Jewish out-group and its relation to Peterson.

15   "Jordan Peterson Asked to Answer the Jewish Question: 'I Can't Do It'", *YouTube*, video uploaded by RexMode, 31 January 2018, https://www.youtube.com/watch?v=mbZZyVyEHGo; see also: [username], "Jordan Peterson said 'I can't do it' when asked about Jewish Influence. I wonder why that is", *Reddit*, 16 May 2019, https://www.reddit.com/r/JordanPeterson/comments/bpixpr/jordan_peterson_said_i_cant_do_it_when_asked.

also through a long pause of silence, as well as, subsequently, using irony—that he considered the question to express a resentful and distorted worldview that has no place in the public debate. After several half-hearted attempts to deconstruct this worldview, Peterson finally responded with "I can't do it". Knowing the longevity and persistence of antisemitic images of POWER and CONSPIRACY in all sorts of contexts of expression, many audience members will have interpreted his response as an attempt to banish a clearly anti-Jewish admission from the public space of this event. However, the Netanyahu interview seems to have prompted commenters to reinterpret Peterson's inability to answer the question clearly as lack of permission to tell the truth or not wanting to address the so-called "Jewish question" because of his own bias. The same pattern is suggested in the following statements:

23. "Remember when Jordan Peterson would actually engage in intellectual argument rather than ad hominem smears of anyone who criticizes his hypocrisy with anonymity? Notice how Peterson will not address the JQ. All he has is sophistry"

24. "Remember the video where someone asked Jordan Peterson if the bankers are a threat to freedom, JP said no, now we know why he has that answer".

25. A: "Question. Does anyone here remember when an audience member asked Matt Walsh about the large Jewish influence on gender ideology and Matt basically just stared down at the floor and insulted the guy? I think that playing that sort of game, as many conservatives do, is what has allowed for this whole Kanye thing to occur. If conservatives were not so spineless and willing to hold all groups equally accountable we would have no need for Kanye's theatrics". B: "They cry out in pain as they strike you".

The statement in (23) paints the picture of Peterson's avoidance strategy as soon as the Jewish Question ("JQ") is addressed. In (24), the commenter seems to accuse Peterson of continuous submissive behaviour in his dealings with both bankers and Netanyahu, thus establishing an equivalence between the two distinct groups—Israel and "the bankers"—ostensibly read from Peterson's attitude. This indirectly activates the antisemitic CONSPIRACY MYTH that the two are allied and that

Peterson would be obedient to both parties.[16] In (25), reference is first made to the (right-wing) political commentator Matt Walsh, who is said to have a similarly biased approach. The bias, according to the comment, is a specific feature of the conservative spectrum in the USA that thinks Jews enjoy special treatment—a defect that was only brought into focus by the Kanye West scandal. User B responds by reproducing a popular line among white nationalists and antisemitic milieus. It is based on a proverb that translates as "The Jew cries out in pain as he strikes you" and has become a popular antisemitic slogan in the context of the subreddit 'TheDonald'.[17] Underpinning it is the idea that Jews claim to be victims of an act because they secretly want to harm the non-Jewish in-group.

The bias and lack of demanded responses addressing the role of Jews in world affairs today are juxtaposed with commenters' own justifications and fake quotes, which further emphasise the fundamental bias on Peterson's part:

26.   A: "I must have missed your 'Message to Jews' video, you were so eager to lecture Christians and Muslims"
      B: "It will never happen unless it is some kind of apology to them for everyone else's shortcomings".

27.   "Jordan Peterson be like: 'We must secure the existence of our people and a future for jewish children.'"

28.   "JP: Message to the Jews – 'On behalf of the rest of the world, we are so sorry for how you've been treated. You guys are so smart, man. Sniff. We just..we just ...want to do whatever we can to help you all out. And golly, maybe just one day we'll deserve you all. Sniff.'"

---

16   Research in recent years on antisemitism in online debates related to Brexit has revealed interestingly similar indirect conflations of domains that, though separate, are interpreted differently when linked together. For example, referring to an antisemitic incident in France, a British commenter said: „And our bankers really believe that they are better off in France?" The comment is not problematic in itself, but, as part of a discourse event related to an incident directed against Jews, it establishes an equivalence relationship between the domains *Jews* and *bankers*. The negative orientation created by the linking is an example of everyday antisemitism.

17   'r/The_Donald' was a subreddit wherein participants created discussions and Internet memes in support of former U.S. President Donald Trump.

This section shows how subtle and coded the accusation of Peterson's SERVILITY TO A JEWISH POWER is. However, such insinuations are not communicated exclusively via allusions, semiotic markers and slogans. In some places, although much less frequently comments resort to more direct patterns of communication by explicitly addressing the Jewish out-group or Israel by proxy (for example, via rhetorical questions):

29. "Peterson's great logic and analytical reasoning suspends when it comes to Israel. I wonder why"

30. "Maybe JP is being blackmailed by the jewish mafia"

4.4 The intellectual showing his true colours (*Group C*)

So far, the analysis has examined the notions of Peterson's self-inflicted incompetence on the one hand and his externally or Jew-induced victim status on the other. Next, I will briefly describe the attributions of character traits that dominate the *YouTube* thread and that identify Peterson as a self-responsible subject who has gone astray or has strong character deficits. In comments with such an orientation, corresponding statements can certainly be associated with antisemitic projections such as GREED, IMMORALITY and HYPOCRISY; however, corresponding conclusions cannot be drawn as references to Jewish identity are missing (see, by contrast, the following section).

What first stands out is the image of greed. Users claim that Peterson got carried away with the interview and other undertakings in order to enrich himself. Behind this stands the insinuation that the interview was not motivated by an interest in the Middle East conflict from an Israeli perspective but by pecuniary considerations:[18]

31. "Jordan Peterson loves money, this is what love for money does to a man".

---

18 Insinuations like these are particularly common in online comment sections about documentaries or articles that denounce conspiracy theories related to the Jewish philanthropist George Soros. The idea that Jews supposedly BENEFIT FROM SUCH CRITICISMS of hate speech directed against them is often carried by the insinuation that they were the funders of these publications (INFLUENCING PUBLIC OPINION) or want to capitalise on them (INSTRUMENTALISING ANTISEMITISM) (cf. Becker, Troschke, and Allington 2021, Becker and Troschke 2022).

32. "He was a gatekeeper from the very beginning, he never really fought globalism to begin with. Globalism is great when you're paid handsomely for just talking in to a microphone for a living".

33. "It is not worth trading your decency, intellect, truthfulness for a small amount of benefit Mr. Peterson. But it seems this one hour of podcast of yours sheds an illuminating light on many followers mind on what you truly hide deep in your heart..."

In (33), a user refers, again, to the relationship between Peterson and his followers. Although the comment's last part is semantically ambiguous as to what exactly is assumed to be at the heart of the intellectual (the feature that distinguishes him from his fans), the gap can be filled by the allusion to financial advantage in the first line ("for a small amount of benefit").

Observations of Peterson's supposed general moral depravity and mendacity, particularly with regard to his perceived withholding of empathy for the suffering of actual victims, are evident in the *YouTube* thread:

34. "I thought your tears of compassion for humanity were authentic Mr. Peterson. I felt repulsed by your apathy towards real suffering of innocent people because I have invested so much time in listening to you, reading your books, crying with you etc. Power and high status really do show ones true colors, and turns out you're not ALL THAT, after all..."

Finally, commenters claim that Peterson has not only made a pact with the evil side but represents evil itself. Here, again, are references to the devil, as mentioned earlier:

35. "'If someone says i am all good than look for the opposite, because either he is Jesus Christ and all angels combined or there is the dark side which he is hiding. Devil is somewhere.' Jordan Peterson Thank you for correcting yourself and unveiling your devil. You are no more a honest man in my opinion."

36. A: "And when, exactly, did Jordan Peterson claim he is all good?"
    B: "his reputation was like this. But now he has revealed his dark side".

In this brief overview, analysis shows that the qualities of greed, lying, immorality and wickedness attributed to Peterson are closely linked to the repertoire of antisemitic ideas. This interpretation of the discourse about a non-Jew may seem surprising, but it is underscored by other passages in the *YouTube* thread in which Peterson himself becomes the object of antisemitism.

4.5 The 'judaisation' of the interviewer (*Group D*)

The insinuation that Peterson is showing his true colours and behaving in at least morally questionable ways is, in some cases, heightened by association with clearly antisemitic terms. This section presents contributions in which Peterson is positioned as an active, self-directed actor within an alliance with a group described as Jewish, or in which he himself is characterised as Jewish.

37. A: "When do you think Jordan will realize that he is now a gatekeeper for globalism?"
    B: "Oh he knows... That's his main purpose anyway ..."

In this dialogue, A proposes a connection between the Netanyahu interview and globalism. Peterson is presented as the "gatekeeper" of the latter, while, in his role as interviewer and initiator of this media event, he is also regarded as a supporter of Netanyahu. In this respect, the two spheres of Israel's government and globalism are linked through Peterson. The comment draws an antisemitic image in which Peterson plays the role of the right-hand man of an alleged Jewish-Israeli internationalist CONSPIRACY (see also the link between "bankers" and the Israeli government in (24)). This allegation is particularly interesting in light of Peterson's positioning as a supporter of ethno-nationalism and the politicians who represent it.

38. C: "Definitely universalism. Absolutely something that Judaism preaches and pushes for the world expect for Israel".
    D: "Globalism worldwide but nationalism in Israel is what he [Peterson] wants".

In (38), two other commenters responding to the previous dialogue refer to the idea of Judaism as a promoter of "universalism"—a claim that, in accordance with the antisemitic concept of PRIVILEGE, would not apply to Israel's nationalism. This double standard is used to illustrate Peterson's alleged bias.

In addition to insinuating a close relationship between Peterson and Jews or Israel—one desired by both sides—the interviewer himself is constructed as a Jewish person. This is performed linguistically in various ways. For example, commenters use allusions to a central motif from Christian anti-Judaism:

39. "I'll respect him [Peterson] when he repents and gives up his 30 pieces of silver".

Applying cultural knowledge, the phrase "30 pieces of silver" is commonly interpreted as a reference to bribery. However, within a thread focussing on a famously Jewish person and on Peterson's involvement in allegedly whitewashing Israel's reputation, it refers to the biblical account of Judas betraying Jesus in exchange for thirty pieces of silver.[19] By invoking other sources of knowledge, the interpretation of the overarching meaning can be extended in two ways. First, the comment draws on three core concepts of Christian anti-Judaism, namely GREED, BETRAYAL and DEICIDE. Secondly, it appeals to the concept of INFLUENCE ON THE MEDIA. Both additional meanings are communicated via the applied allusion. According to the comment, Peterson indirectly becomes Judas: his role as interviewer re-enacts the latter's treachery and immorality. Moreover, use of this rhetorical device associates Netanyahu with the notion of opinion control. The implication is that Peterson can regain his reputation only if he returns the thirty pieces of silver, that is, abandons the alleged alliance with Netanyahu and/or an invisible JEWISH POWER.

Another very popular form of Peterson's 'judaising' exclusion is the rhetorical device of puns, in which the intellectual's name is changed by means of references to conventional, universally known Jewish names:

40. "Juden Peterstein"

41. "Judas Peterson"

---

19 For comparable references to Soros, see Becker, Troschke and Allington 2021, Becker and Troschke 2022.

It is striking how often users resort to irony and wit, expressing a false appreciation and support for Peterson, to emphasise the effect of the pun as well as to communicate their contempt and disdain:

42. "Juden Peterstein is my hero"

43. "Rabbi Judas Peterstein has a nice ring to it".

44. "Stop hating on my hero Juden Peterstein!"

In conjunction with these rhetorical devices, stereotypes regularly arise in which Peterson is juxtaposed with a JEWISH POWER (see 4.3) and once again exposed to ridicule:

45. "Jewdon Peterson sure won't bite the hand that feeds him".

46. "Judas Peterson; 'Yes master, please don't hurt me'"

47. "Yes, PeterSTEIN is being fairly biased in his shilling for Israel. Yes, Peterson has been quite cringe lately".

While the first two of these comments remain unspecific regarding the identity of the power, the commenter in (47) explicitly link Peterson's subservience to Israel. The concept of DUAL LOYALTY is a popular antisemitic stereotype used to indirectly accuse Jews worldwide of a SECONDARY or LACK OF LOYALTY TO THEIR OWN (US, British, German, etc.) HOMELAND and a (too) strong ATTACHMENT TO ISRAEL (see Troschke 2024). In (47), precisely this accusation is levelled against Peterson, who was previously conceived as a Jew by means of wordplay.

Overall, the exclusion of Peterson by means of wordplay is very popular: "Peterstein" appears 33 times in this sample alone, "Judas" in combination with Peterson's name twelve times. Due to the research design of this case study, not all puns involving Peterson's name could be taken into account; the total number, including those which were not picked up by the chosen search terms, is probably much higher. Nevertheless, it is significant that, in this online milieu, these mocking rhetorical devices, which virtually turn Jewish names into swear words, find unchallenged acceptance.

5. Conclusion and outlook

This contribution examines the reactions to Jordan Peterson's interview with Israeli PM Benjamin Netanyahu in December 2022. The qualitative linguistic case study takes a closer look at about 800 viewer comments that refer directly to the interviewer by name and focuses on the overwhelming subset in which negative and even antisemitic attitudes towards the conservative, non-Jewish intellectual are voiced. It is interested in understanding how antisemitism, triggered by Netanyahu's participation, is able to break the intimate bond between influencer and followers. The analysis showed that a high number of comments from Peterson's supporters, who thus appear to be influenced by a mainstream conservative stance, contained antisemitic concepts, especially notions of JEWISH POWER and CONSPIRACY THEORIES.

The analysis is divided into four main parts that discuss two conflicting strains of response. It notes that comments, on one hand, openly express disappointment with Peterson in a sometimes Jew-hostile way and insinuate that he is acting under the influence of an imagined external, partly JEWISH POWER; on the other hand, it observes attributions of negative character traits (which, in other contexts, often serve as ingredients of antisemitic discourses) to Peterson but also statements in which Peterson himself is discursively constructed as Jewish. These phenomena take place implicitly—through semantic gaps, puns, the use of malice, irony and references to other scenarios and prominent figures—but also through directly expressed hatred.

The insults, devaluations and conspiracy theories eruptively expressed in the thread shine a light on the presence of antisemitism within the conservative camp online. They also highlight the frictions and compatibilities between this faction and the extreme right—dynamics that are far too little examined in recent research. This deficiency must be addressed through consistent analyses, this study proposes, since, especially in the USA, fragments of antisemitic conspiracy theories cultivated in the far-right end of the spectrum threaten to enter the mainstream. If allowed to do so, they will decisively determine the shape of a normalised antisemitism in large parts of society.

References

ADL (Anti-Defamation League), 2022. "5 of Kanye West's Antisemitic Remarks, Explained", https://www.ajc.org/news/5-of-kanye-wests-antisemitic-remarks-explained

Basaure, Mauro, Alfredo Joignant, and Rachel Théodore, 2023. "Public Intellectuals in Digital and Global Times". *International Journal of Politics, Culture, and Society*, 36, 139–161, https://doi.org/10.1007/s10767-022-09417-y

Becker, Matthias J., 2019. "Understanding Online Antisemitism: Towards a New Qualitative Approach". *Fathom: For a deeper understanding of Israel and the region*, 09 October 2019, https://fathomjournal.org/understanding-online-antisemitism-towards-a-new-qualitative-approach

Becker, Matthias J., 2021. *Antisemitism in Reader Comments: Analogies for Reckoning with the Past*. London: Palgrave Macmillan/Springer Nature, https://doi.org/10.1007/978-3-030-70103-1

Becker, Matthias J. and Matthew Bolton, 2022. "The Decoding Antisemitism Project—Reflections, Methods, and Goals". *Journal of Contemporary Antisemitism*, 5 (1), 121–126, https://doi.org/10.26613/jca/5.1.105

Becker, Matthias J. and Hagen Troschke, 2022. "How Users of British Media Websites Make a Bogeyman of George Soros". *Journal of Contemporary Antisemitism*, 5 (1), 49–68, https://doi.org/10.26613/jca/5.1.100

Becker, Matthias J., Hagen Troschke, and Daniel Allington, 2021. *Decoding Antisemitism: An AI-driven Study on Hate Speech & Imagery Online*. *Discourse Report 1*. Technische Universität Berlin. Centre for Research on Antisemitism, https://doi.org/10.14279/depositonce-14976

Becker, Matthias J., Hagen Troschke, Matthew Bolton, and Alexis Chapelan (eds), 2024. *Decoding Antisemitism: A Guide to Identifying Antisemitism Online*. London: Palgrave Macmillan, https://link.springer.com/book/9783031492372

Bolton, Matthew, 2024. "Evil/The Devil". In: Matthias J. Becker, Hagen Troschke, Matthew Bolton, and Alexis Chapelan (eds). *Decoding Antisemitism: A Guide to Identifying Antisemitism Online*. London: Palgrave Macmillan, https://link.springer.com/book/9783031492372

Chapelan, Alexis, 2024. "Repulsiveness and Dehumanisation". In: Matthias J. Becker, Hagen Troschke, Matthew Bolton, and Alexis Chapelan (eds). *Decoding Antisemitism: A Guide to Identifying Antisemitism Online*. London: Palgrave Macmillan, https://link.springer.com/book/9783031492372

Chapelan, Alexis, Laura Ascone, Matthias J. Becker, Matthew Bolton Pia Haupeltshofer, Jan Krasni, Alexa Krugel, Helena Mihaljević, Karolina Placzynta, Milena Pustet, Marcus Scheiber, Elisabeth Steffen,

Hagen Troschke, Victor Tschiskale, and Chloé Vincent, 2023. *Decoding Antisemitism: An AI-driven Study on Hate Speech and Imagery Online*. *Discourse Report 5*. Technische Universität Berlin. Centre for Research on Antisemitism, https://doi.org/10.14279/depositonce-17105

Dahlgren, Peter, 2012. "Public Intellectuals, Online Media, and Public Spheres: Current Realignments". *International Journal of Politics, Culture, and Society*, 25 (4), 95–110, https://doi.org/10.14279/depositonce-17105

Ebner, Julia, 2023. *Going Mainstream: How Extremists are Taking Over*. London: Bonnier Books

Finlayson, Alan, 2021. "Neoliberalism, the Alt-Right and the Intellectual Dark Web". *Theory, Culture & Society*, 38 (6), 167–190, https://doi.org/10.1177/02632764211036731

Fleishman, Cooper and Anthony Smith, 2016. (((Echoes))), "Exposed: The Secret Symbol Neo-Nazis Use to Target Jews Online" [archive]. *Mic*, 1 June 2016, https://www.mic.com/articles/144228/echoes-exposed-the-secret-symbol-neo-nazis-use-to-target-jews-online

Kelsey, Darren, 2020. "Archetypal Populism: The 'Intellectual Dark Web' and the 'Peterson Paradox'". In: Michael Kranert (ed.). *Discursive Approaches to Populism Across Disciplines*. London: Palgrave Macmillan, 171–198, https://doi.org/10.1007/978-3-030-55038-7_7

Königseder, Angelika, 2022. "Arthur Langerman's Collection of Visual Antisemitica at the Center for Research on Antisemitism, Technische Universität Berlin". In: Dossin, Kazerne (ed). *#FakeImages. Unmask the Dangers of Stereotypes*, Metropol, 108–112

Lynskey, Dorian, 2018. "How dangerous is Jordan B Peterson, the rightwing professor who 'hit a hornets' nest'?". *The Guardian*, 7 February 2018, https://www.theguardian.com/science/2018/feb/07/how-dangerous-is-jordan-b-peterson-the-rightwing-professor-who-hit-a-hornets-nest

Mayring, Philipp, 2015. "Qualitative content analysis: Theoretical background and procedures". In: *Approaches to Qualitative Research in Mathematics Education*. Dordrecht: Springer, 365–380, https://doi.org/10.1007/978-94-017-9181-6_13

Miller, Noam, 2020. "Public Intellectuals in the Digital Age". *The Prog*, 11 January 2020, https://theprincetonprogressive.com/public-intellectuals-in-the-digital-age

Nagle, Angela, 2017. *Kill All Normies: Online Culture Wars from 4Chan and Tumblr to Trump and the Alt-Right*. Winchester: Zero Books

Peters, Michael A., 2022. "Public intellectuals, viral modernity and the problem of truth". *British Journal of Educational Studies*, 70 (5), 557–573, https://doi.org/10.1080/00071005.2022.2141859

Rich, Dave, 2016. *The Left's Jewish Problem. Jeremy Corbyn, Israel and anti-Semitism.* Hull: Biteback Publishing

Schwarz-Friesel, Monika, 2019. "'Antisemitism 2.0'—The Spreading of Jew-hatred on the World Wide Web'. In: Lange, Armin et al. (eds). *Volume 1: Comprehending and Confronting Antisemitism: A Multi-Faceted Approach.* Berlin: De Gruyter, 311–338, https://doi.org/10.1515/9783110618594-026

Schwarz-Friesel, Monika and Jehuda Reinharz, 2017. *Inside the Antisemitic Mind: The Language of Jew-hatred in Contemporary Germany.* Waltham, MA: Brandeis University Press, https://doi.org/10.26530/oapen_625675

Solomon, Daniel, K., 2023. "Kanye and the new Far West of American Antisemitism". *La Revue*, 05 January 2023, https://k-larevue.com/en/kanye-and-the-new-far-west-of-american-antisemitism

Trachtenberg, Joshua, 2002. *The Devil and the Jews: The Medieval Conception of the Jew and Its Relation to Modern Anti-Semitism.* Philadelphia, PA: Jewish Publication Society

Troschke, Hagen, 2024. "Disloyalty, Dual Loyalty". In: Matthias J. Becker, Hagen Troschke, Matthew Bolton, and Alexis Chapelan (eds). *Decoding Antisemitism: A Guide to Identifying Antisemitism Online.* London: Palgrave Macmillan, https://link.springer.com/book/9783031492372

Troschke, Hagen and Matthias J. Becker, 2019. "Antisemitismus im Internet. Erscheinungsformen, Spezifika, Bekämpfung". In: Jikeli, Günther/ Glöckner, Olaf (eds). *Das neue Unbehagen. Antisemitismus in Deutschland heute.* Hildesheim: Olms, 151–172

Wendling, Mike, 2018. *Alt-Right: From 4Chan to the White House.* London: Pluto Press

Wilson, Jason, 2022. "Kanye's Antisemitic Hate Speech Platformed by Enablers in Tech, Media, Politics", Southern Poverty Law Center, 7 December 2022, https://www.splcenter.org/hatewatch/2022/12/07/kanyes-antisemitic-hate-speech-platformed-enablers-tech-media-politics

3. 'Pop' Antisemitism and Deviant Communities

An Analysis of French Social Media Users' Reactions to the Dieudonné (2020) and Kanye West (2022) Antisemitism Controversies

Alexis Chapelan

Social media platforms and the interactive web have had a significant impact on political socialisation, creating new pathways of community-building that shifted the focus from real-life, localised networks (such as unions or neighbourhood associations) to vast, diffuse and globalised communities (Finin et al. 2008, Rainie and Wellman 2012, Olson 2014, Miller 2017). Celebrities or influencers are often focal nodes for the spread of information and opinions across these new types of networks in the digital space (see Hutchins and Tindall 2021). Unfortunately, this means that celebrities' endorsement of extremist discourse or narratives can potently drive the dissemination and normalisation of hate ideologies.

This paper sets out to analyse the reaction of French social media audiences to antisemitism controversies involving pop culture celebrities. I will focus on two such episodes, one with a 'national' celebrity at its centre and the other a 'global' celebrity: the social media ban of the French-Cameroonian comedian Dieudonné M'bala M'bala in June–July 2020 and the controversy following US rapper Kanye West's spate of antisemitic statements in October–November 2022. The empirical corpus comprises over

 https://doi.org/10.11647/OBP.0406.03

4,000 user comments on *Facebook*, *YouTube* and *Twitter* (now X). My methodological approach is two-pronged: a preliminary mapping of the text through content analysis is followed by a qualitative Critical Discourse Analysis that examines linguistic strategies and discursive constructions employed by social media users to legitimise antisemitic worldviews. We lay particular emphasis on the manner in which memes, dog-whistling or coded language (such as allusions or inside jokes popular within certain communities or fandoms) are used not only to convey antisemitic meaning covertly but also to build a specific form of counter-cultural solidarity. This solidarity expresses itself in the form of "deviant communities" (see Proust et al. 2020) based on the performative and deliberate transgression of societal taboos and norms.

1. Introduction

Social media platforms and the interactive web have had a significant impact on political socialisation, creating new pathways of community-building that shifted the focus from real-life, localised networks (such as unions or neighbourhood associations) to vast, diffuse and globalised communities (Finin et al. 2008, Rainie and Wellman 2012, Olson 2014, Miller 2017). Celebrities or influencers are often focal nodes for the spread of information and opinions across these new types of networks in the digital space (Hutchin and Tindall 2021). Unfortunately, this means that celebrities' endorsement of extremist narratives can potently drive the dissemination and normalisation of hate ideologies. Not only do celebrity influencers benefit from an outsized personal media salience (Bantimaroudis 2021), which gives them an agenda-setting power; they can also leverage an affective capital from their fan communities (Mansor et al. 2020, Dong 2022). Therefore, influencers can act as "ambassadors of ideology" (Rothut et al. 2023) who bypass the gatekeeping filters of mainstream media and significantly impact the public's consumption of political information (Newman et al. 2021). However, we identify a gap in existing scientific literature concerning the role of parasocial opinion leaders in the spread of hate ideologies, with most studies focusing on the 'supply' side of the issue (Gaden and Dumitrica 2014, Stehr et al. 2015, Winter et al. 2020, Rothut et al. 2023). We aim to address this by shifting the emphasis from the vertical (top-down) agenda-setting power of celebrities to the communication strategies used by their audience across a range of social media networks (*Facebook, Twitter* (now *X*), *YouTube*) in reaction to exclusionary and discriminatory influencer communication.

This paper sets out to analyse the reaction of French social media audiences to antisemitism controversies involving pop culture celebrities. I focus on two such episodes, one with a 'national' celebrity at its centre and the other a 'global' celebrity: the social media ban of the French-Cameroonian comedian Dieudonné M'bala M'bala in June and July 2020 and the controversy following American rapper Kanye West's spate of antisemitic statements in October and November 2022. The focus on user-generated discourse and on comment sections as crucial loci of linguistic struggle (see Loke 2012, Toepfl and Piwoni 2015, Calabrese 2019, Lee et al. 2020) sheds light on the role of audience agency in the performance of 'anti-system' conspiracist and antisemitic narratives. I highlight in particular the linguistic strategies of minimisation, justification and legitimation through which social media users publicly negotiate support for pop culture figures accused of antisemitism. At the juncture of traditional Jew-hatred and pop culture, 'pop' antisemitism emerges as a novel configuration—one co-constructed top down by influencers as well as bottom up by web users from their communities, and as a major driver of hate ideology in society.

2. Methodological approach

My contribution largely builds on the methodology and the data used within the research project *Decoding Antisemitism*; however, given the smaller and more focused corpus, I rely for the analysis phrase on qualitative tools such as Critical Discourse Analysis and the Discourse Historical Approach. The empirical corpus comprises over 4,000 user comments on the *Facebook, YouTube* and *Twitter* accounts of leading French news outlets (see Table 3.1) reporting critically on Dieudonné and West's statements. My methodological approach is two-pronged. I first conduct a preliminary thematic mapping of the text through qualitative content analysis (Mayring 2015) enriched with categories from antisemitism studies, using a complex codebook developed within the Decoding Antisemitism project and comprising over 80 items derived from the International Holocaust Remembrance Alliance (IHRA)'s definition of antisemitism (IHRA 2023, Becker et al. 2024). The codebook takes into account multiple levels of analysis, such as the conceptual level (antisemitic concepts comprising stereotypes, analogies and self-references), the linguistic level (figures of speech, argumentation, etc.) and the semiotic level (punctuation, icons, emoticons, text-image relations, etc.). The qualitative content-analysis stage is followed by a more granular qualitative Critical Discourse Analysis which examines linguistic strategies and discursive constructions employed by social media users to legitimise antisemitic worldviews. Within the field of critical discourse studies, Ruth Wodak's Discourse Historical Approach (DHA) offers some of the most efficient analytical tools to systematically deconstruct such utterances (Wodak/Reisigl 2009). Building on the DHA, I have designed a framework that takes into account multiple heuristic levels of analysis, synthesised in Figure 3.1:

Dieudonné subcorpus (2020)	Kanye West subcorpus (2022)
Le Monde	Le Monde
Le Figaro	Le Figaro
Libération	Le Point
Marianne	Nouvel Obs
Valeurs Actuelles	Les Echos
Le Parisien	Le Parisien
L'Express	BFMTV
Les Inrockuptibles	LCI
Numerama	TFI
	Les Inrockuptibles
	French Rap_US
	France GQ

Table 3.1. Analysed media outlets

Level of analysis	What is analysed	Direction of decoding
Micro level Textual sub-units (phrases, clauses, tropes, lexemes, icons or emojis)	**Rhetorical devices:** rhetorical questions, metaphors, puns, euphemisms, hyperboles, etc. **Linguistic and semiotic markers of a 'coded language' of antisemitism:** memes, dog-whistles, allusions or inside jokes popular within certain communities or fandoms	
Meso level Text as a whole	**Global discursive strategies:** nomination (construction of in-groups and out-groups) predication (labelling social actors more or less positively) argumentation (justification of positive and negative attributions) perspectivisation (construing a certain frame of interpretation for an event) intensification and mitigation	
Macro level Broader sociopolitical and historical context	**Media practices:** impact of social media communication practices on antisemitic discourse, with a focus on influencer communication as a potential catalyst of virality for hate speech (see section 2.2). **Cultural, ideological and normative practices:** evolution of antisemitic narratives and imagery in France and the United States in the post-Holocaust era; cross-pollination between traditional anti-Jewish tropes and other discursive formations, such as anti-imperialism, anti-colonialism, anti-elitism or anti-feminism (see sections 2.2 and 2.3)	

Figure 3.1. Levels of discourse analysis

In order to understand how online support for controversial influencers can map onto and reinforce patterns of anti-Jewish prejudice, the following research questions are asked: Is there a correlation between support for Kanye West and Dieudonné and expressions of antisemitic prejudice? Which antisemitic stereotypes or concepts are used to legitimise West's and Dieudonné's positions? How explicit is antisemitic rhetoric in this context and what are the functions of coded language in the discursive construction of the 'us/them' dichotomy?

2.1 Antisemitism and (online) virality: The role of influencers

Virality is defined as the probability of an entity—such as a message—being passed along (Hansen et al. 2011). While virality is an anthropological fixture in human society, only recently, with the advent of the interactive web, has it became a major research focus in social sciences (Arjona-Martín et al. 2020). A growing body of literature has highlighted the perverse effects of viralisation mechanisms, which allow extremism, disinformation and hate speech to leverage some of the inbuilt features of the internet's mass-sharing infrastructures: the lack of gatekeeping, the algorithmic amplification of highly engaging content regardless of its quality, the creation of echo chambers, etc. (Cooper 2012, Mathew et al. 2019, Paris and Donovan 2019, Ananthakrishnan and Tucker 2021, Finkelstein 2022). Antisemitism offers a good vantage point to observe such phenomena: polymorphic, adaptable and syncretic in nature, it is perfectly suited for an age of mass flow of information.

Since the late twentieth century, the internet has become the lifeblood of antisemitic propaganda distribution (Weitzman 2022). Far-right networks in anglophone countries were the first to organise online, using this channel to bypass institutional gatekeeping in mainstream media. At their heart, these online ecosystems were interactive, decentralised portals, such as the forums *Stormfront* and *The Right Stuff*, or Wikipedia-like archives such as *Jew Watch*. In this respect, the far-right anticipated the 'participatory turn' in digital communication. Since the 2000s, a 'revolution within the revolution' has taken place in communication, with Web 2.0 (or the interactive web) marking a transition from linear mass media (such as newspapers and the radio, or even the first websites) to user-driven creation and dissemination of content. This unprecedented democratisation of speech has had a dark side: a dissemination of hate ideologies and antisemitism on a hitherto unknown scale (Hübscher and von Mering 2022). A central feature of content-sharing platforms such as *Facebook, Twitter, YouTube, Instagram* or *TikTok* is the use of automated sets of rules, called algorithms, that make decisions about what users see on the platform. Algorithms promote high-engagement content and, in doing so, risk amplifying outrageous content, including Holocaust-denial or conspiracy theories, because it generates reactions (likes, dislikes, comments and shares). These dynamics also fuel what Ebner (2020) dubs "radicalisation machines": algorithms tend to recommend content based on users' past viewing behaviour, thus creating 'echo chambers' and radicalisation pipelines, often without (or with minimal) external human involvement. This is why self-radicalisation is now a significant focal point of counter-extremism studies (see Archetti 2013, Bradbury et al. 2017). Machine-driven virality proves to be much harder to control and track than the human-driven virality of the past.

However, algorithms do not negate the fundamental verticality embedded into media discourse spaces. Wu et al. (2011) note that, while members of the general public now share the same access to social media that a celebrity does, information flows have not become egalitarian by any means. Personal salience (Bantimaroudis 2023) is still a key—and very unequally distributed—commodity in the attention economy (Marshall 2021, Hendricks and Mehlsen 2022). Although it is far from new or unique to social media, the figure of the *influencer* occupies a prominent position within information ecosystems and is a powerful driver of virality. Influencers—whether they are digitally native celebrities or have amassed their symbolic capital as artists, entertainers or journalists—act as "superspreaders" in networks who can set and proliferate socio-political agendas (Hendricks/Mehlsen 2022). The Covid pandemic foregrounded the agency of influencers in the spread of disinformation, conspiracy theories and hate speech (Baker 2022).

The interest of studying the role of online influencers in the spread of antisemitism is twofold. First and foremost, influencers act as bridges between digital networks and the broader social conversation. They are relevant as "ideological entrepreneurs" (Hyzen and Van den Bulck 2021) of hate speech, who produce and circulate the stereotypes, analogies and discursive strategies that structure contemporary antisemitic discourse. Secondly, they possess resources of "affective capital" (Dong 2022), which can be channelled into building communities of supporters or fandoms (Stevenson 2018). The emotional and affective dimension that can be embedded into parasocial relations by charismatic celebrities is an interesting blind spot in the study of antisemitic discourse.

2.2 Between the 'old' and the 'new': Dieudonné and French antisemitism

The first such influencer we will be focusing upon is the French comedian and actor Dieudonné M'Bala M'Bala, who became famous for his comedy routines in the 1990s and early 2000s. Dieudonné was born in a Parisian suburb to a mixed-race middle-class family. He achieved a breakthrough in the world of entertainment with his long-time friend, the comedian Élie Semoun (who has Jewish origins), by performing anti-racist, left-leaning comedy routines. However, in the early 2000s, in a context marked by the post-9/11 rhetoric of the 'clash of civilisations' and an uptick in violence in the Israeli-Palestinian conflict, he split with Semoun and started promoting a form of 'Black consciousness' tinged with antisemitism and third-worldism (Jobard 2017). Despite being marginalised in the mainstream entertainment industry, Dieudonné managed to structure around him a dense network of alternative media. He re-established himself on his flagship website *Dieudosphère* (with on-demand video service and an e-shop), the streaming and news website *Quenel+*, as well as through his *Twitter* (150,000 followers), *Facebook* (1.3 million followers) and *YouTube* (400,000 followers) accounts. In 2020, *YouTube, Facebook* and *Instagram* decided in quick succession to ban his accounts, further cutting him off from the mainstream (Le Monde 2020). Today, he remains an active figure in far-right circles, trying to capitalise on various anti-establishment movements, such as the yellow vests and anti-lockdown and anti-vaccine protests.

Dieudonné is highly representative of the new ideological synthesis described as 'new antisemitism' (Taguieff 2004, Peace 2009, Bruneteau 2015, Weitzmann 2019). His appeal rests on a trinity of classical antisemitic tropes (such as GREED, CONSPIRACY or POWER), radical anti-Zionism and a more diffuse anti-globalism that aligns with a rejection of the 'cosmopolitan elites' and Western liberal modernity. Dieudonné's core antisemitic views cluster around a few basic key themes:

The rejection of Israel

Anti-Zionism serves as the gateway towards a more radical form of antisemitism. Dieudonné engages in a demonisation of Israel, notably through the use of the NAZI ANALOGY (expressed through puns such as 'Israheil') or COLONIALISM ANALOGIES. His anti-Israeli discourse is not rooted in geopolitics or human rights but in what Taguieff (2004) dubs "fantasy-world Zionism": a belief that Israel and Zionists are plotting against the world; that they are omnipotent and demonic; that they are controlling and manipulating the global (and particularly Western) political, financial and media establishment.

The topos of JEWISH POWER

See Becker et al. 2024 on the topos of JEWISH POWER. Dieudonné's anti-Zionism maps onto the canonical narrative of a Jewish plot to take over the world. Dieudonné builds on the notion—developed by his long-time political ally Alain Soral—of the 'Empire', an alleged global oligarchic regime secretly run by the Jewish elite (Collectif des 4 2018). A French counterpart of the Zionist Occupied Government (ZOG) conspiracy theory, this narrative is often hinted at by Dieudonné in his shows. For example, he uses his one liner "Au dessus c'est l'soleil" ["Above there's only the sun"], accompanied by a finger pointing upward, alongside references to Jews. This builds on CONSPIRACY narratives and tropes of alleged JEWISH POWER, suggesting that Jews sit at the very top of power hierarchies and receive orders from no one, unlike politicians or governments, which project an appearance of power but lack true agency. A corollary of this topos is

The topos of the TABOO OF CRITICISM

This posits that Jews will supposedly use their networks of influence to silence any critical opinion about them or the State of Israel. Dieudonné, using his legal troubles and his exclusion from the mainstream entertainment industry, *performs* on stage his alleged victimisation and silencing at the hands of the Jews and their accomplices. He jokes that he cannot make jokes about Jews, designating them instead through allusions and detour communication (Proust et al. 2020). Dieudonné frames other comedians—especially if they are also from minority backgrounds—who decide to remain 'politically correct' as traitors, cowards and sell-outs: public figures who choose material comfort over truth.

Jews as ontological oppressors of non-White minorities

Borrowing from the discourse of the antisemitic *Nation of Islam* in the United States (with which the French comedian has strong links), he relentlessly describes Jews as slavers. This pattern of oppression is today perpetuated, according to him, in the Israeli treatment of Palestinians. This brings a distinct radicality to his anti-Zionist stances: if Palestinian suffering is not a result of an unfortunate geopolitical context but supposedly a natural consequence of Jewish nature, any peaceful cohabitation between the two peoples is impossible.

Denial and/or instrumentalisation of the Holocaust

See Becker et al. 2024 on this trope. Dieudonné's position on the Holocaust is a clear example of the ways contemporary Holocaust denial is formulated in contemporary discourse through the use of detour communication. Although he gives a platform in his shows to Holocaust deniers such as Robert Faurisson, Dieudonné has never explicitly denied the genocide of the Jewish people. Rather, he frequently adopts a pseudo-intellectual posture of radical scepticism; Dieudonné's 'doubt' aligns with a specific kind of Holocaust denial based on a hypertrophic form of rationality—one which claims to prolong the French tradition of Cartesianism (Jobard 2017). However, Dieudonné is more open in articulating the concept of the instrumentalisation of the holocaust by the Jews. He calls Holocaust commemoration "memorial pornography" and alleges that it has been weaponised by Jews to achieve their (Zionist) agenda. Classical antisemitic stereotypes like greed and avarice are hybridised with themes specific to secondary antisemitism in sketches such as when he portrays the Jewish philosopher Bernard-Henri Lévy trying to haggle with a greengrocer for a bag of potatoes: "With six million dead, you can at least give me a good price". He also mocks the Holocaust through puns and wordplay, such as with the song "Hot Pineapple" ("Chaud Ananas" in French, which is phonetically close to the word Shoah, a Hebrew word referring to the Holocaust).

Dieudonné's syncretic antisemitism merges anti-imperialism, anti-capitalism, support of Palestinian movements, HOLOCAUST DENIAL and systematic suspicion of historical accounts. With millions of followers on social media, Dieudonné is the jutting prow and the public face of contemporary anti-Jewish prejudice in the French-speaking world.

2.3 The "Paranoid Style" of Kanye West: The Ambiguities of American Antisemitism

Unlike European nations, the United States has no significant history of institutionalised federal antisemitism. Under the 1790 Nationality Act, Jews were considered "free white persons" eligible for citizenship (Library of Congress n.d.). Nevertheless, anti-Jewish prejudice developed in the folds of racial science, social Darwinism (popular in the Anglo-Saxon world in the late nineteenth century) and/or Christian fundamentalism. In the interwar period, American populism borrowed heavily from fascism and national socialism: Reverend Charles Coughlin blamed Jews for the spread of communism, while at the same time railing against the 'international bankers' and 'money changers' of the world. He also asserted that Nazism was a "national mechanism of self-defence against Communism" (Dinnerstein 1995). Through its extensive use of modern mass media, notably radio broadcasts, Coughlin represents a sort of 'proto-influencer' who used technology and showmanship to amplify his message, building a parasocial bond with his audience. In post-war America, antisemitism was politically weak, but it could still be an effective force within broader anti-establishment coalitions. Latent anti-Jewish narratives were a structural element of what historian Richard Hofstadter (1967) called the "paranoid style" in American politics: a form of siege mentality and a fantasy of victimisation and moral decay that animates populist and radical ideologies. Later, McCarthyism was infused with antisemitic innuendo, and this anti-communist crusade helped to revive the anti-Jewish sentiment of former Coughlinites. Antisemitism is also a subtext for Christian fundamentalism, despite followers' articulated support for Israel. The Cultural Marxism conspiracy theory, prevalent in most hardline conservative circles, retains elements of structural antisemitism in its allegation that the predominantly Jewish thinkers of the Frankfurt School have been systematically enacting a subversion of traditional American values and morality (Braune 2019).

But one of the most debated aspects of post-war antisemitism has been the rise of anti-Jewish prejudice in some Black communities. Dinnerstein (1995) suggests, quite pertinently, that the cultural legacy of evangelical Christianity had already created a predisposition towards antisemitism in Black communities in the deeply religious American South. However, the emergence of a coherent 'Black antisemitism' is rooted in disillusionment following the Civil Rights Movement, which led some activists to become radicalised. A 'martyrological competition' was established between slavery and the Holocaust, driven by belief that Jewish suffering is acknowledged while Black suffering is marginalised (Sundquist 2009). This resentment hardened into an even stronger allegation: that Jews are fundamentally oppressors that bear a major responsibility for the transatlantic trade. *Nation of Islam* leader Louis Farrakhan alleged that Jews have an "undeniable record" of "anti-Black behavior starting with the horror of the trans-Atlantic slave trade, plantation slavery, Jim Crow, sharecropping, the labour movement of the North and South, the unions and the misuse of our people that continues to this very moment" (Farrakhan 2010). The Black Power movement embraced Islam, third-worldism and, with these, anti-Zionist attitudes. Black antisemitism in America has been just as syncretic as the 'new antisemitism' in France, rehashing old tropes such as the supposed global Jewish plot, greed or usury. It also produced original outputs, such as the bizarre Black Hebrew Israelites myth, according to which Black people are the rightful descendants of Biblical Hebrews, and contemporary Jews have usurped this genealogy (Southern Poverty Law Center n.d.).

Kanye West's political trajectory is, contrary to Dieudonné's, far from linear and coherent. One of the most recognizable faces in the global entertainment and music industry, the Chicago-born rapper, singer, songwriter, record producer and fashion designer started off as a quintessential Black icon. Since then, his political stances radicalised and increasingly attracted controversy. His embrace of religion and of social conservatism (on themes such as abortion) was mirrored by a more sinister promotion of far-right ideology, whether through selling Confederate flags on tour, donning a "White Lives Matter" T-shirt or issuing a spate of antisemitic comments on social media (ADL 2022). While still inchoate, West's antisemitism matters. First and foremost, as an international celebrity spanning multiple industries, West potentially reaches an unprecedented global audience. Secondly, like Dieudonné, his specific strand of 'intersectional' antisemitism sits at the juncture of multiple ideological traditions. West has cultivated strong links to the *Nation of Islam* and Farrakhan, who he called "sensei" (ADL 2022). More recently, West has also been active in right-wing networks: he has been a guest on the conservative *Fox News* talk show "Tucker Carlson Tonight", dined with white supremacist Nick Fuentes and former *Breitbart* editor Milo Yiannopoulos at Donald Trump's Mar-a-Lago residence and appeared on conspiracy theorist Alex Jones's *InfoWars* show (ADL 2022). West's antisemitic statements cluster around a few prominent themes:

Tropes about Jewish POWER AND CONTROL—particularly in the entertainment and media industry—as well as tropes about Jewish GREED and EXPLOITATION

West has espoused conspiracy narratives such as the '300 families'[1] or ZOG, which claim that a (Jewish) oligarchy controls the economic system, the world's governments and media corporations: "The Zionist control—the 300 in control of the media and in control of the governments—they don't want us to connect to each other..." ("The Alex Jones Show" on *InfoWars*, 1 December 2022); "[...] the Jewish people have their hand on every single business that controls the world" ("Drink Champs", 16 October 2022). Such statements map onto the notion of a Jewish takeover of Hollywood and the entertainment

---

1   The '300 families' is a conspiracy theory that claims a powerful group of interconnected oligarchs, often presented as Jewish, are controlling politics, finance, banking and the military.

industry, which has been embedded into American antisemitism since the 1920s—a time when Jews, amongst others, were accused of using film to weaken the moral fibre of the country with increasing violent and sexual content (Carr 2001). The Cultural Marxism narrative, as well as more recent QAnon phenomenon[2], sees Hollywood and the creative industries as focal points for the dissolution of the American traditional order. Kanye's allegations articulate two distinct narratives from different sides of the political spectrum: that parasitic Jewish elites have captured the heart of the country and that they use their cultural capital to exploit marginalised groups (Black artists) for profit. He has said, "Jewish people have owned the Black voice... The Jewish community, especially in the music industry, in the entertainment [industry], they'll take one of us, the brightest of us [...] and milk us till we die". ("Drink Champs", 16 October 2022). Re-activating the language of 'ownership' of Black people by Jews also connects back to the narrative, popular within certain Black Power milieus, of Jews supposedly organising the transatlantic slave trade.

Questioning Jewish identity through the Black Hebrew Israelite ideology

The Black Hebrew Israelite (BHI) narrative, which West has espoused alongside another high-profile celebrity, basketball star Kyrie Irving, not only erases Jewish identity but also maps onto the stereotype of Jewish deceitfulness and even greed, as it alleges Jews are unfairly benefitting from a usurped status. It can also serve, in West's rhetoric, as a line of defence against antisemitic allegations: "We are Semite, we Jew, so I can't be antisemite" ("Drink Champs", 16 October 2022).

Holocaust denial and affirmation of Hitler and Nazism

West has stated that "The Holocaust is not what happened. Let's look at the facts of that. And Hitler has a lot of redeeming qualities". ("The Alex Jones Show" on *InfoWars*, 1 December 2022). He also suggests that the negative portrayal of Nazis is a result of the purported Jewish monopoly on media: "The Jewish media has made us feel like the Nazis and Hitler

---

2   The QAnon conspiracy theory posits that the world is controlled by a cabal of Satan-worshipping paedophiles.

have never offered anything of value to the world". ("The Alex Jones Show" on *InfoWars*, 1 December 2022).

The topos of the TABOO OF CRITICISM

West has asserted: "I crossed the antisemite line. I crossed the gun line. I stood in front of the tank in Tiananmen Square". ("Drink Champs", 16 October 2022). He also often makes a parallel between the social opprobrium over antisemitic beliefs and the genocide of the Jewish people, thus engaging in a trivialisation of the Holocaust: "There's Jewish people that are basically hiding me under their floorboards right now—under the wooden floors. It's like a reverse version of the Holocaust" ("The Alex Jones Show" on *InfoWars*, 1 December 2022).

3. Empirical analysis: Comparative case study of web user reactions in French media

In the first stage of the empirical analysis, we attempt to gauge the level of support for Dieudonné and Kanye West expressed in the comment sections. I am operating with three broad categories: antisemitic speech, non-antisemitic speech and counter speech. Non-antisemitic speech includes any comment which does not contain an antisemitic concept, while counter speech is defined more specifically as communicative action that seeks to actively problematise and refute antisemitic tropes, or, more generally, Dieudonné's and Kanye West's behaviour.

In the Dieudonné subcorpus of 1,464 user comments, 58% (n=850) has been labelled non-antisemitic or unclear; 19% (n=284) has been labelled as counter speech. The remaining 23% (n=331) were labelled as antisemitic following the IHRA definition. Only a minority (13%, or 45) of those 331 antisemitic comments were explicit. The vast majority (86%, or 286) relied on implication, detour communication or prior cultural knowledge for the decoding of the antisemitic meaning. In the Kanye West subcorpus, composed of 1,953 comments, 82% (n=1,607) were classified as non-antisemitic or unclear, only 4% (n=69) were deemed to constitute counter speech and 14% (n=276) were of an antisemitic nature. Once again, most of the comments in this final subset (79%, or

220) make use of contextual forms of antisemitic speech, with only 56 comments being explicit.

Of the 3,417 comments analysed in total, therefore, 607, or 17% were antisemitic. These are split unevenly across the two subcorpora (23% and 14% respectively). I hypothesise that the disparity in the percentage of antisemitic comments between the two subcorpora can be explained by the fact that Dieudonné has a highly politicised nucleus of supporters, who fully engage not only with his comedic content but also with his ideological worldview. Meanwhile, West's supporters are often depoliticised and express admiration for the rapper's artistic achievement while distancing themselves from his controversial political stances. A common distancing strategy is the separation of the art from the artist or questioning his mental capacity. Following the codebook developed in the project Decoding Antisemitism, praise for Dieudonné or West's artistic achievements, without reference to their political stances, was classified as non-antisemitic.

A similar dynamic might be an important factor for the dramatic disparity in counter speech observed (19% in the Dieudonné subcorpus to slightly under 4% in the West subcorpus). The polarising and highly politicised nature of Dieudonné means that most of the backlash in the comment sections explicitly targets and problematises his antisemitism. Web users often address and contest allegations of censorship, highlighting for example the private nature of Big Tech companies (which have their own standards outlined in the terms of use) or the illegal nature, under French law, of antisemitic speech. This is not the case in the West subcorpus, where most of the criticism levelled against the rapper is vaguer and encompasses, beyond his political opinions, other aspects of his eccentric persona.

Despite these differences, the most prominent antisemitic topoï were strikingly similar. Unsurprisingly, the concepts and strategies articulated by web users mirror Dieudonné's and West's own discourse against Jews. On the most basic conceptual level, comments convey antisemitism by expressing support for the two influencers and reinforcing their social and political worldview. Support is articulated through conventional phrases such as "Full support to Kanye 💪 💪"[3] (LCI.F-FB[20221026]),

---

3   "Soutien à Kanye 💪 💪".

"Sending support and strength, Dieudo"[4] (LEFIG-FB[20200630]), "GO DIEUDO" (LEFIG-FB[20200630]) and also through iconographic elements, such as hearts, clapping hands or flexed-arm emojis. The choice of attributes—"brave", "courageous", "free-thinking"—has an embedded political dimension, reinforcing the narrative that Dieudonné and West are dissenters or martyrs persecuted by society for their beliefs: "They [Dieudonné and his ally Alain Soral] are the two most courageous men in France"[5] (MARIA-FB[20200806]); "YE's bluntness and free spirit is bothering the conspirators"[6] (BFMTV-FB[20221027]). Sexual metaphors such as "bending over", implying submission and servility, are also used in predication strategies, distinguishing them from 'sell-out' mainstream entertainers who do not question the system: "At least Kanye kept his pants on unlike those wet rags"[7] (BFMTV-FB[20221027]).

Support for these influencers is also articulated in implicit ways, through allusions and detour communication. The slogan "Je suis Kanye" or "Je suis Dieudonné" ["I am Kanye" or "I am Dieudonné"] has, in this context, a threefold function: first, to express solidarity with the allegedly silenced celebrity; second, to politicise this support by portraying them as victims of a brutal censorship attempt, which is compared to terrorism; third, it levels an accusation of double standards and hypocrisy against liberal democracies, which are accused of promoting the values of free speech yet cracking down on anti-Jewish offensive speech. One example is, "Je suis Charlie, that does not work for these people as they pick on the poor Jews... what a double standard... disgusting"[8] (LEPAR-FB[20200707]).

This maps onto another highly salient topos: the topos of the TABOO OF CRITICISM. In synergy with the topos of JEWISH POWER, it enacts an effective argumentation macro-strategy, because it appeals to the consensual liberal ethos of freedom of expression and conscience: "The best comedian in France is persecuted for daring to make jokes about a group that shall not be named. Freedom of speech is just hypocrisy

---

4 "Soutien et courage Dieudo".
5 "C'est les 2 hommes les plus courageux de France."
6 "Cette liberté d'expression et d'esprit de YE dérange la théorie du complot".
7 "Au moins Kanye a su garder son pantalon contrairement à tt ces serpillières".
8 "Je suis Charlie , ca ne marche pas pour ces gens car ici sa rabaisse les pvres juifs ....deux poids deux mesurs ...deguelasse Tout sa".

and double standards"[9] (LEFIG-FB[20200709]). The Jewish out-group is rarely mentioned directly but is regularly alluded to through phrases such as the "chosen people", "the untouchables" or "the community that shall not be named". Intensification strategies and hyperboles are also used, through claims that "there are first-class citizens, and those who are not permitted to look at them or talk about them"[10] (LEFIG-FB[20221025]). Feeding into broader anti-elitist and populist frames, this comment manufactures a dichotomy between an alleged corrupt (Jewish) elite and the pure people, kept by the taboo of criticism into a state of submission. Other comments use literary allusions to George Orwell's novel *1984* to create, based on an alleged suppression of free speech, a metaphorical parallel between Orwell's brutal dystopia and Western societies: "The Ministry of Truth strikes again. They are not even hiding it anymore"[11] (LEFIG-FB[20200709]). The taboo of criticism triggers what Ruth Wodak (2015) dubbed an ideological *"perpetuum mobile"*, a rhetorical strategy which involves legitimising a controversial statement by means of shifting the optics and reframing the debate. In this case, the antisemitic nature of Dieudonné's and West's stances are being obfuscated by a debate about civil freedoms. Another such argumentation strategy built on re-framing attempts to shift the attention towards the treatment of other discriminated minorities alleges that there is a pervasive societal double standard which shields Jews from any criticism while tolerating attacks on other ethnic and religious groups. While not systematically antisemitic, these remarks frequently intersect other antisemitic stereotypes, such as Jewish power and privilege or accusations of instrumentalising the Holocaust.

The most prominent concepts found in the corpus analysed are listed in Table 3.2 below:

---

9   "Le meilleur humoriste de France qui est persécuté parce qu'il a osé faire des sketchs sur une communauté qu'on a pas le droit de citer. Comme quoi la liberté d'expression c'est de l'hypocrisie de deux poids deux mesures"

10   "Il y a les citoyens de première zone et ceux qui ne peuvent les regarder ou parler d'eux".

11   "Le Ministere de la vérité a frappé. Ils ne se cachent même plus".

Topos	Percentage (of all antisemitic comments)		Definition	Examples
	Dieudonné Subcorpus	Kanye West Subcorpus		
Affirmation of antisemitism	26%	26%	Support, praise, legitimation or justification of an antisemitic person, act or concept	"Full support to Kanye 👏 👏" (LCI.F-FB[20221026]) "Sending support and strength, Dieudo" (LEFIG-FB[20200630]) "JE SUIS DIEUDONNE" (MARIA-FB[20200806])
TABOO OF CRITICISM	34%	31%	The idea that all opinions critical of Jewish people are being systematically supressed and persecuted	"Strangely, only those who criticise the J*** are done away with, treated worse than murderers or child rapists!!!"[12] (LEPOI-FB[20221212]) "To learn who rules you, find out who you are not allowed to criticise"[13] (LEFIG-FB[20221208]) "Dieudonné is censored, which is shameful, in a country which pretends to be the land of freedom!"[14] (LEFIG-FB[20200711]) "The Ministry of Truth strikes again. They are not even hiding it any more" (LEFIG-FB[20200709])

---

12 "Bizarrement il n'y a que ceux qui critiquent les j**** qui finissent au placard, présenté comme des assassins pire que les vrais violeurs de gosses !!!"
13 "Pour savoir qui vous gouverne, regardez qui vous ne pouvez pas critiquer"
14 "Dieudonné est censuré, ce qui est une honte dans un pays qui se revendique être celui de la liberté!"

Topos	Percentage (of all antisemitic comments)		Definition	Examples
	Dieudonné Subcorpus	Kanye West Subcorpus		
CONSPIRACY	9%	17%	The allegation that Jews exercise a secret control over society	"The dude spoke against the world order, he's getting shot down by the rulers of the rulers"[15] (BFMTV-FB[20221027]) "And then they say that it's not true, (((they))) don't control everything"[16] (BFMTV-FB[20221027]) "This comes from very very high-up, from Tel-Aviv"[17] (LEFIG-FB[20200630])
CONTROL OVER MEDIA	6%	3%	The allegation that Jews exercise control over media institutions and public opinion	"He's in the crosshairs of the community that represent the 500.000 who control the media in France"[18] (LEFIG-FB[20200711])

---

15 "Le mec a parlé contre l'ordre mondial, il se fait abattre par les dirigeants des dirigeants".
16 "Et après on nous dit que ce n'est pas vrai, (((ils))) ne contrôlent pas tout".
17 "Ça vient d'en haut de très haut, du côté de Tel-Aviv"
18 "Il est dans le viseur de la communauté qui représente 500.000 personnes en France qui contrôlent les médias françaises".

Topos	Percentage (of all antisemitic comments)		Definition	Examples
	Dieudonné Subcorpus	Kanye West Subcorpus		
SELF-VICTIMISATION	4%	7%	Construction of victimhood of the non-Jewish in-group at the hands of the Jewish out-group	"If you are not like them, they'll squish you like a bug"[19] (BFMTV-FB[20221208]) "He's been CRIFicied (pardon this neologism)[20]" (LEPAR-FB[20200707])

Table 3.2: The most prominent concepts found in the corpus

4. Detour communication, pop culture and community-building

Another crucial insight of the empirical study concerns the more subtle encoding mechanisms that occur within comment sections. Following Stuart Hall's (2010) influential model of communication, we conceptualise discourse as fundamentally dialogical and interactive: the intersubjectivity of the encoding/decoding process means that communication establishes a recognitive relationship between the sender and the receiver of a message. This dynamic applies also to hate speech and, particularly, to antisemitism. Various authors (Bergmann and Erb 1984, Milbradt 2013, Schwarz-Friesel 2019, Richards et al. 2023) highlight that antisemitic speech increasingly relies on "detour communication" and dog whistles to circumvent the social taboo associated with crude anti-Jewish prejudice. Dog whistles, which can be defined as coded or suggestive language understood by the in-group but hard to decode for the out-group (Richards et al. 2023), are a

---

19 "C est comsa ,ils sont ,si tu n est pas les leurs il sont pres a t ecrasé comme un caffart".
20 "Il a été CRIFicié (permettez-moi le néologisme)". CRIF is the acronym of the *Conseil Représentatativ des Institutions Juives de France*, one of the main bodies representing the Jewish minority in France.

particularly interesting form of implicit communication. All implicit communication requires contextual or cultural knowledge to some extent. For example, the allegation in one comment that the order to terminate Dieudonné's social media accounts came from "very very high up, from Tel-Aviv" (LEFIG-FB[20200630]) demands cultural information about the Jewish state and its most populous city, but this information is superficial and very easily accessible. A dog whistle mobilises deeper strata of subcultural knowledge, the meaning of which is opaque to the uninitiated. For example, the triple parentheses (seen in a comment in Table 3.2) or references to "celestial dragons" (see below) will not make sense to someone who is not familiar with the vernacular of online antisemitism. Dog whistles are in a constant state of fluctuation, as new meanings emerge and replace the old.

The corpus exhibits, amongst antisemitic comments, a high level of reliance of coded languages and dog whistles. Some of them, like the echoes (triple parentheses), are well-established in the international language of antisemitism. The echoes, believed to originate from the neo-Nazi American blog *The Right Stuff*, are used to encase a name, institution or category—for instance (((Soros))) or (((bankers)))—to identify it as Jewish; originally, it was a visual pun signifying that Jewish names and actions "echo throughout History" (Smith and Fleishman 2016). They appear a few times in our corpus, often in the context of accusations of an alleged Jewish conspiracy: "And then they tell us that (((they))) don't control everything" (BFMTV-FB[20221027]). While the echoes represent a form of the globalisation of antisemitic vernacular, other dog whistles are specific to the French context and suggest that processes of encoding and decoding are still mainly taking place within each language community, even if there is, naturally, an increased level of cross-pollination between them.

Dieudonné's success in antisemitic milieux was due to his ability to create viral slogans, puns and catchphrases that are perfectly suited to the internet ecosystem. Unsurprisingly, web users repeat these slogans in their comments as a way of covertly conveying approval of Dieudonné's worldview or to manufacture new communication patterns. The one-liner "Above there's only the sun" (see section 2.2), often accompanied or visually represented by the sun emoji, enacts a metaphor for Jewish power: "Then they tell you they are not above the sun. So unfair. They do as they please in this country²¹" (LEFIG-FB[20200630]); "When you touch the sun ☀ you get burnt"²² (BFMTV-FB[20221208]). The fact such comments show up consistently in our West subcorpus demonstrate they go beyond in-jokes within Dieudonné's fandom and belong to the vernacular of antisemitism in France. Other elements borrowed from Dieudonné's shows include the pineapple symbol—from the "Hot Pineapple" ["Chaud ananas"] jingle—or the phrase "How much does it cost?". The former does not have a fixed meaning, but it is often used to mock accusations of antisemitism or Jewish identity in general, therefore functioning as a knowing wink to other web users familiar with this symbolism. The latter has more conceptual depth, as it maps onto traditional tropes of Jewish greed but also recent accusations of instrumentalising antisemitism: in Dieudonné's sketches, public figures seeking forgiveness for having offended the Jewish community enquire about the amount of financial compensation they need to offer to be 're-admitted' into public life. Commenters now allude that it is Dieudonné and West who will need to pay up to ensure they will be allowed back in the entertainment industry. The meaning is sometimes reinforced by other allusions. For example, one commenter states that Dieudonné will have to pay his compensation in shekels, Israel's currency, thus implying the beneficiaries of this alleged financial "extorsion" scheme (VALEU-FB[20200701]).

Dog whistles are in constant flux, and new meanings and codes emerge as old ones fade out of relevancy. In the French space, the West subcorpus reveals a new pattern. Drawing on anime culture, Jews are often referred to as "celestial dragons" ["dragons célestes"]. In the manga *One Piece* by Eiichiro Oda, "celestial dragons" refer to the greedy, arrogant and cruel aristocracy in that fictional universe. Embedding antisemitic stereotypes into pop-culture vernacular ensures that old antisemitic repertoires (such as concepts of GREED, EVIL or GLOBAL POWER) are more easily transferred to contemporary times, able to find new audiences, especially amongst young people who are not otherwise familiar with the ideological tenets of antisemitism. It can also increase

---

21 "Après on nous dira qu'ils sont pas au-dessus du soleil. Belle injustice, ils font ce qu'ils veulent dans ce pays".

22 "Quand tu touches le soleil ☀ tu te brules".

the virality of the message, by reducing complex concepts to shareable hashtags and by circumventing moderation filters.

But coded antisemitism is not only a strategic move to evade content moderation efforts. It cuts to the core of the in-group/out-group dynamic upon which antisemitism (amongst other hate ideologies) is premised. Coded language functions as a tool for community-building, creating what psychoanalytical theorist Jacques Lacan (1966: 80 ff) dubbed a social process of "reciprocal recognition" between the actors in the communication act. Being able to understand and decode the inside jokes (and, more broadly, the crypted references) reinforces the sense of belonging. In the case of antisemitism, the social opprobrium adds a new dimension to such processes of community-building. The pleasure of taking part in transgressive "prohibitions" is a strong component that fuels identification with the in-group, while increasing the (moral) gap with the out-group (Proust et al. 2020). As both Dieudonné and West have created a public persona around their alleged victimisation at the hands of the Jewish out-group, expressions of support for the two influencers draw on the same repertoire of performative transgression. Due to their high level of media salience and their extensive sympathy capital, the two influencers have become focal points for the creation of such deviant online communities, however diffuse they may be.

5. Conclusions

This paper sets out to understand the way web users try, in mainstream discourse spaces, to negotiate support for highly controversial public figures accused of antisemitism. Despite the strong moral stigma attached to antisemitism in Western societies, we found both Dieudonné and Kanye West received strong support from, respectively, 23% and 17% of web users in comment sections of major French media outlets. A qualitative empirical analysis of these comments showcases a clear ideological parallel between the antisemitic repertoire of the two influencers and the one mobilised by their supporters. This fact highlights the centrality of influencer speech on the spread of antisemitic tropes. Both Dieudonné and West are products of their social, political and ideological context, and, as such, they are recipients of entrenched traditions of antisemitic thinking in France and the United States. But they also possess a considerable agency: they are not merely 'amplifiers' of antisemitism but also 'ideological entrepreneurs' who actively create and refine new concepts, putting them into circulation in the ideological marketplace. These concepts, fuelled and boosted by the influencer's own personal media salience, achieve viral status before 'trickling down' and entering everyday discourse.

Another key of the success of such 'pop' antisemitism is its heavy use of coded language. Harbouring yet hiding antisemitic meaning, this coded language serves as a medium for passing elements of antisemitic ideology under conditions of social opprobrium. But it can also enhance a sense of belonging and of community within the in-group, by adding a ludic dimension to social and discursive transgression. This raises a set of questions—notably on the dynamics of virality of such antisemitic content on social media and the role of influencers or other 'nodes' in its spread—that would need to be addressed in further empirically grounded research on antisemitism, hate speech and digital culture.

References

Ananthakrishnan, Uttara M. and Catherine E. Tucker, 2022. "The drivers and virality of hate speech online", https://doi.org/10.2139/ssrn.3793801

Anti-Defamation League, 2022. "Ye (Kanye West): What ou need to know", https://www.adl.org/resources/blog/ye-kanye-west-what-you-need-know

Archetti, Cristina, 2013. *Understanding Terrorism in the Age of Global Media: A communication approach*. London: Palgrave Macmillan, https://doi.org/10.1057/9781137291387

Arjona-Martín, José-Borja, Alfonso Méndiz-Noguero and Juan-Salvador Victoria-Mas, 2020. "Virality as a paradigm of digital communication. Review of the concept and update of the theoretical framework". *El Profesional de La Información*, 29 (6), 1–18, https://doi.org/10.3145/epi.2020.nov.07

Baker, Stephanie Alice, 2022. "Alt. health influencers: How wellness culture and web culture have been weaponised to promote conspiracy theories and far-right extremism during the COVID-19 pandemic". *European Journal of Cultural Studies*, 51 (1), 3 –24, https://doi.org/10.31235/osf.io/jt2ha

Bantimaroudis, Philemon, 2021. "Agenda selfying and agendamelding. Advancing the salience of the self". *The Agenda Setting Journal*, 5 (2), 115–133, https://doi.org/10.1075/asj.20008.ban

Bantimaroudis, Philemon, 2023. "Influencers and their salience: Public perceptions of individual agendas on Instagram". *Media Watch*, 14 (2), 217–237, https://doi.org/10.1177/09760911231163281

Becker, Matthias J., Hagen Troschke, Matt Bolton and Alexis Chapelan, (eds), 2024. *Decoding Antisemitism: A Guide to Identifying Antisemitism Online*. London: Palgrave Macmillan, https://link.springer.com/book/9783031492372

Bergmann, Werner and Rainer Erb, 1984. „Kommunikationslatenz, Moral und öffentliche Meinung: theoretische Überlegungen zum Antisemitismus in der Bundesrepublik Deutschland". *Kölner Zeitschrift für Soziologie und Sozialpsychologie*, 38, 223–246, https://doi.org/10.15203/99106-015-4-04

Bradbury, Roger, Terry Bossomaier, and David Kernot, 2017. "Predicting the emergence of self radicalisation through social media: A complex systems approach". In: Maura Conway et al. (eds). *Terrorists' Use of the Internet*. Amsterdam: IOS Press, 379–389

Braune, Joan, 2019. "Who's afraid of the Frankfurt School? 'Cultural Marxism' as an antisemitic conspiracy theory". *Journal of Social Justice*, 9 (1), https://transformativestudies.org/wp-content/uploads/Joan-Braune.pdf

Bruneteau, Bernad, 2015. "Les permanences de l'antisémitisme antimondialiste (fin XIXe-début XXIe siècle)". *Revue d'histoire moderne & contemporaine*, 62 (2–3), 225–244, https://doi.org/10.3917/rhmc.622.0225

Calabrese, Laura (ed), 2020. *Le commentaire, du manuscrit à la toile*. Roubaix: EME Editions

Carr, Steven Alan, 2008. *Hollywood and Anti-Semitism: A cultural history up to World War II*. Cambridge: Cambridge University Press, https://doi.org/10.1017/CBO9780511612633

Carter Olson, Candi, 2016. "#BringBackOurGirls: Digital Communities Supporting Real-World Change and Influencing Mainstream Media Agendas". In: *Feminist Media Studies*, 16 (5), 772–787, https://doi.org/10.1080/14680777.2016.1154887

Cooper, Abraham, 2012. "From Big Lies to the Lone Wolf: How Social Networking Incubates and Multiplies Online Hate and Terrorism". In: Alan Baker, Ha-Yerushalmi Le-'inyene Tsibur U-Medinah Merkaz and Konrad-Adenauer-Stiftung (eds). *The Changing Forms of Incitement to Terror and Violence: The Need for a New International Response*. Jerusalem: Jerusalem Center For Public Affairs

Collectif des 4, 2018. *Le cas Alain Soral. Radiographie d'un discours d'extrême-droite*. Lormont: Le Bord de l'eau

Dinnerstein, Leonard, 1995. *Antisemitism in America*. Oxford: Oxford University Press, https://doi.org/10.1093/acprof:oso/9780195101126.001.0001

Dong, Wei, 2022. *The Cultural Politics of Affect and Emotion*. Bielefeld: Transcript Verlag

Ebner, Julia, 2020. *Going Dark: The Secret Social Lives of Extremists*. London: Bloomsbury Publishing Ltd, https://doi.org/10.1515/9783839462843

Farrakhan, Louis, 8 July 2012. "Minister Louis Farrakhan's Letter to ADL's Abraham Foxman", https://www.finalcall.com/artman/publish/Minister_Louis_Farrakhan_9/article_7116.shtml

Finin, Tim, Joshi Anupam, Kolari Pranam, Java Akshay, Kale Anubhav and Amit Karandikar, 2008. "The Information Ecology of Social Media and Online Communities". In: *AI Magazine*, 29 (3), 77–92, https://doi.org/10.1609/aimag.v29i3.2158

Finkelstein, Joel, 2022. "Memes, viruses, and violence: A nation guide to managing contagious threats". In: *The Journal of Intelligence, Conflict, and Warfare*, 5(1), 85–89, https://doi.org/10.21810/jicw.v5i1.4250

Gaden, Georgia and Delia Dumitrica, 2014. "The 'Real Deal': Strategic Authenticity, Politics and Social Media". In: *First Monday*, 20 (1), http://dx.doi.org/10.5210/fm.v20i1.4985

Hall, Stuart, 2010 [1980]. "Encoding-Decoding". In: Chris Greer (ed). *Crime and Media*. Abingdon: Routledge, 44–55

Hansen, Lars Kai, Adam Arvidsson, Nielsen, A. Finn, Elanor Colleoni, Michael Etter, 2011. "Good Friends, Bad News - Affect and Virality in Twitter". In: James J. Park et al. (eds). *Future Information Technology. Communications in Computer and Information Science*, 185. London: Springer, 34–43, https://doi.org/10.1007/978-3-642-22309-9

Hendricks, Vincent F. and Camilla Mehlsen, 2022. *The Ministry of Truth*. London: Springer

Hofstadter, Richard, 1967. *The Paranoid Style in American Politics and Other Essays*. New York: Vintage Books

Hübscher, Monika and Sabine Von Mering, 2022. *Antisemitism on Social Media*. Abingdon: Routledge, https://doi.org/10.4324/9781003200499

Hutchins, Amber L. and Natalie T. J. Tindall, 2021. *Public Relations and Online Engagement: Audiences, Fandom and Influencers*. Abingdon: Taylor & Francis Group

Hyzen, Aaron and Hilde Van den Bulck, 2021. "Conspiracies, Ideological Entrepreneurs, and Digital Popular Culture". In: *Media and Communication*, 9 (3), 179–188, https://doi.org/10.17645/mac.v9i3.4092

International Holocaust Remembrance Alliance (IHRA), 2023. "Working Definition of Antisemitism", https://www.holocaustremembrance.com/resources/working-definitions-charters/working-definition-antisemitism

Jobard, Fabien, 2017. "Dieudonné M'Bala M'Bala: Between Anti-Racism, Antisemitism, and Holocaust Denial". In: Jacob Eder et al. (eds). *Holocaust Memory in a Globalizing World*. Göttingen: Wallstein Verlag, 98–113, https://doi.org/10.5771/9783835340114-95

Lacan, Jacques, 1966. *Écrits*. Paris: Éditions du Seuil

Le Monde, 3 August 2020. "Facebook supprime la page de Dieudonné, ainsi que son compte instagram, pour 'discours de haine'", https://www.lemonde.fr/pixels/article/2020/08/03/facebook-interdit-a-dieudonne-toute-presence-sur-facebook-et-instagram_6048019_4408996.html

Lee, Eun-Ju, Jang Yoon Jae and Chung Myojung, 2020. "When and How User Comments Affect News Readers' Personal Opinion: Perceived Public Opinion and Perceived News Position as Mediators". In: *Digital Journalism*, 9 (1), 1–22, https://doi.org/10.1080/21670811.2020.1837638

Library of Congress. "Constitution Annotated. ArtI.S8.C4.1.2.3 Early U.S. Naturalization Laws", https://constitution.congress.gov/browse/essay/artI-S8-C4-1-2-3/ALDE_00013163/

Loke, Jaime, 2012. "Public Expressions of Private Sentiments: Unveiling the Pulse of Racial Tolerance through Online News Readers' Comments". In:

Howard Journal of Communications, 23 (3), 235–252, https://doi.org/10.1080/10646175.2012.695643

Marshall, P. David, 2021. "The commodified celebrity-self: industrialized agency and the contemporary attention economy". In: *Popular Communication*, 19 (3), 164–177, https://doi.org/10.4324/9781003383512-2

Mathew, Binny, Ritam Dutt, Pawan Goyal and Animesh Mukherjee, 2019. "Spread of Hate Speech in Online Social Media". In: *WebSci '19: Proceedings of the 10th ACM Conference on Web Science.* New York, NY: Association for Computing Machinery, 173–182

Mayring, Philipp, 2015. *Qualitative Inhaltsanalyse: Grundlagen Und Techniken*, 12th Edition. Weinheim: Beltz

Milbradt, Bjoern, 2013. "Antisemitic Metaphors and Latent Communication". In: Charles A. Small, (ed). *Global Antisemitism: A Crisis of Modernity.* Leiden: Brill, 45–49, https://doi.org/10.1163/9789004265561_006

Miller, Ryan, 2017. "'My Voice Is Definitely Strongest in Online Communities': Students Using Social Media for Queer and Disability Identity-Making". In: *Journal of College Student Development*, 58 (4), 509–525, https://doi.org/10.1353/csd.2017.0040

Newman, Nic, Richard Fletcher, Anne Schulz, Andi Simge, Craig T. Robertson and Rasmus K. Nielsen, 2021. *Reuters Institute Digital News Report*, 10th Edition. Reuters Institute for the Study of Journalism, https://reutersinstitute.politics.ox.ac.uk/sites/default/files/2021-06/Digital_News_Report_2021_FINAL.pdf

Nur, Aliah Mansor, Abdul Razak Rizalniyani, Zuriyati Mohamad Zam, Din Norrina and Abdul Razak Arbaiah, 2020. In: Norazah Mohd Suki and Norbayah Mohd Suki (eds). *Leveraging Consumer Behavior and Psychology in the Digital Economy.* Hershey, PA: Business Science Reference, https://doi.org/10.4018/978-1-7998-3042-9

Paris, Britt and Donovan, Joan, 2019. *Deepfakes and Cheap Fakes. The manipulation of audio and visual evidence.* Data & Society, https://datasociety.net/library/deepfakes-and-cheap-fakes/

Peace, Timothy, 2009. "Un Antisémitisme Nouveau? The Debate about a 'New Antisemitism' in France". In: *Patterns of Prejudice*, 43 (2), 103–121, https://doi.org/10.1080/00313220902793773

Proust, Serge, Jérôme Michalon, Marine Maurin and Camille Noûs, 2020. "Dieudonné: Anti-Semitism, Moral Panics and Deviant Community". In: *Déviance et Société*, 44 (3), 383–419, https://doi.org/10.3917/ds.443.0041

Rainie, Harrison and Barry Wellman, 2012. *Networked: The New Social Operating System.* Cambridge, MA: MIT Press

Richards, Abbie, Robin O'Luanaigh and Lea Marchl, 2023. "How 'Gnome Hunting' Became TikTok's Latest Antisemitic

Dog Whistle", https://gnet-research.org/2023/06/09/how-gnome-hunting-became-tiktoks-latest-antisemitic-dog-whistle/

Rothut, Sophia, Heidi Schulze, Julian Hohner and Diana Rieger, 2023. "Ambassadors of ideology: A conceptualization and computational investigation of far-right influencers, their networking structures, and communication practices". In: *New Media & Society*, 0 (0), https://doi.org/10.1177/14614448231164409

Schwarz-Friesel, Monika, 2019. "'Antisemitism 2.0'—The Spreading of Jew-hatred on the World Wide Web". In: Armin Lange et al. (eds). *Comprehending and Confronting Antisemitism*. Berlin: De Gruyter, 311–337, https://doi.org/10.1515/9783110618594-026

Smith, Anthony and Cooper Fleishman, 2016. "(((Echoes))) Exposed: The Secret Symbol Neo-Nazis Use to Target Jews Online". MIC, 1 June 2016, https://www.mic.com/articles/144228/echoes-exposed-the-secret-symbol-neo-nazis-use-to-target-jews-online#.ss1GX29cQ

Southern Poverty Law Center. "Radical Hebrew Israelites", https://www.splcenter.org/fighting-hate/extremist-files/group/radical-hebrew-israelites

Stehr, Paula, Patrick Rössler, Friederike Schönhardt and Laura Leissner, 2015. "Opinion Leadership| Parasocial Opinion Leadership Media Personalities' Influence within Parasocial Relations: Theoretical Conceptualization and Preliminary Results". In: *International Journal of Communication*, 9 (1), 982–1001

Stevenson, Nick, 2018. "Celebrity, fans and fandom". In: Elliott, Anthony (ed.), *Routledge Handbook of Celebrity Studies*. Abingdon: Routledge, 99–115, https://doi.org/10.4324/9781315776774-9

Sundquist, Eric J., 2005. *Strangers in the Land: Blacks, Jews, Post-Holocaust America*. Cambridge, MA: Harvard University Press, https://doi.org/10.4159/9780674044142

Taguieff, Pierre-André, 2004. *Rising from the Muck: The New Anti-Semitism in Europe*. Chicago: Ivan R. Dee

Toepfl, Florian and Eunike Piwoni, 2015. "Public Spheres in Interaction: Comment Sections of News Websites as Counterpublic Spaces". In: *Journal of Communication*, 65 (3), 465–488

Mark Weitzman, 2022. "Antisemitism in Social Media and on the Web". In: Stephan Katz (ed). *The Cambridge Companion to Antisemitism*. Cambridge: Cambridge University Press, 481–496, https://doi.org/10.1017/9781108637725.032

Weitzmann, Marc, 2019. *Hate: The Rising Tide of Anti-Semitism in France (and What It Means for Us)*. Boston, MA: Houghton Mifflin Harcourt

Winter, Charlie, Peter Neumann, Alexander Meleagrou-Hitchens, Magnus Ranstorp, Lorenzo Vidino and Johanna Fürst, 2020. "Online Extremism:

Research Trends in Internet Activism, Radicalization, and Counter-Strategies". In: *International Journal of Conflict and Violence (IJCV)*, 14 (2), 1–20, https://doi.org/10.4119/ijcv-3809

Wodak, Ruth, 2020. *The Politics of Fear: What Right-Wing Populist Discourses Mean*. Los Angeles: Sage, https://doi.org/10.4135/9781446270073

Wodak, Ruth and Martin Reisigl, 2009. "The Discourse-Historical Approach (DHA)". In: Ruth Wodak and Michael Meyer (eds). *Methods of Critical Discourse Studies*. London: Sage.

Wu, Shaomei, Jake Hofman, Winter Mason and Duncan Watts, 2011. "Who Says What to Whom on Twitter". In: *Proceedings of the 20th International Conference on World Wide Web*, March 2011, 701–714, https://doi.org/10.1145/1963405.1963504

Sources

LEFIG-FB[20221025] *Le Figaro*, 25 Octobre 2022, "Adidas rompt son partenariat avec Kanye West après des remarques antisémites", https://www.facebook.com/lefigaro/posts/pfbid0TF7f6AiJeA48jvRaoxNLZx2kTxwQUBE3rh43r7U BZKZgpH5HjxGtPmmX6CA7ca95l

LEFIG-FB[20200630] *Le Figaro*, 30 June 2020, "FLASH - YouTube bannit la chaîne de Dieudonné", https://www.facebook.com/lefigaro/posts/10157900362821339

VALEU-FB[20200701] *Valeurs Actuelles*, 01 July 2020, Dieudonné banni de YouTube, il dénonce des "pressions israéliennes", https://www.facebook.com/valeursactuelles.page/posts/2686501424784330

LEPAR-FB[20200707] *Le Parisien*, 07 July 2020, "Après Dieudonné, YouTube supprime les chaînes d'Alain Soral", https://www.facebook.com/leparisien/posts/10159203904639063

LEFIG-FB[20200709] *Le Figaro*, 09 July 2020, "Soral et Dieudonné vont devoir se réinventer totalement", https://www.facebook.com/lefigaro/posts/10157928661686339

LEFIG-FB[20200711] *Le Figaro*, 11 July 2020, "Comment Dieudonné file entre les doigts des autorités", https://www.facebook.com/lefigaro/posts/10157933638861339

MARIA-FB[20200806] *Marianne*, 06 August 2020, "Quand les Gafam jouent les inquisiteurs et font un joli cadeau à Dieudonné et Soral", https://www.facebook.com/Marianne.magazine/posts/10164034969505445

LCI.F-FB[20221026] *LCI*, 26 October 2022, "Propos antisémites : et si c'était (aussi) la fin de la carrière musicale de

Kanye West ?", https://www.facebook.com/LCI/posts/
pfbid0tL1iFLvzDchxRts2re5RnNimFfe6t5ub8ia5N8FoJYfYiKgEU
MW253iEDk9N84MFl

(BFMTV-FB[20221027]) *BFMTV*, 27 October 2022, "La statue
de cire de Kanye West retirée du musée Madame Tussauds
à Londres", https://www.facebook.com/BFMTV/posts/
pfbid0pgh35wsyzC7ekaQxe1iKEr7ntp7nU3SAX23ep9QsWFC
4soqbFy4e4R5igi94fgJGl

LEFIG-FB[20221208] *Le Figaro*, 08 December 2022, "Après Balenciaga,
Adidas rompt son partenariat avec Kanye West après des remarques
antisémites", https://www.facebook.com/lefigaro/photo
s/a.375133496338/10159677190596339

BFMTV-FB[20221208] *BFMTV*, 08 December 2022, "La statue de cire de Kanye
West retirée du musée Madame Tussauds à Londres", https://www.
facebook.com/BFMTV/posts/pfbid0pgh35wsyzC7ekaQxe1iKEr7ntp7nU
3SAX23ep9QsWFC4soqbFy4e4R5igi94fgJGl

LEPOI-FB[20221212] Le Point, 12 December 2022, "Remarques antisémites
: Kanye West aurait perdu 2 milliards de dollars jeudi", https://www.
facebook.com/lepoint.fr/photos/a.389816860702/10158763855725703

4. "More Like Genocide"

The Use of the Concept of Genocide in UK Online Debates About Israel

Matthew Bolton

Accusations that Israel has committed, or is in the process of committing, genocide against the Palestinian population of the Middle East are a familiar presence within anti-Israel and anti-Zionist discourse. In the wake of the Hamas attacks of 7 October 2023 and the subsequent Israeli military invasion of Gaza, claims of an Israeli genocide reached new heights, culminating in Israel being accused of genocide by South Africa at the International Court of Justice. Such claims can be made directly or indirectly, via attempts to draw an equivalence between Auschwitz or the Warsaw Ghetto and the current situation in the Palestinian territories. This chapter examines the use of the concept of genocide in social media discussions responding to UK news reports about Israel in the years prior to the 2023 Israel-Hamas war, thereby setting out the pre-existing conditions for its rise to prominence in the response to that war. It provides a historical account of the development of the concept of genocide, showing its interrelation with antisemitism, the Holocaust and the State of Israel. It then shows how accusations of genocide started being made against Israel in the decades following the Holocaust, and argues that such use is often accompanied by analogies between Israel and Nazi Germany and forms of Holocaust distortion. The chapter then qualitatively analyses comments referencing a supposed Israeli genocide posted on the *Facebook* pages of major

https://doi.org/10.11647/OBP.0406.04

British newspapers regarding three Israel-related stories: the May 2021 escalation phase of the Arab-Israeli conflict; the July 2021 announcement that the US ice cream company Ben & Jerry's would be boycotting Jewish settlements in the West Bank; and the rapid roll-out of the Covid-19 vaccine in Israel from December 2020 to January 2021.

1. Introduction[1]

In December 2023, South Africa formally issued proceedings against Israel at the International Court of Justice (ICJ). This court was set up following World War II as one of the principal organs of the new United Nations, as a means of settling legal disputes between member states. South Africa claimed that Israel was committing, and intended to commit, genocide against the Palestinian population of the Gaza Strip, as part of the Israeli military's response to the Hamas attacks in southern Israel on 7 October 2023. It called for the court to enforce a series of "provisional measures" against Israel, principally the cessation of military activity in Gaza. In January 2024, the ICJ made an initial ruling, which did not adjudicate on the question of whether Israel had committed, or was committing, genocide. Rather, it recognised—as Joan Donoghue, President of the ICJ for the hearing, later explained—that "the Palestinians had a plausible right to be protected from genocide, and that South Africa had the right to present that claim in the court" (BBC Hardtalk, 2024). The court did order that Israel should apply some "provisional measures" to prevent the possibility of genocide, primarily securing access to aid and basic services, and preventing statements from Israeli politicians and public figures which could be viewed as incitement to genocide (International Court of Justice 2024). However, the court did not rule that Israel should cease its military activity in Gaza, a "provisional measure" that would presumably be of the utmost urgency if Israel was indeed viewed as being in the process of committing genocide.

---

1 The chapter was conceived before Hamas attacks on 7 October and subsequent Israeli military actions in Gaza, but has been significantly revised since.

The ICJ's initial ruling did not, then, back up the claim of Israeli genocide in Gaza. While the final ruling is not expected for a number of years, the absence thus far of any legally certified allegations of genocide did not prevent the idea of an Israeli "genocide" becoming a widespread, if not dominant, way of depicting the war by pro-Palestinian and anti-Israel supporters, particularly online.[2] This chapter seeks to show that the choice of the concept of "genocide" to describe Israel's response to the 7 October attacks was not based on a disinterested appraisal of the actual situation on the ground in Gaza, nor a universally applied concern with genocide. As the Holocaust historian Tal Bruttmann notes, there has been a clear disparity in the use of "genocide" in relation to the 2023–24 Israel-Hamas conflict. While Israel's critics wasted no time in "jump[ing] over the "war crime" and then "crime against humanity" boxes to label Israel's actions as "genocide", Hamas's indiscriminate violence against any Jew or Israeli they could find on 7 October—precisely the marker of genocidal intent—remains for such observers only at the level of "war crime" (Bruttman and Bou 2024). Moreover, one need only note that on 4 January 2024, the South African President Cyril Ramaphosa warmly welcomed Sudanese militia leader General Mohamed Hamdan Dagalo (Hemedti) for a "courtesy" visit to the country. In 2023, Hemedti was accused of leading a genocidal attack on the Masalit group in Western Darfur, in which at least 15,000 died. He has also been implicated in genocidal acts in the early 2000s (Copelyn 2024). Similarly, in 2015, South Africa refused to arrest the then-president of Sudan Omar al-Bashir when he visited the country for an African Union summit—despite his being subject to an International Criminal Court arrest warrant for crimes against humanity and genocide in Darfur (International Criminal Court 2017). These incidents seem to call into question South Africa's universal concern with preventing and/or punishing genocide.

This disparity in the use of the concept of genocide in discussions of the recent war, driven by what might appear as a singular, *a priori* desire to associate Israel with genocidal actions, can be better understood once the history of the concept of genocide and its relation to Israel is placed in historical context. The charge of genocide has been made of Israel for

---

2   See for example, UK political commentator Owen Jones' claim that Israel was in the grip of a "genocidal mania" made a week after the initial ICJ judgement (Jones, 2024).

decades, and in response to all manner of Israeli actions, long before the 2023 war. The concept was, as it were, already lying "at hand" for use in debates about the Israeli response to the Hamas atrocities, having been in preparation for years. As this article shows, hanging over the history of accusations of Israeli genocide is the spectre of the Holocaust—and the opportunity to accuse Jews of committing the very crime to which they were subjected by the Nazi regime.

This chapter will explore the uses of the concept of "genocide" in online discussions in the UK regarding the State of Israel in the two years preceding the 7 October attacks. In retrospect, these discussions can be seen as laying the discursive groundwork for the concept's ubiquity in 2023 and 2024. The premise of the chapter is that framing the Arab-Israeli conflict through the concept of genocide radically distorts that conflict's origins, historical development and current state. Despite its broader, universal applicability, the concept of genocide is inextricably entwined with antisemitism, the Holocaust and the State of Israel. As such, no use of the concept is free of these historical resonances. This means that charging Israel with committing, or seeking to commit, genocide against the Palestinian population of the West Bank and Gaza is one of the most inflammatory and provocative claims that can be made against Israel as a Jewish state. Moreover, such claims are often accompanied—as frequently seen in online debates about the current conflict—by attempts to equate the Holocaust with the events of the 1947–49 Arab-Jewish/Israeli war, or Auschwitz and the Warsaw Ghetto with contemporary Gaza. The chapter suggests that such comparisons amount to a form of Holocaust distortion, erasing its exterminatory antisemitic character and reducing it to a generic form of state violence.

The chapter begins by summarising the meaning and historical development of the concept of genocide throughout the 1930s, until its adoption by the United Nations in 1948. It then shows why the charge of genocide against Israel is factually unsound, and briefly outlines the political factors which have led to its frequency today, exploring how its adoption by some political leaders and influential academics lends authority to its use by social media commenters in online discussions of Israel. The latter half of the chapter explores the use of the concept online, through qualitative analysis of online responses to three separate UK news stories involving Israel: the escalation phase of the Arab-Israeli conflict in

May 2021, the July 2021 announcement that the US ice cream company Ben & Jerry's would no longer permit their products to be sold in Israeli settlements on the West Bank, and the roll-out of the Covid-19 vaccine in Israel in December 2020 and January 2021. The analysis shows how the concept of GENOCIDE (Bolton 2024a) is used as a means to delegitimise Israel's existence, and often articulated in combination with other antisemitic concepts—such as making analogies between Israel and Nazi Germany (Becker 2024c), the idea of Jewish or Israeli EVIL (Bolton 2024b), and CALLS FOR VIOLENCE (Ascone 2024) or DEATH WISHES against Israelis and/or Jews (Placzynta 2024a).

2. The concept of genocide, the Holocaust and the State of Israel

The concept of genocide was gradually constructed over the 1930s and 40s by the Polish legal scholar Raphael Lemkin. As the Nazi persecution of German Jews ramped up to become the attempted extermination of Jews across Europe, including 49 members of his own family, Lemkin drew parallels with previous incidents of state-led murder of national and ethnic groups, such as the Ottoman Empire's attempt to wipe out the Armenians and the slaughter of Christian Assyrians in Iraq. Arguing that such mass murder based on group identity was a distinct crime from the mass murder of individuals, Lemkin contended that existing legal and political concepts were unable to grasp the specificities of the Nazi persecution and extermination of European Jewry (Lemkin 2012). He struggled for over a decade to convince international legal bodies to make the "destruction of national, religious and racial groups" a crime in international law. In 1942 he coined the neologism "genocide" to describe what had hitherto been a "crime without a name"—"geno-" derived from the Greek *genos*, meaning tribe, and *-cide* from the Latin *caedere*, "to kill". In 1948, the UN adopted the Convention on the Prevention and Punishment of the Crime of Genocide, outlawing "acts committed with intent to destroy, in whole or in part, a national, ethnic, racial or religious group, as such".

The experience of the Holocaust clearly hung over both the forging and juridical adoption of the concept of GENOCIDE, while the State of Israel was established the same year as the Genocide Convention was adopted. Although Israel's founding was neither a direct consequence nor cause of the legal recognition of genocide, the experience of the Holocaust had given a new moral urgency to the Zionist project for a Jewish nation-state. The failure of other states to allow Jews to escape their fate via immigration, and the need to provide a home for thousands of Jewish displaced persons, seemingly made the case for a Jewish state in Mandatory Palestine inarguable.

The concept of genocide thus carries the history of Jewish persecution and attempted extermination within it as a "sedimented layer" (Koselleck 2018), such that it is not possible to use the concept without evoking, in some sense, that history. In the same way, the existence of the State of Israel and the Jewish experience of genocidal violence are, in historical terms, inextricably entwined. Nevertheless, that concept was not a mirror image of the Holocaust: from the outset, Lemkin sought a broader concept that was able to contain a multiplicity of historical experiences, with each able to shed light on the others. There were downsides to this abstraction: something of the historically unprecedented nature of the Holocaust is lost when it is reduced to the concept of genocide. But there are upsides too. By seeking to make visible a mode of state violence against groups that had previously been hidden, Lemkin's concept acts as what Walter Benjamin described as kind of temporal "shock" (1999: 262). It explodes the ceaseless forward march of "homogenous, empty time" (262) and opens up a new vantage point upon experiences and memories of suffering previously lost in the depths of a forgotten or repressed past. This potential to "arrest [...] the flow of thought" (262) and bring the past to the present remains potent. Today, an accusation of genocide against a state continues to be one of the most powerful and morally charged that can be made, bringing all of that retrieved history to bear. Despite recent critiques of its prominence (Moses 2021), genocide is still widely regarded as the "crime of crimes" and claims of genocide continue to carry a grave weight.

Given this history, and the interrelation of the concept with the Holocaust and the State of Israel, the claim that Israel has committed, is committing, or intends to commit genocide upon the Palestinian population across the Middle East—that Israel seeks to "wipe the Palestinians from the face of the earth"—is one of the most incendiary charges that can be made of the Jewish state. It is true that claims of genocide are, to an extent, a routine presence within passionate online political debate in the UK—witness the claims that Boris Johnson's Conservative government was seeking to commit genocide by delaying the introduction of Covid-19 lockdowns (Shaw 2020). But when aimed at Israel—so that the victims of the most extreme genocide in history become the perpetrators—it represents an aggravating factor which goes beyond the frenzied hyperbole that characterises much political discourse online. The accusation of Israeli genocide is often combined with disapproval of Jews' supposed moral failure to "learn the lessons" of their past (Placzynta 2024b).

Claims that Israel has perpetrated or is perpetrating a genocide upon the Palestinians can be debunked on a purely empirical basis. As Philip Spencer notes, they are "without foundation in relation to what the Genocide Convention specifies; there is no evidence of an intent on the part of the Israeli state to annihilate the Palestinians as a group" (Spencer 2010: 146). The Palestinian population has not shrunk or disappeared over the course of Israel's existence—quite the opposite. According to the World Bank, in 1990 the Palestinian population in the West Bank and Gaza was around two million. By 2019, it stood at around 4.9 million— more than a 100% rise over a period which included the Second Intifada and numerous violent conflicts between Israel and Palestine (World Bank 2019). No political party in Israel advocates for the extermination of the Palestinian people—there are extreme factions which argue for the transfer of the Palestinian population, but this has never been a serious policy, nor has it gained any serious support amongst either Israeli politicians or public. There is no programme for the removal of Palestinian children from their parents to Israeli families, as was the case in colonial genocides such as that of Aboriginal Australians. There is no systematic destruction of Palestinian, Arab or Islamic cultural or religious artefacts, as would be needed to substantiate the weaker claim of "cultural genocide".

A description of the 2023–24 Israeli military actions in Gaza as "genocidal"—that is, a military campaign with the express intent to destroy the Palestinian population as such—relies on a similar distortion of the historical record. In the first place, it means downplaying or ignoring what could rationally be depicted as the genocidal nature of Hamas's 7 October attacks themselves, in which the clear purpose was to kill as many people as possible—regardless of civilian or military status, age or sex—in the time available (van Aaken et al. 2023). If Hamas's actions are, on the contrary, understood as being motivated by genocidal intent, then Israel would fall foul of the Genocide Convention by *not* taking action against the group (Mor 2024). Second, it means redescribing what is a war between the Israeli army and Hamas military units as a one-sided bombardment of civilians by Israel. It further entails ignoring Israeli attempts to warn civilians prior to attacks and to encourage them to move out of targeted areas, and failing to examine whether Hamas is preventing them from doing so. Third, it means dismissing without consideration the Israeli claim that the ratio of civilians to combatants killed by Israel in Gaza is much lower than other equivalent conflicts, and a long way from the total destruction implied by the concept of genocide—while accepting at face value the death figures provided by Hamas-run health agencies (Aizenberg 2023). Fourth, it means ignoring any role Hamas has played in commandeering food and aid meant to be distributed to civilians. Finally, it means removing any responsibility for the continuation of the war from the leaders of Hamas, who could immediately end the fighting by releasing the remaining Israeli hostages and handing themselves in to the International Criminal Court. Thus, as with the more general accusation of Israeli genocide, the specific accusation in the case of 2023–24 war can only be made through a long series of historical and conceptual distortions—although the final ICJ decision may, of course, impact this analysis.

Understanding the origins and spread of the idea of a supposedly genocidal Israeli state therefore entails leaving the world of empirical fact behind and entering the realm of political and symbolic orders. The concept of Israeli genocide sits within a constellation of related antisemitic stereotypes and analogies, particularly those which seek to posit an equivalence or identity between Israel or Zionism and Nazi Germany (Becker 2021). One strain of origin lies in the reception of the Holocaust within the Arab world in the post-war period, as tensions between the Jewish and Arab populations of Mandatory Palestine rose with the prospect of partition and a Jewish state on the horizon, eventually spilling over into war. As Esther Webman and Meir Litvak (2012) have argued, across the post-war period Arab politicians, intellectuals and publics generally regarded the Holocaust as solely a European affair, for which Arabs have paid the ultimate price through the establishment of Israel. Some went a step further and suggested that Jews had exaggerated or fabricated the Holocaust in order to justify a Jewish state (Becker 2024a). This latter position was often combined with comparisons or analogies between Israel and the Nazis, underpinning narratives in which "the Palestinians are [...] represented as the Holocaust's true victims" (Webman and Litvak 2012: 2). The building blocks were thus set in place for "the transformation" of Jews "from victims" of genocide "to culprits" (2).

The shifts in narratives around the Nakba, or "the catastrophe"—the expulsion and flight of Arabs from what would become Israel during the Jewish-Arab war of 1947–48—were marked by the impact of these ideas. While the "catastrophe" in the immediate post-war period was understood in terms of the failure of the collected Arab armies to defeat the Israeli military forces (Mor 2023), over time "the Nakba" become the foundation upon which was built a "politics of memory" clearly "modelled [...] after Israeli Shoah commemorations" (Bartov 2014: 19). By seeking to make a direct equivalence between the circumstances surrounding the establishment of the State of Israel and the Holocaust, a path is opened not just to the delegitimisation of Israel but to HOLOCAUST DISTORTION and even DENIAL (Troschke 2024). The Holocaust here is reduced to an abstract universal (Fine and Spencer 2018), drained of its specific content so that it can be conflated with any number of other forms of political and state violence, thereby making claims of a "Palestinian Holocaust" possible.

The same tendency to equate Israel with the Nazis in order to demonise the former reappears in the narratives of the political left across Europe and the US, particularly in periods of intensified conflict in the Middle East. As Izabella Tabarovsky has shown, much of the conceptual architecture used by the Western left today to demonise Israel—from claims of apartheid to genocide and analogies between Israel and Nazi Germany—originated in the antisemitic anti-Zionist campaigns instigated by the Soviet Union from the 1950s onwards, the terms of which were taken over wholesale by European Communist parties and their "fellow travellers" in the 1970s and 80s (Tabarovsky 2022). By the time of the Second Intifada, claims that Gaza represented a continuation or return of Auschwitz, or was akin to the Warsaw Ghetto, were a frequent presence in Palestinian solidarity movements and marches—again, radically distorting the historical reality of the gas chambers and of the Ghetto (Bob from Brockley 2014). Accusations of Israeli genocide continue to be made in response to Israeli military attacks within the West Bank and Gaza, while the international isolation of Hamas, after their takeover of Gaza following Israeli withdrawal in 2005, is often framed as a step on the road to genocide. This is despite that isolation being a result of Hamas's refusal to agree to the conditions for recognition (most notably full acknowledgement of Israel's right to exist) set out by the Middle East Quartet, as well as Hamas's continued indiscriminate rocket fire at Israeli towns and cities (Reuters 2007).

Throughout the 2000s and 2010s, left-led campaigns in the UK sought to abolish Holocaust Memorial Day, or rename it "Genocide Memorial Day", winning support from leading politicians including Jeremy Corbyn, the now former leader of the British Labour Party. The campaigns' ostensible argument was that by focusing on the Holocaust alone, the history and experiences of other genocides were being blotted out. This argument is on shaky ground given that Holocaust Memorial Day events and literature do not solely focus on the Holocaust, but rather commemorate and provide educational information on the history of genocidal violence from the Armenians and the Sinti to atrocities in Cambodia, Srebrenica, Rwanda and Darfur. Indeed, to a great extent the only time when these events gain any public traction in Britain is through Holocaust Memorial Day publicity. Rather, the underlying motive for the campaigns against the name "Holocaust Memorial Day" was the desire to make an equivalence between the Holocaust and the Israeli treatment of Palestinians, a desire in clear evidence when Corbyn hosted an event entitled "Never Again for Anyone: Auschwitz to Gaza" in Parliament on Holocaust Memorial Day in 2010 (Zeffman 2018).

These narratives have been lent legitimacy by the academic discipline of Genocide Studies itself. In order to condemn Israel in the language of the "crime of crimes", some scholars have sought to extend the concept of genocide so that it now includes the Allied bombing of Dresden during World War II, the forced transfer of ethnic Germans from Eastern Europe in the aftermath of the German defeat, and multiple partition and population transfer polices of the post-colonial era, including, crucially, those of the wars that led to the establishment of the State of Israel (Shaw 2010). In so doing, the concept of genocide is deprived of its specific meaning and, as Omer Bartov notes, it becomes impossible to distinguish between different modes of violence "in a manner that would help us understand similarity and difference" (2010: 252). Much as with the use of the apartheid and colonial analogies to describe contemporary Israel by leading NGOs (see Bolton et al. 2023) then, by providing spurious claims of Israeli genocide with the imprimatur of scholarly authority, such works bolster the confidence of those who wish to wield the concept of genocide as a weapon in online debates about Israel. It is likely that the ICJ case on the 2023–24 Israel-Hamas war, and the way its initial judgement has been (mis)interpreted by anti-Israel activists and web users, will only intensify this process of authorisation. Given the proximity of the genocide concept to that of the Nazi analogy, it is at least possible that the latter will be the next concept to be granted scholarly and institutional authority in this way.

3. Qualitative analysis

To explore in more depth the way that the concept of genocide is used in online debates around Israel, and to see how the conceptual history laid out above impacts upon the contemporary use of the concept, the rest of this chapter will focus on the online reactions to three Israel-related new stories over the course of 2020 and 2021. Given that these stories and reactions took place prior to the 2023–24 war, analysing this discourse provides an opportunity to trace the pre-conditions for the concept of genocide's rise to prominence following the war.

To this end, three separate corpora were built of comments posted on the *Facebook* pages of major British newspapers in response to reports of:

a. The May 2021 escalation phase of the Arab-Israeli conflict, sparked by a long-running legal dispute over housing in the Sheikh Jarrah area of East Jerusalem conflict, sparked by a long-running legal dispute over housing in the Sheikh Jarrah area of East Jerusalem;

b. The US ice cream company Ben & Jerry's July 2021 announcement;[3]

c. The rapid roll-out of a Covid-19 vaccine across Israel from December 2020 to January 2021.

---

3   https://www.benjerry.com/about-us/media-center/opt-statement.

These stories were chosen because they cover a range of angles on Israel: one directly related to the conflict with the Palestinians; another focused on political campaigns against Israel; and the last a story that was not directly conflict-related, and which drew significant positive coverage of Israel.

Each corpus consisted of 10–15 *Facebook* threads. These threads were analysed qualitatively using the MAXQDA content analysis programme with the antisemitic stereotypes, analogies and linguistic structures used by commenters classified according to the guidelines set out in the Decoding Antisemitism project's "guidebook" (Becker et al. 2024). All comments coded with the "genocide" code where then analysed. In the following, I will set out details of the data set and results of the analysis for each of the three discourse-triggering events in a separate section.

3.1 The May 2021 escalation phase of the Arab-Israeli conflict[4]

In May 2021, a long-standing legal case regarding the ownership and tenancy of properties in Jerusalem's Sheikh Jarrah district descended into violence. After protestors at the Al-Aqsa Mosque clashed with Israel police, Hamas militants in Gaza sought to capitalise on the unrest by firing hundreds of rockets at Israeli towns and cities. Israeli forces retaliated through airstrikes on targets in Gaza, leading to many civilian casualties. Intercommunal violence spread within Israel itself, while large anti-Israel demonstrations took place across Europe and the US. These were followed by multiple incidents of physical and verbal attacks on Jewish people, Jewish-owned businesses and synagogues. The escalation phase received substantial coverage in the UK media, and a large number of web-user comments posted in response. As an event directly concerned with the conflict, emotional and at times extreme language and argumentative strategies are to be expected (Becker, Ascone and Troschke 2021).

The corpus for this event consisted of 10 threads taken from the *Facebook* pages of a range of British newspapers across the political spectrum, from *The Times*, *Telegraph* and *Daily Mail* to the *Guardian* and *Independent*. In total, 1,504 comments were analysed. Of these, 422 were

---

4　For a more general analysis of online reactions to this event, see Becker et al. 2021.

classed as antisemitic, either directly or in the context of the thread—28% of the total comments. Within the antisemitic comments, 26 expressed or activated the accusation of an Israeli genocide, equalling 6% of the antisemitic comments.

The relatively small number of comments invoking genocide might be explained by the nature of the "discourse trigger"—very few observers, even those most ideologically committed to the Palestinian cause and/or highly distorted images of Israel, could fail to notice that Israeli attacks on Gaza were responding to a barrage of rockets aimed at Israeli cities from Gaza. In the popular interpretation of the concept of genocide, the notion that a group is undergoing genocide sits uneasily with that group's political and military wing engaging in military activity that poses a serious threat to the supposed perpetrators of that genocide. Thus, to use the concept of genocide in such a context entails downplaying the success or effectiveness of the "resistance", something which it appears many pro-Hamas commentators are loath to do.

(1) "Totally deserved and appropriate!!!Israel deserves MUCH more than this. Fascist, Genocidal state!!!!" (IND-FB[20210511])

(1) was posted in response to a report of more than 80 rockets being fired at Tel Aviv from Gaza by Hamas militants. Such rocket attacks are indiscriminate and are directly targeted at civilian populations. The web user not only praises such attacks on civilians as being "deserved" but calls for further and more effective attacks, using a capitalised "MUCH" to emphasise the extent of the destruction and death that Israelis supposedly deserve to suffer and for which they hope. The justification for this death wish appears in the final line of the comment, where Israel as a state is described in essentialised terms as both "Fascist" and "Genocidal".[5] Exclamation marks reaffirm the strength of the web user's destructive feelings towards Israel.

---

5   'Essentialised' here means presenting an ascribed characteristic as inherent, without any specification or limitation. Thus, a comment describing a particular Israeli politician as 'fascist' would not automatically be classed as antisemitic. Describing the state of Israel as 'fascist' in its totality makes fascism an innate (and therefore not temporally limited) characteristic of Israel as such, and this is regarded as an antisemitic ascription.

(2) "Not sure you can call it 'full scale war' when only one side is properly armed? More like genocide". (MIR-FB[20210511])

Here the web user disputes another commenter's description of the escalation phase as tipping into "full scale war", arguing that because only "one side"—i.e. Israel—is "properly armed", the conflict is in fact no such thing, but rather "genocide". Denying that the Palestinians have access to arms—often by portraying Iran-supplied weapons as almost child-like "homemade rockets"—is a common means of attributing SOLE GUILT FOR THE CONFLICT (Vincent and Bolton 2024) to Israel. Similarly, denying that there is a conflict between Israel and Palestine at all, or rejecting the idea that there are "two sides", and instead using one-sided terminology such as "oppression", and, at its extreme, "genocide", to describe the situation in the Middle East is an increasingly popular framing device within social media discussions. This logic is precisely that which has been at play in discussions of the 2023–24 Israel-Hamas war, in which, as notes above, the nature and significance of the 7 October attacks is downplayed or ignored, and use of the term "war"— which signifies two combatants—is replaced by "genocide", which, in popular usage, implies a binary aggressor-victim relation.

(3) "Sick telling only one side of the story, and it is the story of the oppressor, genocidal occupier. The Independent deserves being gagged. Sick". (IND-FB[20210511])

(3) aims its ire at the media reporting of the escalation—in this case, reports of rocket fire from Gaza. The web user describes reporting of the experience of Israelis under rocket fire as "sick", and the—presumably distorted, if not fictional—"story of the oppressor, genocidal occupier". The comment implies that the news outlet is deliberately suppressing the Palestinian "story" and as such should be "gagged", i.e. censored. While such comments can often come close to attributions of JEWISH POWER AND INFLUENCE (Becker 2024b) over the media, here the implication is rather that the media are, through their own political choice, servile to Israeli interests.

(4) "you do realise Palestine was there before Israel. Is real was created after ww2. So the people persecuted in ww2 have gone on to persecute others the same way. You really need to educate yourself. Actually do some history you plank" (TEL-FB[20210511])

(5) "The fact remains that they are commuting genocide on Palestine what in turn has caused the conflict. Israel wasn't there before ww2" (TEL-FB[20210511])

Both of these comments were posted in quick succession by the same web user in response to reports of Israeli airstrikes on Gaza. The first (4) implies that the creation of Israel following World War II marks the point at which "the people persecuted in ww2" have begun "persecute[ing] others the same way". This not only implies an accusation of genocide and creates an analogy between Israel and the Nazis, but through the use of "the same way" amounts to a form of HOLOCAUST DISTORTION or relativisation. The second comment, (5), makes explicit what was implicit in the first, by directly accusing Israel of "commuting [sic] genocide on Palestine". The entire conflict is explained by the supposed "genocide" and the fact that Israel did not exist as a state prior to World War II, thus attributing all guilt for the conflict onto the Israeli side.

(6) "So if some one come and take ur home and ask u to leave .will u . Just leave ? . Or fight back ? . And I already know your answer isn't how white America built with taking ppl home and killing 80 million america native . So I'm not surprised you back isreal crimes ". (TEL-FB[20210511])

(6) begins with a rhetorical question aimed at a previous commenter, asking how they would respond to "some one...tak[ing] ur home", and suggesting that "fight[ing] back" is an appropriate response. The idea of "fighting back" here is broad, with no distinction being drawn between, for example, non-violent civil disobedience and suicide bombings targeting civilians. The comment then makes the genocide accusation implicitly, through an analogy with the destruction of the Native American population during the European colonisation of North America. The deaths of "80 million america native" are cited as an equivalent to Israeli "crimes", effectively accusing Israel of a genocide that in numerical terms surpasses the Holocaust.

3.2 Ben & Jerry's boycott of Israeli settlements on the West Bank

On 19 July 2021, the American ice cream producer Ben & Jerry's announced through its website that it would no longer sell its ice cream in Israeli settlements on the West Bank, saying that it was inconsistent with its values. Priding itself on its politically radical image, the company's decision had been influenced by criticism of its continued operation in the region from "fans and trusted partners". The move was met with a positive reception from sections of Israel civil society and pro-Palestinian groups, but also fierce criticism, including from Israel's foreign minister Yair Lapid, who called it "capitulation to anti-Semitism, to BDS, to all that is evil in the anti-Israeli and anti-Jewish discourse".

The claim that the Ben & Jerry's boycott was antisemitic seems to elide the difference between the State of Israel (as such) and the settlements—an elision that in other contexts could itself be categorised as antisemitic. Indeed, Ben & Jerry's openly declared that they were not boycotting Israel as a state, nor did they support the BDS movement, but rather distinguished between the State of Israel and settlements in the West Bank.[6] As such, in contrast to comments like Lapid's, within this analysis the event itself was not considered to be an act of antisemitism. This had an effect on the classification of comments responding to reports of the boycott—comments which merely stated support for the boycott were not classed as antisemitic.[7]

This corpus consisted of 12 threads taken from the *Facebook* pages of *The Guardian*, *The Times*, *Telegraph*, *Financial Times*, *The Independent* and *The Spectator*. A total of 794 comments were analysed, with 176 (or 22%) categorised as directly or contextually antisemitic. Of the antisemitic comments, 12—or, as with the May escalation corpus, just

---

6   Ben & Jerry's decision led to a prolonged conflict with its parent company, *Unilever*, over whether the Israeli licence could be separated from the rest of the business. The dispute was reported as being "settled" in December 2022, although the details remain opaque (https://www.theguardian.com/business/2022/dec/15/unilever-ben-and-jerrys-ice-cream-israel-west-bank, last accessed on 11 July 2023).

7   By contrast, a comment affirming the author Sally Rooney's boycott of Israeli publishers and translators – which she explicitly linked to BDS and the state of Israel as a whole, rather than just the settlements, would be classed as antisemitic. See Karolina Placzynta's chapter in this volume, and Becker et al. 2021b.

over 6%—expressed claims of, or references to, Israeli genocide. The majority of these references appeared in *Facebook* threads responding to articles in *The Guardian*. The relatively low level of references to genocide in this corpus might be explained by the innocuous or even faintly comical image of an ice cream company seeking to intervene in a complex conflict. Nevertheless, the above average level of antisemitic comments overall—the average proportion of antisemitic comments in UK comment threads examined across the course of the Decoding Antisemitism project is around 10–12%—clearly shows that substantial numbers of web users looked to capitalise on the story in order to make antisemitic statements, with the concept of GENOCIDE part of the topoi utilised to that end.

(7) "'Settlers'? I think you mean perpetrators of genocide😒"
(GUARD-FB[20210723])

Responding to a report on the reactions of residents on an Israeli settlement on the West Bank to the boycott, (6) reframes their identity from "settlers" to "perpetrators of genocide", in a question-and-answer format laden with irony. The ostensible world-weary calmness of the comment is emphasised by the use of an eye-rolling emoji, yet disguises an attribution that creates a monstrous, murderous image of the "settlers" which moves far beyond legitimate critique of the practice of settlement.

(8) "The genocideof Palestinian will never be forgotten and when time change israiel will pay for every brutality it's committed and committing against poor Palestinians... and Anti Israiel is not anti semitism the whole world know they can't hide any more behind this ". (GUARD-FB[20210723])

In (7), the Israeli "genocide" of the Palestinians is presupposed, such that the comment's focus is on the future consequences Israel will suffer in response. The web user predicts that Israel will "pay for every brutality" when "times change"—an indirect threat, with an undertone of approval for violent reprisals. This message is combined with an attempt to pre-empt the accusations of antisemitism the web user seems to expect, writing that "anti Israiel is not anti semitism"—but they go further, implicitly making an accusation that Israel INSTRUMENTALISES ANTISEMITISM (Becker 2024a) by making false claims to deflect legitimate criticism of their actions. As with the supposed genocidal actions, the web user suggests that this strategy no longer works as it presumably once did, as "the whole world know they can't hide any more behind" such claims.

> (9) "Hamas is just an excuse for the genocide of Palestinians women children's and men's. Where on earth you can see that ghaza is live human jail made by terrorist israiel and then even there Israiel killing innocent humans. Israiel illegally grabbed Palestinians lands houses and farms and made many Palestinians homeless. And after all that terrorist israiel supporters blaming Palestinians. Only humans can understand this". (GUARD-FB[20210723])

Here, the web user argues against other commenters who sought to highlight Israeli security concerns in the face of the fundamentalist, authoritarian and indiscriminate violence of Hamas. (8) contends that references to the nature of Hamas are merely "an excuse" for the Israeli "genocide" of Palestinian society—women, children and men. Gaza is presented as a "live human jail" created by "terrorist" Israel, thereby again removing any political or moral responsibility for the current state of the region from Hamas, the rulers of Gaza. The comment ends by declaring that "only humans can understand this", implicitly attributing a form of immorality and/or evil to Israel and its supporters, depicting them as inhuman and thus morally deficient.

> (10) "I think we're well past the point of solely defending human rights there. The very existence of an entire people is at stake so every little bit helps" (GUARD-FB[20210720])

This comment expresses urgency in the face of the imminent destruction of "the very existence of an entire people"—the comment itself is based on an allusion which in the context, is a clear reference to the Palestinian population, and thus an implicit reference to Israeli genocide. Actions and campaigns to defend human rights in the West Bank and Gaza are declared insufficient, implicitly suggesting support for violent resistance. Given that "every little bit helps", there is no distinction made here between boycotts by an ice cream company, violent resistance against the Israeli military, and the targeting of Israeli civilians. This offhand comment therefore implies support for any form of "resistance" against Israel, however indiscriminately violent—a reaction that was, indeed, commonplace in the wake of the 7 October attacks (Becker et al. 2023).

3.3 The roll-out of the Covid-19 vaccine in Israel[8]

In December 2020, Israel launched its Covid-19 vaccination programme, the first state in the world to do so. The speed of Israel's roll-out of the vaccination programme across its population drew plaudits and positive media coverage, with other countries looking to see what could be learnt from the Israeli experience. But this generally favourable coverage was swiftly followed by media stories focusing on the question of Israel's supposed responsibility for distribution of the vaccine to Palestinians in the West Bank and Gaza. For some, Israel as an occupying power in the West Bank was obliged to distribute the vaccine to Palestinians in the area over which they hold control. Israeli ministers argued that the Oslo Accords gave responsibility for healthcare to the Palestinian Authority, and that it was legitimate for Israel—as for any other nation-state—to prioritise its own citizens (including Israeli Arabs) before donating vaccines elsewhere (Trew 2021). In the event, Israel did donate 5,000 vaccine doses to Palestinian healthcare workers in January 2021, and further donations and swap deals followed later in the year (BBC 2021).

The corpus consisted of 15 threads of comments taken from the *Facebook* pages of all major British national newspapers, with a total of 1,522 comments analysed. Of these, 259 (or 17%) were classified as antisemitic. Out of the antisemitic comments, 32 (or 12%) articulated claims of genocide against Israel.

These results therefore stand out from those of the previous two corpora. Reports on the speed and success of the vaccine roll-out were, unlike the other two discourse events, not directly connected to either the Israel-Palestine conflict or political campaigns against Israel, and this may explain why the overall level of antisemitic comments was significantly lower, dropping by around 5–10%. Yet despite the lower overall level, the percentage of the comments referencing Israeli genocide within those classed as antisemitic was almost double that within the escalation phase and Ben & Jerry's threads.

Reasons for this surprising result—which would need to be explored in further research—might include a general increase in references to genocide and/or deliberate state killing during the most intense and

---

8   For further analysis of the reactions to this event, including those from France and Germany, see Becker et al 2021.

fear-ridden periods of the Covid-19 era, or that positive, non-conflict-related stories about Israel motivated some web users to draw on more extreme concepts to express their antipathy to Israel. On the other hand, stories specifically focusing on the question of Israel's responsibility for Palestinian healthcare did open up a potential pathway to speculation about Israel's motives for not immediately supplying Palestinians with the vaccine. It is possible that the medieval antisemitic depiction of Jews as "well-poisoners", while a rarity in contemporary antisemitic discourse, may have played a more-or-less unconscious role here. For those already motivated by anti-Israel or anti-Jewish animus, it thus only took a small step to begin accusing Israel of deliberately withholding the vaccine for political ends—including, at its most extreme, the end of genocide.

> (11) "How is the world silent about this continued genocide. Its insanely inhumane!" (IND-FB[20210108])

This comment presupposes Israeli genocide, and as such portrays the absence of an immediate vaccine distribution programme to the Palestinians as a mere "continuation" of an ongoing extermination policy. Via the use of a rhetorical question, the web user evokes ideas of Jewish privilege or a "free pass" by bemoaning "the world['s]" silence about this supposedly self-evident genocide. The comment concludes with an indeterminate claim that either the genocide itself, or the silence about it, is "insanely inhumane"—implicitly presenting Israel as standing opposed to humanity as such.

> (12) "Yet another Israeli crime .... if this isn't intended genocide I don't know what is!!!!!" (IND-FB[20210108])

> (13) "They just want the Palestine people dead and gone shame on them" (IND-FB[20210108])

> (14) "The only time Zionists wanna be hands-off is when it leads to the genocide of the native Palestinian population" (TEL-FB[20210124])

Each of these comments present the decision of the Israeli government to vaccinate its own population before distributing vaccines elsewhere as a deliberate, "intentional" attempt to kill (if not entirely wipe out) the Palestinian population. Example (12) begins with the identification of "yet another Israeli crime", accompanied by an ellipsis which indicates graphically the never-ending series of supposed crimes. The self-evidence of the supposed "intended genocide" represented by the dispute over vaccine distribution is then indicated by the web user through the claim that if it is not "genocide" then nothing can be classed as genocide. Comment (13) makes a similar argument in more direct fashion, positing that Israel (or Israelis) "just want[s] the Palestinian people dead and gone". Comment (14) approaches the issue from an act/omission angle, suggesting that "Zionist" inaction in this case stands in contrast to a presupposed over-intervention that characterises Israel's normal position vis-à-vis the Palestinian territories. The only explanation, according to this web user, is that through this omission, "Zionists" hope for the genocide of the "native" population— here perhaps alluding to the colonial genocides that accompanied the founding of the US and Australia.

(15) A: "it would only cause a conspiracy that israel is trying to poison them".
     B: "they probably where" (DM-FB[20201230])

In the first comment of this interchange, a web user justifies Israel's decision to not immediately distribute Covid vaccines to the Palestinians by suggesting that doing so would only lead to a conspiracy theory that Israel was trying to "poison" the population of the West Bank and Gaza—in effect, that even distributing vaccines would lead to accusations of Israeli genocide. In response, B replies by confirming the proposed conspiracy theory (which carries echoes of the aforementioned "well-poisoner" calumny), writing that "they"—the Israelis—"probably where [sic]". In so doing, they express the GENOCIDE concept indirectly through affirmation of a conceptual frame initially presented as a form of critique.

(16) "That way they wont have any foreigners there to watch them commit more mass genocide on the Palestinians". (DM-FB[20210125])

(17) "How to be a racist apartheid state that commits genocide on the indigenous people, commits daily war crimes, and human rights abuses. But the tories already do that". (TEL-FB[20210112])

Both of these comments respond to two news stories that are not directly related to the conflict or to the question of Palestinian vaccine distribution—the first responds to a report of Israeli plans to close their borders to foreign travel; the second to an opinion piece asking what other countries could learn from the Israeli roll-out of the vaccine. Despite the benign nature of both stories, these web users nevertheless use them as a vehicle to accuse Israel of genocide. In (16) the comment suggests that there is an ulterior motive to the border closures, namely that Israel will be able to "commit more mass genocide" safe from the prying eyes of foreign observers. (17) combines the concepts of Israel as an innately "racist state" and the apartheid analogy with the claim of genocide, adding to this depictions of Israeli evil ("war crimes" and "human rights abuses"). The final sentence of the comment suggests that the same phenomena are characteristic of the British government, demonstrating how concepts such as genocide, war crimes and abuse of human rights are routinely deprived of concrete meaning through frequent use as generic intensifiers in everyday online communication.

> (18) "you clearly support the genocide and holocaust of Palestinians too". (TIMES-FB[20210103])

> (19) "so you're denying the Palestinian Holocaust?" (TEL-FB[20210124])

Both (18) and (19) use news stories about the success of the vaccine roll-out to draw a direct equivalence between Israel's treatment of Palestinians and the Holocaust. Example (18) accuses a previous pro-Israeli commenter of "clearly support[ing]" genocide and "holocaust of Palestinians". And, (19) uses language normally associated with the identification of HOLOCAUST DENIAL to suggest that denying that Israel's relations with the Palestinians are comparable to the Holocaust is akin to Holocaust denial. In so doing, both comments indirectly distort the Holocaust themselves. By using the terminology of the Holocaust as a linguistic weapon against Israel—or rather against those, potentially Jewish, web users who support or do not automatically condemn Israel—such comments amount to an aggravated form of antisemitic harassment.

> (20) "Genocide started after the birth of Israel and this is the Jewish peoples thanks to all those people who sacrificed their lives to liberate them in the second world war". (DM-FB[20201230])

This comment again evokes the image of the Nazi genocide to demonise Israel as genocidal—but adds to this a further attack on "the Jewish people" more broadly. The web user suggests that by supposedly committing genocide—and thereby replicating the Nazi crimes against the Jews—"the Jewish people" have displayed an immoral ingratitude to "all those people who sacrificed their lives to liberate them" in World War II. This gross historical falsehood—no nation entered the war to "liberate" Jews, and many refused entry to Jewish refugees fleeing Nazi persecution—is evoked solely in order to magnify the genocide charge and create an implicit Nazi analogy.

> (21) "apologists for slow genocide like you make mynscin crawl. Pure demonic evil" (TEL-FB[20210112])

Responding to an opinion piece on what the British National Health Service could learn from the Israeli experience, comment (21) describes Israel as committing a "slow genocide", and uses dehumanising language—"you make [my skin] crawl" to demonise those who refute such a depiction of Israel. This ascription is intensified by a final clause in which either the posited "slow genocide" itself, or those who support such actions—or both—represent "pure demonic evil". In so doing, the comment activates classical Christian antisemitic stereotypes which associate Jews with the DEVIL and the presence of EVIL.

4. Conclusion

This chapter has explored the uses of the concept of GENOCIDE in online discourse about Israel in the UK. It traces the concept's history, showing how it has been deeply connected with antisemitism, the Holocaust and the State of Israel from the outset. As such, it represents one of the most incendiary concepts that can be used in disputes about Israel. The chapter sets out why the concept of GENOCIDE in relation to Israel is factually inaccurate and distorts the historical reality of the conflict. Moreover, it is often a gateway to forms of HOLOCAUST DISTORTION if not outright DENIAL. Qualitatively analysing comments posted online in response to three separate events involving Israel across 2020 and 2021, it has found that references to a supposed Israeli GENOCIDE are a continual, if relatively minor, presence within antisemitic comments.

In both the May 2021 escalation phase and the Ben & Jerry's boycott corpora, comments referring to Israeli GENOCIDE made up just over 6% of the antisemitic comments. In the Covid-19 vaccine roll-out corpus, 12% of antisemitic comments referenced genocide. In each corpus, comments referencing Israeli GENOCIDE also expressed other antisemitic concepts, including notions of Jewish/Israeli EVIL and IMMORALITY, NAZI ANALOGIES, and DENIALS OF JEWISH SELF-DETERMINATION.

While the data set analysed here—comprising a total of 3,820 comments—is not large enough to draw concrete conclusions, it is nevertheless striking that, rather than a story directly related to the Arab-Israeli conflict, it was the one unambiguously positive news story—the speedy roll-out of the Israeli vaccine—that contained the highest percentage of usage of the GENOCIDE concept, more than double the level of the other two corpora. This may be due to the heightened emotional atmosphere during the most intense periods of the Covid-19 era, but it may also be that the generally positive nature of the coverage of this event meant web users were forced to reach for more extreme concepts to express their antipathy towards Israel. Further research comparing the uses of the concept in response to different non-conflict-related stories about Israel would be needed to test this hypothesis. Other potential research questions raised by this analysis include testing how levels of HOLOCAUST DISTORTION in online discussions relate to the frequency of attributions of Israeli GENOCIDE.

References

Aizenberg, Salo. 2023. "The battle over casualty counts in Gaza". *Honest Reporting* (11 December), https://honestreporting.com/ the-battle-over-casualty-counts-in-gaza/

Ascone, Laura. 2024. "Calls for violence". In: Becker, Matthias J., Hagen Troschke, Matthew Bolton and Alexis Chapelan (eds). *Decoding Antisemitism: A Guide to Identifying Antisemitism Online*. London: Palgrave Macmillan, https://link.springer.com/book/9783031492372

Bartov, Omer. 2010. "On definitions". In: Shaw, Martin and Omer Bartov (eds). "The question of genocide in Palestine, 1948: An exchange between Martin Shaw and Omer Bartov". *Journal of Genocide Research*, 12 (3–4): 243–259, https://doi.org/10.1080/14623528.2010.529698

Bartov, Omer. 2014. "Genocide and the Holocaust: Arguments over history and politics". In: Earl, Hilary and Karl A. Schleunes (eds). *Lessons and legacies XI: Expanding perspectives on the Holocaust in a changing world*. Evanston, IL: Northwestern University Press: 5–28, https://doi.org/10.2307/j.ctv47wb5x.5

BBC. 2021. "Covid: Israel to transfer 5,000 vaccine doses to Palestinians". *BBC* (31 January 2021), https://www.bbc.co.uk/news/ world-middle-east-55879337

BBC HARDtalk, 2024. "Joan Donoghue - Former President of the International Court of Justice". *BBC HARDtalk*, 25 April, https://www.bbc.co.uk/iplayer/ episode/m001yplc/hardtalk-joan-donoghue-former-president-of-the-international-court-of-justice

Becker, Matthias J. 2021. *Antisemitism in Reader Comments: Analogies for reckoning with the past*. London: Palgrave Macmillan/Springer Nature, https://doi.org/10.1007/978-3-030-70103-1

Becker, Matthias J. 2024a. "Instrumentalisation of antisemitism and the Holocaust". In: Becker, Matthias J., Hagen Troschke, Matthew Bolton and Alexis Chapelan (eds). *Decoding Antisemitism: A Guide to Identifying Antisemitism Online*. London: Palgrave Macmillan, https://link.springer. com/book/9783031492372

Becker, Matthias J. 2024b. "Power". In: Matthias J. Becker, Hagen Troschke, Matthew Bolton and Alexis Chapelan (eds). *Decoding Antisemitism: A Guide to Identifying Antisemitism Online*. London: Palgrave Macmillan, https:// link.springer.com/book/9783031492372

Becker, Matthias J. 2024c. "The Nazi analogy". In: Matthias J. Becker, Hagen Troschke, Matthew Bolton and Alexis Chapelan (eds). *Decoding Antisemitism: A Guide to Identifying Antisemitism Online*. London: Palgrave Macmillan, https://link.springer.com/book/9783031492372

Becker, Matthias J., Laura Ascone, Matthew Bolton, Alexis Chapelan, Jan Krasni, Karolina Placzynta, Marcus Scheiber, Hagen Troschke and Chloé Vincent. 2021. *Decoding Antisemitism: An AI-driven study on hate speech and imagery online. Discourse Report 2.* Technische Universität Berlin. Centre for Research on Antisemitism, https://doi.org/10.14279/depositonce-15310

Becker, Matthias J., Laura Ascone, Matthew Bolton, Alexis Chapelan, Pia Haupeltshofer, Alexa Krugel, Karolina Placzynta, Marcus Scheiber and Victor Tschiskale. 2023. *Celebrating Terror: Antisemitism online after the Hamas attacks on Israel: Preliminary results I.* Technische Universität Berlin. Centre for Research on Antisemitism, https://doi.org/10.14279/depositonce-19143

Becker, Matthias J., Laura Ascone, Matthew Bolton, Alexis Chapelan, Jan Krasni, Karolina Placzynta, Marcus Scheiber, Hagen Troschke and Chloé Vincent. 2022. *Decoding Antisemitism: An AI-driven study on hate speech and imagery online. Discourse Report 3.* Technische Universität Berlin. Centre for Research on Antisemitism, https://doi.org/10.14279/depositonce-15310

Becker, Matthias J., Laura Ascone and Hagen Troschke. 2022. "Antisemitic comments on Facebook pages of leading British, French, and German media outlets". *Humanities and Social Sciences Communications, 9* (1): 1–10, https://doi.org/10.1057/s41599-022-01337-8

Becker, Matthias J., Hagen Troschke, Matthew Bolton and Alexis Chapelan (eds). 2024. *Decoding Antisemitism: A Guide to Identifying Antisemitism Online.* London: Palgrave Macmillan, https://link.springer.com/book/9783031492372

Ben & Jerry's, 2021. "Ben & Jerry's Will End Sales of Our Ice Cream in the Occupied Palestinian Territory". *Ben & Jerry's,* https://www.benjerry.com/about-us/media-center/opt-statement

Benjamin, Walter. 1999. *Illuminations.* London: Pimlico

Bob from Brockley. 2014. "Gaza/Warsaw Ghetto". *Bob from Brockley* (24 July 2014), https://brockley.blogspot.com/2014/07/gazawarsaw-ghetto.html

Bolton, Matthew, Matthias J. Becker, Laura Ascone and Karolina Placzynta. 2023. "Enabling concepts in hate speech: The case of the apartheid analogy. In: Ermida, Isabel (ed.). *Hate Speech in Social Media.* London: Palgrave Macmillan, https://doi.org/10.1007/978-3-031-38248-2_9

Bolton, Matthew. 2024a. "Genocide". In: Becker, Matthias J., Hagen Troschke, Matthew Bolton and Alexis Chapelan (eds). *Decoding Antisemitism: A Guide to Identifying Antisemitism Online.* London: Palgrave Macmillan, https://link.springer.com/book/9783031492372

Bolton, Matthew. 2024b. "Evil/the devil". In: Becker, Matthias J., Hagen Troschke, Matthew Bolton and Alexis Chapelan (eds). *Decoding Antisemitism: A Guide to Identifying Antisemitism Online.* London: Palgrave Macmillan, https://link.springer.com/book/9783031492372

Bruttman, Tal and Stéphane Bou. 2024. "Interview with Tal Bruttmann. Holocaust Historian facing October 7". *K-larevue* (3 February), https://k-larevue.com/en/ interview-with-tal-bruttmann-holocaust-historian-facing-october-7/

Copelyn, Jesse, 2024. "Why did Cyril Ramaphosa gladhand a genocidal general?". *Mail & Guardian*. 5 Feburary, https://mg.co.za/ africa/2024-02-05-why-did-cyril-ramaphosa-gladhand-a-genocidal-general/

Fine, Robert and Philip Spencer. 2018. *Antisemitism and the Left*. Manchester: Manchester University Press, https://doi.org/10.7765/9781526104960

International Criminal Court. 2017. "Al-Bashir case: ICC Pre-Trial Chamber II decides not to refer South Africa's non-cooperation to the ASP or the UNSC". *International Criminal Court News* (6 July), https://www.icc-cpi. int/news/al-bashir-case-icc-pre-trial-chamber-ii-decides-not-refer-south-africas-non-cooperation-asp-or

International Court of Justice. 2023. "Application of the Convention on the Prevention and Punishment of the Crime of Genocide in the Gaza Strip (South Africa v. Israel)—Provisional measures". *International Court of Justice* (26 January), https://www.icj-cij.org/case/192/provisional-measures

Jones, Owen. 2024. "Israel's genocidal mania is becoming contagious". *The National* (2 February), https://www.thenational.scot/politics/24094988. owen-jones-israels-genocidal-mania-becoming-contagious/

Koselleck, Reinhart. 2018. *Sediments of Time: On possible histories*. Stanford, CA: Stanford University Press, https://doi.org/10.1515/9781503605978

Lemkin, Raphael. 2012. *Lemkin on Genocide* (ed. Steven Leonard Jacobs). Lanham, MD: Lexington Books

Mor, Shany. 2023. "The UN is distorting the meaning of the Nakba". *Unherd* (15 May 2023), https://unherd.com/thepost/ the-un-is-distorting-the-meaning-of-the-nakba

Moses, A. Dirk. 2021. *The Problems of Genocide*. Cambridge: Cambridge University Press, https://doi.org/10.1017/9781316217306

Placzynta, Karolina. 2024a. "Death wishes". In: Becker, Matthias J., Hagen Troschke, Matthew Bolton and Alexis Chapelan (eds). *Decoding Antisemitism: A Guide to Identifying Antisemitism Online*. London: Palgrave Macmillan, https://link.springer.com/book/9783031492372

Placzynta, Karolina. 2024b. "Jews have not learned from the past". In: Becker, Matthias J., Hagen Troschke, Matthew Bolton and Alexis Chapelan (eds). *Decoding Antisemitism: A Guide to Identifying Antisemitism Online*. London: Palgrave Macmillan, https://link.springer.com/book/9783031492372

Reuters. 2007. "Quartet deeply concerned by Palestinian violence". *Reuters* (9 August), https://www.reuters.com/article/idUSN02225618/

Shaw, Martin. 2010. "Palestine in an international historical perspective on genocide". *Holy Land Studies, 9* (1): 1–25, https://doi.org/10.3366/hls.2013.0056

Shaw, Martin. 2020. "'Herd immunity and let the old people die'—Boris Johnson's callous policy and the idea of genocide". *Discover Society* (23 March), https://archive.discoversociety.org/2020/03/23/herd-immunity-and-let-the-old-people-die-boris-johnsons-callous-policy-and-the-idea-of-genocide

Spencer, Philip. 2010. "The left, radical antisemitism, and the problem of genocide". *Journal for the Study of Antisemitism, 2* (1): 133–152

Tabarovsky, Izabella. 2022. "Demonization blueprints: Soviet conspiracist antizionism in contemporary left-wing discourse". *Journal of Contemporary Antisemitism, 5* (1): 1–20, https://doi.org/10.26613/jca/5.1.97

Trew, Bel. 2021. "Israel rebuffs WHO vaccine request for Palestinian medics, amid outcry over disparity". *The Independent* (8 January 2021), https://www.independent.co.uk/news/world/middle-east/israel-palestine-coronavirus-vaccine-b1784474.html

Troschke, Hagen. 2024. "Holocaust distortion and denial". In: Becker, Matthias J., Hagen Troschke, Matthew Bolton and Alexis Chapelan (eds). *Decoding Antisemitism: A Guide to Identifying Antisemitism Online*. London: Palgrave Macmillan, https://link.springer.com/book/9783031492372

Van Aaken, Anne et al. 2023. *Public Statement by International Law Experts*, https://docs.google.com/forms/d/e/1FAIpQLSd4lrsDRg3HbJqoAf0BlAe7BHJuzpQB_Le27Iureq9vpCoBkw/viewform

Vincent, Chloé and Matthew Bolton. 2024. "Israel's sole guilt for the conflict". In: Becker, Matthias J., Hagen Troschke, Matthew Bolton and Alexis Chapelan (eds). *Decoding Antisemitism: A Guide to Identifying Antisemitism Online*. London: Palgrave Macmillan, https://link.springer.com/book/9783031492372

Webman, Esther and Meir Litvak. 2012. *From Empathy to Denial: Arab responses to the Holocaust*. London: Hurst Publishing

World Bank. 2019. *Population, Total—West Bank and Gaza*, https://data.worldbank.org/indicator/SP.POP.TOTL?locations=PS

Zeffman, Henry. 2018. "Jeremy Corbyn hosted event likening Israel to Nazis". *The Times* (1 August 2018), https://www.thetimes.co.uk/article/jeremy-corbyn-hosted-event-likening-israel-to-nazis-6sb5rqd5x

Sources

DM-FB[20201230] *Daily Mail* (30 December 2020). "Israel vaccinates over 600000 people in just nine days", https://www.facebook.com/DailyMail/posts/6520275314698828

DM-FB[20210125] *Daily Mail* (25 January 2021). "Israel prepares to ban ALL incoming passenger flights", https://www.facebook.com/DailyMail/posts/6617099281683097

IND-FB[20210108] *The Independent* (8 January 2021). "Israel rebuffs WHO vaccine request for Palestinian medics, amid outcry over disparity", https://www.facebook.com/TheIndependentOnline/posts/10159045223066636

GUARD-FB[20210723] *The Guardian* (23 July 2021). "'It's just ice-cream': settlers' chilly response to Ben & Jerry's boycott", https://www.facebook.com/theguardian/posts/10160419085936323

GUARD-FB[20210720] *The Guardian* (20 July 2021). "Ben & Jerry's to stop sales in occupied Palestinian territories", https://www.facebook.com/theguardian/posts/10160411196976323

IND-FB[20210511] *The Independent* (11 May 2021). "Over 80 rockets fired at Tel Aviv from Gaza with security at 'highest alert', police say", https://www.facebook.com/TheIndependentOnline/posts/10159394323906636

MIR-FB[20210511] *Daily Mirror* (11 May 2021). "Israel air strike destroys Gaza tower block with 38 dead and 'full-scale war' feared", https://www.facebook.com/dailymirror/posts/10160040464054162

TEL-FB[20210511] *The Telegraph* (11 May 2021). "Israel unleashed new airstrikes on Gaza early on Tuesday", https://www.facebook.com/TELEGRAPH.CO.UK/posts/10160041119554749

TEL-FB[20210124] *The Telegraph* (24 January 2021). "Israel expands vaccination drive to include 16 to 18-year-olds in bid to save exams", https://www.facebook.com/TELEGRAPH.CO.UK/posts/10159767727909749

TEL-FB[20210112] *The Telegraph* (12 January 2021). "Five things the NHS can learn from Israel", https://www.facebook.com/TELEGRAPH.CO.UK/posts/10159738195734749

TIMES-FB[20210103] *The Times* (3 January 2021). "Vaccine success in a small country: "What we could learn from Israel", https://www.facebook.com/timesandsundaytimes/posts/4190971667598750

5. Countering Antisemitism Online

A Discursive Analysis of *Facebook* and *Twitter/X* Comments

Laura Ascone

Since their emergence on the web, social networks have elicited diverging reactions and opinions. If they are appreciated for helping create new forms of social relations, they are also criticised for facilitating both the emergence and circulation of hate speech. On a macro-level, different European countries have been taking a step forward to counter hate speech, but on a micro-level online comment sections show that some users try to counter it as well, namely by taking part in a discussion and/or reporting hate content. This chapter investigates the way users of French media counter antisemitic discourse in both *Facebook* and *Twitter* (now *X*) comment sections.

The analysis was conducted on 4,230 comments posted on the official *Facebook* and *Twitter* pages of French mainstream media such as *Le Monde* and *Le Figaro*. The comments were divided in three sub-corpora according to the event they refer to. This way, it was possible to examine the specificities of the comments countering antisemitism in these three different contexts. The annotation and the analyses performed with the software MAXQDA shed light on the connections between the comments conveying antisemitism and those countering them, as well as on

    https://doi.org/10.11647/OBP.0406.05

how counter speech can sometimes fuel antisemitism and other forms of hate speech.

1. Introduction

The number of laws that have recently been enacted across Europe (among others, the *NetzDG* in Germany or the *Loi Avia* in France) are evidence of the European countries' willingness to both limit and counter hate speech. If, on a macro-level, different European countries have been taking a step forward, on a micro-level, online comment sections show that some users try to counter hate speech as well, namely by taking part in a discussion and/or reporting hate content.

This chapter investigates the way users of French media counter antisemitic comments in both *Facebook* and *Twitter* (now *X*) comment sections. This study aims to determine to what extent counter speech is content-dependent, as well as to identify the specificities of the comments countering antisemitism online. The analysis will focus on the argumentative strategies (Perelman and Olbrecht-Tyteca 1988) that are adopted by users in order to both deconstruct the different concepts mobilised in antisemitic comments (Becker 2021) and make their point of view incontestable by creating an authoritative ethos (Amossy 2010).

The first part of this chapter will present the theoretical background, the corpus and the methods used. The second part will deal with the comments countering antisemitism in *Facebook* and *Twitter* comment sections. To conclude, attention will be paid to the argumentative strategies adopted by users to counter antisemitic comments.

2. Towards a linguistic analysis of antisemitic discourse and counter speech

2.1 Delimiting hate speech and counter speech

The wide range of hateful expressions makes it difficult to establish a universally accepted definition of hate speech. Even though academic and institutional definitions share the core elements of hate speech, none of them seems to encompass all its facets. For this study the following definition was adopted:

Hate speech is defined as bias-motivated, hostile, malicious speech aimed at a person or a group of people because of some of their actual or perceived innate characteristics. It expresses discriminatory intimidating, disapproving, antagonistic, and/or prejudicial attitudes towards those characteristics, which include gender, race, religion, ethnicity, colour, national origin, disability, or sexual orientation. Hate speech is intended to injure, dehumanize, harass, intimidate, debase, degrade, and victimize the targeted groups, and to foment insensitivity and brutality against them (Cohen-Almagor 2011: 1–2).[1]

Othering plays a crucial role in hate speech. The notion of otherness was defined by Staszak (2008: 2) as "the result of a discursive process by which a dominant in-group ("Us", the Self) constructs one or many [...] out-groups ("Them", Other) by stigmatizing a difference—real or imagined—presented as a negation of identity and thus a motive for potential discrimination". By creating an antonymic *Other*, hate speech has a double function: it creates or reinforces the bonds within the in-group (Bernard-Barbeau 2012) while establishing a conflictual link with the out-group.

This link can be reinforced by the phenomenon of "group polarisation" that is facilitated by the internet (Madden 2008): people tend to interact with users sharing the same interests and point of view. This may lead users to perceive their point of view as widely accepted even in cases of hate and extremist ideologies. Likewise, this phenomenon may intensify a sense of identity built in opposition to the out-group.

In this study, I analyse representations of Jews and Israelis as the out-group and consider verbal antisemitism to be "all linguistic elements by means of which Jews are debased, stigmatised, discriminated against and defamed as Jews, i.e. with which anti-Jewish stereotypes are coded and resentments are conveyed" (Schwarz-Friesel/Reinharz 2017: 48). Among the most common stereotypes seen are characterisations of Jews as a community striving for wealth (GREED) and having the POWER to

---

1   Contrary to Cohen-Almagor's definition, the one adopted in the Decoding Antisemitism project comprises unintentional devaluation and/or exclusion as well.

influence the media, politicians and economy. These are long-standing representations of Jews, but new antisemitic concepts have emerged in the last decades. For instance, the NAZI ANALOGY—used to target Israel by comparing it to Nazi Germany—has become one of the most prevalent allegations (Becker 2021).

Counter speech is understood here as a discourse countering, in an explicitly antagonistic way, what has been stated elsewhere (Mouffe 2010). In this study, I considered only the comments explicitly countering antisemitic discourse to form a counter speech. We will see, in this context, if counter speech constitutes a "peripheral discourse" within the discursive system (that is, a discourse putting forward a radical break with the dominant ideas and values (Angenot 1989: 22)), or if this understanding of counter speech is problematic since the ideas and values that are dominant in our society are actually advanced and defended by the comments countering antisemitism. Likewise, this chapter investigates the rhetorical (Reboul 1991) and argumentative strategies (Perelman and Olbrecht-Tyteca 1988) adopted by users to verbalise and legitimise this break with the dominant discourse.

2.2 The corpus

The analysis was conducted on 4,230 comments posted in the *Facebook* and *Twitter* pages of French mainstream media: *Le Monde, Le Figaro, Libération, Le Parisien, L'Express, Le Point, France Info, Marianne, France Bleu, Valeurs Actuelles* and *20 Minutes*. The rationale for focusing on mainstream media is twofold: on the one hand, "[the media] are a powerful site for the production and circulation of social meanings, i.e. to a great extent the media decide the significance of things that happen in the world for any given culture, society or social group" (Thornborrow 2004: 56). On the other hand, mainstream media represents an ideological apparatus that frames the society's way of thinking and acting. It is for this reason that the spread of antisemitic content in this milieu—in opposition to extremist contexts—can lead to the normalisation of antisemitism and other hate ideologies. Furthermore, the free-to-access *Facebook* and *Twitter* comment sections allowed examination of the media outlets that require a subscription to read and/or comment on articles on their websites, and that post the same articles on their social networks pages.

The comments were divided into three sub-corpora according to the event dealt with by the articles. The first sub-corpus, which consists of 1,500 comments, is about an escalation of the Arab-Israeli conflict in May 2021. In response to the publication of these articles, web users criticised and sometimes demonised Israel.

The second sub-corpus comprises 1,000 comments related to the Pegasus case in July 2021. The spyware Pegasus, developed by the Israeli enterprise NSO Group, allows its users to target smartphones. When it was discovered that certain countries used the software to spy on other governments, some web users questioned the innocence of Israel. French mainstream media paid particular attention to the fact that President Emmanuel Macron was targeted by Morocco through the use of this spyware.

The third sub-corpus includes 1,700 comments posted in response to reports of the antisemitic placard shown by right-wing activist Cassandre Fristot in a demonstration against the Covid-19 health pass implementation in August 2021. It bore the slogan "BUT WHO?" ["MAIS QUI?"] surrounded by names of several Jewish personalities and their alleged supporters. Because the rhetorical question refers to the conspiracy theory that holds Jews responsible for the pandemic, the placard was considered antisemitic.

The specificity of this corpus allowed an examination of the way web users of French media counter antisemitism in three different contexts: one involving Israel, one concerning a French news item, and one dealing with an international event that, at first glance, concerns neither Israel nor France.

2.3. The research design

The comments were collected with a custom-designed data-crawling tool and analysed with the MAXQDA software. Detailed coding guidelines were predetermined in order to categorise both the conceptual content of a comment (e.g., the different antisemitic concepts) and the linguistic structures used to convey the antisemitic content (e.g., puns, allusions, threats, etc.). Given the shapeshifting nature of antisemitism, the research team has regularly updated the categories in order to capture the nuances of antisemitic expressions specific to a certain discourse event.

Adopting a qualitative approach made it possible to conduct more in-depth analyses, which focused on the argumentative strategies employed in the comments countering antisemitic content. Particular attention was paid to the way authors of these comments refer to the antisemitic stereotypes they are trying to deconstruct as well as to the arguments they advanced to legitimise their discourse. Moreover, this qualitative approach enabled examination of the reactions triggered by the counter speech comments, allowing us to see whether this form of spontaneous counter speech—that is, counter speech produced by random users rather than by moderators—can be considered effective.

This ability to investigate the connections between the comments conveying antisemitism and those countering them proved crucial in this study. Furthermore, the combination of corpus linguistics and discourse analysis shed light on the characteristics of *Facebook* and *Twitter* comments countering antisemitism in relation to three different contexts.

3. Counter speech as context-related discourse

3.1 The link between antisemitic and counter speech comments

Before examining the link between the comments conveying antisemitism and those countering them, it is necessary to have a general overview of the proportions of both antisemitic and counter speech comments in the three sub-corpora.

The comments relating to Cassandre Fristot, the Arab-Israeli conflict and the Pegasus spyware were found to be antisemitic in 14%, 13% and 4% of cases, respectively. The low amount of antisemitic comments in the Pegasus corpus might be due to the fact that French mainstream media primarily focused on President Emmanuel Macron being spied on by Morocco; only a few articles noted that the spyware was developed by an Israeli enterprise.

This analysis found that the comments countering antisemitism are not as frequent as those spreading antisemitic ideas. In both the Fristot and the Arab-Israeli sub-corpora, 7% of comments are categorised as counter speech. As to the Pegasus sub-corpus, only 1% of comments sought to counter antisemitic content. This suggests that users with antisemitic positions post more freely on the web than those trying to counter these antisemitic ideas. Whether in reaction to the Arab-Israeli conflict, to Fristot's placard or to the Pegasus scandal, antisemitic comments are made twice as frequently as those countering them.

In order to have a better understanding of the way counter speech emerges in *Facebook* and *Twitter* comments, I examined the sequence of comments in the threads under investigation. By looking at the position of counter speech comments in relation to comments marked antisemitic or non-antisemitic, the goal was to test the hypothesis that counter speech would tend to be elicited by antisemitic comments rather than by the news item or the general context.

The Fristot sub-corpus confirmed this hypothesis. Of the 121 comments countering antisemitism, 66 (54%) were posted in reaction to comments expressing antisemitic ideas (see example 1 below); in 32 comments (26%), users reacted to neutral statements, whereas 24 comments (20%) were not posted in reaction to any other comment.

(1) A: "So? Is that antisemitic?
     B: "Quoting some Jews to take them responsible for what others have messed up during the corona, yes that's antisemitism" (LEFIG-FB[20211020])[2]

In this exchange, user A denies that the placard implicitly accuses a group of Jewish individuals of being responsible for the current situation. Therefore, this comment constitutes an indirect form of DENIAL OF ANTISEMITISM (Scheiber 2024). User B then reacts by explaining the message implied by Fristot and why it is considered antisemitic. With this comment, user B counters the idea of an alleged JEWISH POWER (Becker 2024).

A different tendency emerged in the other two datasets. In the Pegasus sub-corpus, most of the comments countering antisemitic stereotypes

---

2   A: « et alors ? C›est être antisémite ? »
     B: « citer des juifs pour leur mettre à dos tout ce que d'autres ont foiré en periode de corona oui c'est de l'antisémitisme »

were posted in reaction to the article rather than in response to other users' comments. In the Arab-Israeli conflict sub-corpus, almost half of the counter speech comments (42 out of 100) were posted in reaction to non-antisemitic statements that nevertheless presented a critique of Israel (see example 2).

> (2) A: "Hamas couldn't stand idly by when the situation was heating up for 1 week [or] 10 days, and leave the initiative to protest to NGOs!"
>
> B: "Hamas couldn't stand idly by? Explain to me on what issue? Hamas, which comes from the Muslim Brotherhood, have been attacking Israel for 70 years. Hamas's only wish is to destroy and annihilate the State of Israel, and do you believe that the State of Israel would stand idly by waiting to be annihilated by Hamas?" (LIBER-FB[20210512])[3]

Since user A explicitly refers to the escalation phase only, this comment cannot be understood to present Israel as the cause and the only guilty actor in the conflict. Therefore, this comment was considered within the definition of this study to be a legitimate critique of Israel's actions and not an antisemitic statement. However, user B seems to perceive it as the latter.

3.2 The link between antisemitic concepts and counter speech comments

In order to examine the link between the concepts expressed in the antisemitic comments and those countered in the counter speech, attention was paid to the comments directly countering antisemitic statements. The Pegasus sub-corpus presents only two comments reacting to antisemitic statements, that is, 15% of the counter speech comments which, as already mentioned, represent 1% of the whole

---

3   A: « Le Hamas ne pouvait pas continuer a rester les bras croises devant un situation qui montait depuis 1 semaine 10 jours, et laisser l'iniative de la contestation a des ONG ! »
  B: « Le Hamas ne pouvait pas rester les bras croisés ? à quel sujet expliquez moi ? Ça fait 70 ans que le Hamas Qui est une émanation des Frères musulmans ne l'oubliez pas agresse l'État d'Israël. la seule volonté du Hamas est de détruire l'état Israël de l'anéantir et croyez vous que l'État d'Israël allait rester les bras croisés à attendre Que le Hamas l'anéantisse ? »

sub-corpus. This is in sharp contrast to the Fristot corpus, wherein 54% of the counter speech comments were posted in reaction to comments expressing antisemitic ideas. The analysis conducted on the Fristot dataset showed that all of them countered the concept expressed in the respective antisemitic comment such as the DENIAL OF ANTISEMITISM (see example 3) and the TABOO OF CRITICISM (Chapelan 2024).

> (3) A: "So, indicating a list of actors in the health crisis whose actions or positions are disapproved is punishable because some of them (7/12 I think) are Jewish? The FN-style ladies aren't my cup of tea but isn't there a problem here?
>
> B: "Please show us the role of Soros and Rotschild in the health crisis. Let's see" (MONDE-TW[20210810])[4]

In this comment, user A questions the accusation of antisemitism for having listed the actors in the health crisis context because only some of them are Jewish. Furthermore, by stipulating that "the FN-style[5] ladies aren't [their] cup of tea", the user seems to argue that the DENIAL OF ANTISEMITISM evident in their comment is not influenced by their political ideas. User B then reacts by addressing user A directly. By asking user A to explain the role of Soros and Rothschild [two names that appear on the placard] in the health crisis, user B indirectly debunks user A's argument that Fristot listed these names without consideration of their [Jewish] identity.

As far as the Arab-Israeli sub-corpus is concerned, only 34% of the counter speech comments were posted in reaction to antisemitic statements (see example 4).

> (4) A: "The problem in your story is that the aggressor and the occupying power is Israel"

---

4   A : « Donc indiquer une liste dˌacteurs de la crise sanitaire dont on désapprouve lˌaction ou les positions est punissable car certains dˌentre eux (7/12 je crois) sont juifs ? Les nénettes style FN C'est pas ma tasse hein mais il n'y aurait pas un soucis là ? »
    B : « Indiquez nous le rôle de Soros et de Rotschild dans la crise sanitaire s'il vous plait. Pour voir. »

5   The speaker refers to the fact that Cassandre Fristot is a right-wing activist having voted Front National, Marine Le Pen's party.

B: "The problem in your story is that Israel is a sovereign and legitimate nation, over the whole Jerusalem and, in the long run, from the sea to the Jordan" (MONDE-FB[20210512])[6]

User A reacts to a comment where Israel was described as the victim by questioning the other user's point of view ("The problem in your story") and presenting Israel as an EVIL (Bolton 2024) entity that is acting against the Palestinian population, which implicitly refers to israel's SOLE GUILT IN THE CONFLICT (Vincent 2024). However, instead of countering this stereotype, user B counters the DENIAL OF ISRAEL'S RIGHT TO EXIST (Vincent 2024), namely by describing Israel as "a sovereign and legitimate nation". Even though the EVIL and the DENIAL OF ISRAEL'S RIGHT TO EXIST are two distinct concepts, user B might have understood "occupying power" as a more indirect way to say that Israel is illegally occupying territories outside the Israeli borders. Furthermore, to turn the argument around, user B repeats user A's opening expression.

In eight further counter speech comments from the Arab-Israeli sub-corpus, the users countered only one of the several concepts evoked in the antisemitic comments. One example:

(5) A: "Gaza is an open-air prison [...] But at the same time, in terms of Israel's state terrorism, I know they're the vice-champions of the world, they have surpassed the segregationist regime of South Africa, well, the next step is to surpass the title holder, that is the Nazi regime"
B: "The terrorism is the use of terror for ideological, political or religious reasons. That's the definition of Hamas, of the Muslim Brotherhood etc, not of Israel, which is just defending itself". (LEPOI-FB[20210512])[7]

---

6   A: « Le problème dans ton histoire c›est que l›agresseur et la puissance occupante est Israël »
B: « Le problème dans ton histoire est qu'Israel est une nation souveraine et légitime, sur la totalité de Jérusalem, et à terme, de la mer au Jourdain »
7   A: « Gaza est une prison à ciel ouvert [...] mais en même temps en matière de terrorisme d'état de la part d'israel, je sais qu'ils sont les vice champion du monde, ils ont dépassé régime ségrégationniste d'Afrique du sud, bah la prochaine étape c'est de dépasser le détenteur du titre à savoir le régime nazis »
B: « Le terrorisme est l'emploi de la terreur à des fins idéologiques, politiques ou religieuses. C est la définition du hamas, des frères musulmans etc, pas d Israël, qui ne fait que se défendre »

In (5), three antisemitic concepts are expressed by user A. Having presented Israel as a TERRORIST STATE, the user cynically compares it to both the South African apartheid system (APARTHEID ANALOGY) and the Nazi regime (NAZI ANALOGY). However, user B counters only the first antisemitic concept: by explaining the definition of terrorism, the user says that Israel does not resort to "the use of terror for ideological, political or religious reasons". Rather, Israel "is just defending itself".

This example suggests that when the antisemitic comments present more than one antisemitic concept, the counter speech comments seem to focus on the first concept only. Yet, the EVIL stereotype is the only one to be countered even when it appears at the end of a comment.

3.3 The link between the discourse event and counter speech comments

In both the Arab-Israeli conflict and the Fristot sub-corpora, the counter speech comments reacting to the articles constitute only a small portion (24% and 20%, respectively), whereas, in the Pegasus corpus, they reach 61%.

(6) "That's obvious that for someone who's close, very close, to Islam Israel can only be guilty all that's bad... 💩 Besides it's hot here at the moment, I think Israel has something to do with that, just like with the floods... 😁" (VALEU-FB[20210721])[8]

In this comment, taken from the Pegasus sub-corpus, the user reacts to the article itself and, in particular, to the French politician Jean-Luc Mélenchon's accusations against Israel mentioned in it. The user disparages Mélenchon by stating that the politician's anti-Israeli stance is affected by his interest in Islam and not by a justifiable reason. Furthermore, with the statement "Besides it's hot here at the moment, I think Israel has something to do with that, just like with the floods", the user derides Mélenchon and all those who blame Israel for any negative event in the world. Using irony in this way, the user implicitly counters the idea that Israel is an EVIL entity responsible for any calamity.

---

8   « Evidemment que pour ce proche , très proche , de l'islam Israël ne peut qu'être coupable de tous les maux ... 💩 D'ailleurs chez nous en ce moment il fait chaud, je pense qu'Israël y est pour quelque chose de même que pour les innondations.... 😁 »

In the following example, extracted from the Arab-Israeli sub-corpus, the commenter makes an explicit reference to the news article and even the outlet:

(7) "But hahahaha we talk about deadly attacks on Gaza!????? Do we talk of 300 rockets launched on Israel tonight???? No no... we talk only of 2/3 rockets launched on Gaza in reaction...Thanks Le Figaro for this publication inciting to hatred against Israel ✌ " (LEFIG-FB[20210510])⁹

This user explicitly reacts to the article by accusing *Le Figaro* of "inciting to hatred against Israel". According to the user, the claim is justified by the fact that the article discusses Israel's "deadly attacks on gaza" without mentioning the "300 rockets launched on Israel tonight". In other words, the user counters the idea that Israel is solely responsible for this conflict (ISRAEL'S GUILT).

4. The impact of counter speech comments

4.1 The argumentative strategies adopted in counter speech comments

In order to counter antisemitic statements, web users often formulate their counter speech comments in a convincing and persuasive way. They need to create an authoritative *ethos* (Amossy 2010) that allows them to present both themselves and their comments as legitimate and, therefore, incontestable. To achieve this, users resort to different argumentative strategies. Here, I will examine the main strategies identified in the three sub-corpora. The counter speech comments posted in reaction to the Pegasus affair include statements presented as incontrovertible facts rather than opinions, as the following example shows:

(8) "NSO is a private company, but like with any defence material they have to obtain their government's approval to sell, That's where

---

9   « Mais mmmmddddr on parle de frappes meurtrière sur gaza !????? On parle de 300roquettes tires cette nuit sur Israël ???? Nan nan... on parle juste de 2/3 roquettes tirés sur gaza en riposte ...Merci Le Figaro pour cette publication incitant à la haine contre Israël ✌ »

the responsibilities of NSO and the Israeli government end, only the software's users are responsible. Nobody would condemn the USA and Microsoft if one Windows user made illegal use of it. What do you think? This intrigue is to exonerate Morocco from its responsibilities and like LFI and accuse the bad Israelis" (VALEU-FB[20211123])[10]

The user implicitly rejects the accusations against Israel and NSO[11], the Israeli company who developed Pegasus, by asserting that the process followed in the case of this spyware is the same as that adopted in the approval and selling of "any defence material". In order to give weight to their argument, the user poses the hypothetical example of the USA and Microsoft, claiming that nobody would condemn them if Windows was used illegally by one user. The parallel emphasises that Israel is often judged in a more severe way than other nations, drawing attention to and countering the DOUBLE STANDARD (Vincent 2024) applied to Israel.

One argumentative strategy that was identified in all three sub-corpora is the appeal to authority (Ducrot 1984). Users refer to legitimate and authoritative sources in order to make themselves appear to be a reliable source, too:

(9) "Hamas launches hundreds of rockets against civilians in Israel, then Hamas puts children near the rocket launchers because they know that the Israeli army will destroy these launchers. [...]: https://www. youtube.com/watch?v=Vl4VaMq3tWc" (LIBER-FB[20210512])[12]

In redirecting readers to a video, this user strives to show that their statement is not simply an opinion or an assumption. Rather, the strategy allows the user to present their comment as based on evidence. Even though the author of the video is not an authoritative source such

---

10 « La société NSO est une société de droit privé, mais comme tout matériel de défense, il doit obtenir l'aval de son gouvernement pour la vente, là s'arrête les responsabilités de la société NSO du gouvernement israélien, seuls sont responsables les utilisateurs de ce logiciel. Il ne viendrait à l'idée de personne de condamner les USA et Microsoft si un utilisateur de Windows en faisait un usage illicite. Qu'en pensez vous? Tout ce micmac pour exonérer le Maroc de ses responsabilités à l'instar de LFI et accuser les méchants israéliens »

11 NSO stands for Niv, Shalev and Omri, the names of the company's founders.

12 « Le hamas tire des centaines de roquettes contre des civils en Israël puis le hamas met des enfants près des lanceurs de roquettes car ils savent que l'armée Israëlienne va détruire ces lanceurs. [...] : https://www.youtube.com/ watch?v=Vl4VaMq3tWc »

as a TV channel, the title of the video, "How HAMAS creates its human shield", suggests that what it shows is a piece of evidence. More precisely, in providing a link to a video that refers to "how" Hamas creates a human shield, the commenter takes for granted that Hamas does use such a defence and then makes this presupposition incontestable. In this indirect way, the user rejects or counters the antisemitic concept of CHILD MURDER (Placzynta 2024).

A different kind of appeal to authority was identified in (10), where the user refers to the law to give weight to their position.

(10) "The law, nothing but the law" (MONDE-TW[20210808])[13]

This comment was posted in one of the threads responding to Fristot's arrest. The user implicitly supports the arrest by referring to the law. Specifically, instead of presenting this support as their own opinion, the user presents it as a general statement—one legitimised by the fact that the arrest is an application of the law. In other words, the user relieves themselves from any responsibility and justifies Fristot's arrest as an enforcement of the law.

Some users counter their interlocutors by involving them in the argumentation. The following example was posted in reaction to an article dealing with the escalation phase of the Arab-Israeli conflict:

(11) "What would you all do if Belgium bombed Paris with more than one thousand missiles and the north of France [bombed] Parisian civilians for 7 days a week 24 hours a day? What would France do in this case? Would it let the Belgian terrorists do it, or would they defend themselves to stop this harassment" (20MIN-FB[20210512])[14]

Here, the user addresses their interlocutors in the argumentation by asking what they would do in a situation similar to the one faced by Israelis. This strategy, which invites identification with the nation, is an effort to legitimise Israel's actions—presented here as defence—and, thereby, to counter the idea that Israel is an EVIL entity.

---

13   « La loi. Rien que la loi »
14   « Que feriez-vous tous si la Belgique bombarde avec plus de Mille missiles sur Paris, et le Nord de la France pendant 7 jours sur 7 les 24 heures sur 24 sur les civils parisiens ? Que ferait la France dans ce cas-là ? Lesser faire les terroristes Belges, ou bien se défendre pour cela cesse ce harcèlement »

4.2 Reactions elicited by counter speech comments

So far, we have examined counter speech comments and whether they were posted in reaction to antisemitic or neutral comments, or to the article. In this section, I investigate the reactions triggered by counter speech comments in order to determine to what extent users succeed in countering antisemitic concepts.

In the Pegasus sub-corpus, eight counter speech comments did not receive any reaction while five comments elicited neutral statements. Different tendencies were observed in the sub-corpora related to the Fristot placard and escalation of the Arab-Israeli conflict. As far as the former is concerned, 43% of the counter speech comments did not receive any reaction, while 33% triggered neutral statements. Some of these responses did not agree with the counter speech comments but did not express any antisemitism. Moreover, 21% of the counter speech comments received antisemitic reactions (including example 12, below), whereas only three comments (2%) received affirming counter speech reactions.

(12) A: "Justice is finally waking up. Even if her sanction is insufficient, especially when it comes to antisemitic placards proudly shown in public".
      B: "Explain where you see antisemitism..." (LEFIG-FB[20211020])[15]

In this extract, taken from one of the threads constituting the Fristot sub-corpus, user A acknowledges the placard's antisemitic character and supports the accusation against Fristot. User B, however, not considering the placard to be antisemitic, asks user A to explain why it would be. The use of ellipsis instead of a question mark suggests that what may appear as a genuine question is actually an expression of DENIAL OF ANTISEMITISM, which proved to be one of the most frequent antisemitic reactions in this corpus.

Similar percentages were identified in the sub-corpus dealing with the Arab-Israeli escalation phase. Most of the counter speech comments received either a neutral reaction (39%) or did not elicit any reaction at

---

15   A: « Enfin la justice se réveille. Et encore sa sanction est insuffisante surtout quand il s'agit de pancartes antisémites brandies avec fièrement en public »
      B: « expliquez où vous voyez l antisémitisme.... »

all. However, as in the Fristot sub-corpus, some of the counter speech comments prompted antisemitic reactions (21%):

(13) A: "The problem in your story is that Israel is a sovereign and legitimate nation, over the whole Jerusalem and, in the long run, from the sea to the Jordan"

B: "According to the international law Israel has no right over Jerusalem. It has been recognised by the whole humanity that its occupation is illegitimate, according to history this state was created in 1948 and was named after a biblical kingdom to spread confusion..." (MONDE-FB[20210512])[16]

In (13), user A's comment countering the DENIAL OF ISRAEL'S RIGHT TO EXIST was rejected by user B, who reaffirms this antisemitic concept. To legitimate their statement, user B resorts to the appeal to authority, namely by evoking the international law as well as history. In this example, one counter speech comment led another user to react and counter with an antisemitic concept.

Furthermore, each sub-corpus presents two counter speech comments that elicited neutral statements in which the users expressed hateful yet non-antisemitic content. User B's statement in example 14, below, demonstrates the verbal violence exhibited in a limited number of responses to counter speech comments:

(14) A: "You seem to insinuate that the 9 million people are so superior that they dominate 2 billion people? You have a very dirty opinion of your co-religionists and yourself"

B: "you're not only stupid, you're stubborn" (MONDE-FB[20220405])[17]

---

16 A : « Le problème dans ton histoire est qu'Israel est une nation souveraine et légitime, sur la totalité de Jérusalem, et à terme, de la mer au Jourdain »
B : « Selon le droit international Israel n'a aucun droit sur Jerusalem. Son occupation est reconnu comme illégitime par l'ensemble de l'humanité dite selon l'histoire cet état qui a été créé en 1948 et qui a pris le nom d'un royaume biblique pour semer la confusion... »

17 A : « Tu sembles insinuer que les 9 millions de personnes sont tellement supérieurs qu'ils dominent 2 milliards de personnes? Tu as une bien sale opinion de tes coreligionnaires et de toi-même »
B : « en plus d'être bête t'es têtu dis donc »

Here, user A rejects the idea that Jews ("9 million people") would have the power to dominate Muslims ("2 billion people"). User B does not reject user A's comment. Rather, they diminish user A through the insult "you're not only stupid, you're stubborn". By delegitimising user A, user B delegitimises user A's statement too.

This analysis has shown that the comments countering antisemitic statements tend to elicit either no reaction or neutral comments. However, antisemitic reactions to counter speech comments occur in the corpora dealing with the Arab-Israeli escalation phase and the antisemitic placard. Likewise, in six cases only, counter speech comments elicited non-antisemitic but nevertheless hateful content.

4.3 The Overlap of Counter Speech and Hate Speech

Not only can counter speech comments trigger antisemitic reactions, but they can also present other forms of hate speech themselves. In the three corpora under investigation, these comments attack and diminish either Islam or Muslims. Not surprisingly, these forms of hate speech are more frequent in the sub-corpus dealing with the escalation phase of the Arab-Israeli conflict. Here, four comments countering antisemitic concepts presented expressions of anti-Muslim racism.

(15) "two states?????Never! No country in the world would share its land and even less with some terrorists!" (LEXPR-FB[20210510])[18]

This comment explicitly presents all Palestinians as terrorists. This generalisation, the goal of which is to diminish the Palestinian population, is combined with a more extreme form of hate speech. By rejecting the possibility of Israel and Palestine's coexistence, the user denies Palestinians' existence and justifies this position by stating that any country would act in the same way as Israel.

In the sub-corpus dealing with the Pegasus case, two counter speech comments present other forms of hate speech. The following is one such example:

---

18 « deux états ?????Jamais !Aucun pays au monde ne partagerai sa terre et encore moins avec des terroristes ! »

(16) "Go and spit your FLNist antisemitism somewhere else. Zionists are 10 million inhabitants, and a GDP that could nourish your shitty country for 50 centuries. Israelis don't throw themselves in the water to reach your old biological mother, France 😃" (MONDE-TW[20210720])[19]

In the Pegasus corpus, the focus is on Morocco's use of the spyware. Therefore, the comments presenting these forms of hate speech tend to attack Morocco itself. In this comment, the user valorises Israel by diminishing the Other: in addition to explicitly insulting Morocco, the user implies that this country would be nothing without France and states that Moroccans even risk their life in order to leave their country.

This last section has shown that even though counter speech comments aim at deconstructing antisemitic concepts, they can also elicit new and stronger antisemitic reactions or, in a few cases, present other forms of hate speech.

5. Conclusion

This study has revealed that the number of comments countering antisemitism in *Facebook* and *Twitter* comment sections is proportionally smaller than the number of antisemitic comments. Moreover, the fact that users produce counter speech not only in reaction to antisemitic comments proves that counter speech is related to the context and, more precisely, to the topic dealt with by the articles. This analysis has also shown that, by putting forward and defending their society's dominant values, the counter speech comments presented in this chapter cannot be considered a "peripheral discourse" within the discursive system (Angenot 1989: 22). As to the efficiency of the comments countering antisemitism online, analysis here has shown that these comments may lead those to whom they are addressed to react and, in some cases, to reaffirm their antisemitic positions. This suggests that, even though online counter speech is needed to prevent one-sided discourse, this form of spontaneous counter speech may paradoxically fuel the

---

19 « Ton antisémitisme FLNiste va le cracher autre part. Les sionistes c'est 10 milliions d'habitant, et un PIB qui peut nourrir ton pays de merde pendant 50 siècles. Cest pas les israéliens qui se jettent en mer pour rejoindre votre ancienne maman génitrice la France 😃 »

emergence of antisemitic comments. Furthermore, the last section has shown that some comments counter antisemitic stereotypes and valorise Israel by diminishing another out-group, as if their goal was to find another scapegoat. These results open the way to more complex questions: is users' spontaneous counter speech efficient enough? Are the positive counter speech effects jeopardised by the negative ones (e.g. the fuelling of hate speech)? Can counter speech be classified as such if it also conveys hate? These questions require further analyses, which would help identify ways of countering hate speech in a more efficient way.

References

Amossy, Ruth, 2010 [2000]. *"L'argumentation dans le discours"*. Paris: Armand Colin

Angenot, Marc, 1989. "Hégémonie, dissidence et contre-discours: réflexions sur les périphéries du discours social en 1889". *Études littéraires*, 22 (2), 11–24

Auger, Nathalie, Béatrice, Fracchiolla, Claudine, Moïse, and Christine, Schultz-Romain, 2010. "Interpellation et violence verbale: Essai de typologisation". *Corela. Cognition, représentation, langage* (*HS-8*), https://doi.org/10.4000/corela.1023

Becker, Matthias J., 2021. *Antisemitism in Reader Comments: Analogies for Reckoning with the Past*. London: Palgrave Macmillan

Bellachhab, Abdelhadi, Galatanu, Olga, 2012. "La violence verbale: représentation sémantique et mécanismes discursifs". *Signes, Discours et Sociétés*, 9, http://www.revue-signes.info/document.php?id=29069

Bernard Barbeau, Geneviève, 2012. "Le bashing: forme intensifiée de dénigrement d'un groupe". *Signes, Discours et Sociétés*, 8, http://revue-signes.gsu.edu.tr/article/-LXz7csbNocGwoCcIp2Z

Bilewicz, Michal, Krzeminski, Ireneusz, 2010. "Anti-Semitism in Poland and Ukraine: The belief in Jewish control as a mechanism of scapegoating". In: *International Journal of Conflict and Violence* (IJCV), 4 (2), 234–243

Cohen-Almagor, Raphael, 2011. "Fighting hate and bigotry on the internet". *Policy and Internet*, 3 (3), 1–26, https://doi.org/10.2202/1944-2866.1059

Ducrot, Oswald, 1984. *"Le dire et le dit"*. Paris: Editions de Minuit

Madden, Christina L., 2008. "Typing TERROR in a Crowded Chat". *Policy Innovations*. 5 February 2008, 31

Mouffe, Chantal, 2000. "Politique et agonisme". *Rue Descartes*, 67 (1), 18–24

Perelman, Chaïm, Olbrecht-Tyteca, Lucie, 1988. *Traité de l'Argumentation*. Bruxelles: Edition de l'Université libre de Bruxelles

Reboul, Olivier, 1991. *Introduction à la rhétorique: théorie et pratique*. Paris: Presses Universitaires de France

Schwarz-Friesel, Monika, Reinharz, Jehuda, 2017. *Inside the Antisemitic Mind: The Language of Jew-Hatred in Contemporary Germany*. Waltham, MA: Brandeis University Press

Staszak, Jean-François, 2008. "Other/otherness". In: Rob, Kitchin and Nigel, Thrift, (eds). *International Encyclopaedia of Human Geography*, 46–47

Thornborrow, Joanna, 2004. "Language and the media". In: Linda Thomas and Shân, Wareing (eds). *Language, Society and Power* (2nd Edition). Abingdon: Routledge, 55–74

Sources

Arab-Israeli conflict

LEFIG-FB[20210510] *Le Figaro*, 10 May 2021, "Frappes meurtrières sur Gaza après des tirs de roquettes", https://www.facebook.com/lefigaro/posts/10158686992106339

LEXPR-FB[20210510] *L'Express*, 10 May 2021, "Frappes israéliennes sur Gaza après des tirs de roquettes, fortes tensions à Jérusalem", https://www.facebook.com/LExpress/posts/10158495051561997

LIBER-FB[20210512] *Libération*, 12 May 2021, "Gaza compte ses morts, la Ligue arabe pèse ses mots", https://www.facebook.com/ Liberation/posts/10159284087887394

MONDE-FB[20210512] *Le Monde*, May 2021, "Proche-Orient : des dizaines de morts après une nouvelle nuit de violences entre Israël et la bande de Gaza", https://www.facebook.com/lemonde.fr/posts/10160012878132590

LEPOI-FB[20210512] *Le Point*, 12 May 2021, "En Israël, la crainte d'un front intérieur", https://www.facebook.com/lepoint.fr/posts/10157898215205703

20MIN-FB[20210512] *20 Minutes*, 12 May 2021, "Mort de plusieurs commandants du Hamas dans des frappes israéliennes", https://www.facebook.com/20minutes/ posts/10159729309828311

Cassandre Fristot

LEFIG-FB[20211020] *Le Figaro*, 20 October 2021, "Six mois de prison avec sursis pour la manifestante anti-passe qui avait défilé avec une pancarte antisémite à Metz", https://www.facebook.com/lefigaro/posts/10159028316021339

MONDE-TW[20210808] *Le Monde*, 8 May 2021, "Une enquête ouverte après qu'une manifestante anti-passe a brandi une pancarte antisémite à Metz", https://twitter.com/lemondefr/status/1424455814593617922

MONDE-TW[20210810] *Le Monde*, 10 October 2021, "Pancarte antisémite à Metz : Cassandre Fristot, la militante d'extrême droite sera jugée pour 'provocation publique à la haine raciale'", https://twitter.com/lemondefr/status/1425125326707957762

Pegasus

MONDE-FB[20220405] *Le Monde*, 5 April 2022, "L'entreprise israélienne NSO poursuivie à Paris pour avoir surveillé un avocat franco-palestinien", https://www.facebook.com/lemonde.fr/posts/10160717732237590

MONDE-TW20210720] *Le Monde*, 20 July 2021, "'Projet Pegasus': Les téléphones d'Emmanuel Macron, d'Edouard Philippe et de quatorze ministres français dans le viseur du Maroc", https://twitter.com/lemondefr/status/1417514491701497858

VALEU-FB[20210721] *Valeurs Actuelles*, 21 July 2021, "Affaire Pegasus : le député insoumis Adrien Quatennens espionné par le Maroc, Mélenchon accuse Israël", https://www.facebook.com/valeursactuelles.page/posts/3730343610400101

6. Multimodal Cognitive Anchoring in Antisemitic Memes

Marcus Scheiber

The ongoing mediatisation and digitalisation of our lives has also resulted in an increasing dissemination of antisemitic concepts. Antisemitic evaluations that have existed for centuries are finding their way into online debates in new semiotic patterns and in innovative communication formats. Memes are one kind of these new communication formats, which prototypically have a text-image structure and can be utilised to realise antisemitic concepts that are anchored in cultural memory. This chapter explores the production and reception processes of these anchored concepts in antisemitic memes by showing the patterns of cognitive processing that allow the integration of verbal and pictorial sign potentials within the meme format via the processes of blending.

1. Introduction

While digital forms of communication, such as the social media or internet fora, offer unlimited possibilities for the distribution of opinions, it is becoming apparent that they can also be used as a breeding ground for antisemitic ideas. Although antisemitic memes do not account for a considerable proportion of popular memes, they can nevertheless be identified in numbers that are sufficiently large to make them relevant with regard to the dissemination of antisemitism. A meme—a popular format of internet content which prototypically combines text and

©2024 Marcus Scheiber, CC BY 4.0   https://doi.org/10.11647/OBP.0406.06

image, usually in a humorous way—has the potential to carry ideas concisely, contributing to their spread and normalisation.

From the point of view of semiotics, an individual meme is configured by the assembly of a format from semiotic resources, which are realised as a functionally organised composition of the participatory sign acts (that is, elements that communicate meaning). This is due to the mutual integration of the pictorial and verbal acts that structure and give rise to the conceptual representation of an antisemitic meme (Scheiber 2019: 150).

Since the interpretation of antisemitic memes is restricted to the conventionalised communicative patterns, these memes can be regarded as sedimentation of discursive practices. The generation of their meaning takes place as a process of cognitive configuration of discursive knowledge, that is, and it is subject to these conventional patterns as well as to the antisemitic projections anchored within society. In such a way, the contextual reference framework evokes a functional matrix. This matrix not only *productively* restricts the communicative and interactive realisation possibilities (of the semiotic surface) but also *receptively* limits the cognitive-semantic conceptual possibilities of an antisemitic meme. Within this chapter, these production and reception processes are analysed with the help of blending theory (Fauconnier and Turner 2002) to show the patterns of cognitive anchoring activated by multimodal antisemitic communication processes online.

2. Data

The following discussion of memes and their analysis are based on a corpus that was compiled with the help of the imageboards—databases of online images—"Know Your Meme", "Quickmeme" and "9Gag" throughout June 2023. Search queries for the terms "antisemitism", "Jews", and "Israel" returned structurally corresponding but thematically different memes from these three imageboards. Selections from this corpus serve as comparative examples to illustrate the respective patterns of the analysed memes.

3. Antisemitic stereotypes

Since the reception process of an antisemitic meme relies on web users' knowledge as well as their communicative expectations related to antisemitic ideas, it is important to explain the antisemitic conceptual structure that the individual memes utilise. Antisemitic beliefs are socially distributed mental constructs that stem from social practice, are based on shared stereotypes and are anchored within a cultural memory. Both antisemitic and non-antisemitic stereotypes can be described as mental representations that are stored in long-term memory and ascribe characteristic features to a specific group. Stereotypes prove to be simplifying, generalising and reductionist schemata that help their users cognitively by making the world both more experienceable and understandable (Quasthoff 1973).

At the same time, stereotypes can also serve as a basis for antisemitism when they conceptualise Jews as alien entities who, by their very nature, represent the absolute EVIL in the world. This is because antisemitism is not based on a flesh-and-blood hatred of Jews but on a systematic projection or mental representation of Jews that has no real-world counterpart. The stereotype is the product of collective schematic attributions; that is, all perceptions and aspects of knowledge—even those that run counter to an antisemitic interpretation—are selected and structured in such a way that they fit into a closed antisemitic conception of the world. This legitimises or constitutes an outlook in which the individual concepts give rise to a relational conceptual structure of Jewish people. Often, the conceptual structure holds Jews responsible for all crises in the world and believes that they profit from them; it allows many to believe that Jews developed both capitalism and communism and that they instrumentalise antisemitism or are themselves responsible for it (Salzborn 2011). The irrational selectivity of antisemitic interpretations overrides reason as well as logic; it is based on a simple dichotomy of good and evil, within which Jews are conceptualised as the root cause of EVIL (Schwarz-Friesel and Reinharz 2017, Bolton 2024). Memes reinforce the antisemite's view of a world that excludes Jews or is seemingly threatened by Jews. Accordingly, analysis of the antisemitic stereotypes found in memes reveals a cognitive narrative about a hostile enemy and an implicit call to fight against it.

4. Patterns of memes

Memes present themselves as a communicative consequence of the diverse semiotic and medial possibilities offered by the technically as well as socio-culturally determined affordances of digital communication. Since the latter enables collaborative practices for participation, memes are realised as formats that function as communicative templates for social interaction. They can be described as patterns of multimodal sign acts that are characterised by

i. collective semiosis (meaning is constituted via multiple sign users);

ii. re-semiotisations (transposing meaning from one context to another) (Iedema 2003: 41);

iii. a functional matrix of production conditions and reception possibilities;

iv. a family resemblance of the individual members; and

v. discourse-semantic network structures (Scheiber, Troschke and Krasni forthcoming).

Based on this list of semiotic properties, (discourse-)semantic conditions and pragmatic usage, the prototypical manifestation of a meme is as a text-image structure.[1] Not every text-image structure within digital communication, however, has the status of a meme: the texts and images in each artefact must follow a recognisable pattern yet exhibit a high degree of variation, and the number of disseminations of individual artefacts must exceed a certain 'tipping point' in order that web users perceive a trend (Breitenbach 2015: 36). Thus, memes emerge via collective-semiosis processes; they are collaborative constructions of meaning that come about through the participation of various users who generate a recurring (multimodal) pattern from a singular artefact

---

1   "Prototypicality", in this article, refers to the prototype theory developed in the cognitive sciences that negates entities' categorical boundaries in favour of a family resemblance. The prototypicality of the property dimensions results from the combination of frequency and distinctiveness of these in relation to other exemplars (Sachs-Hombach 2003: 296).

via its re-semiotisations (reproduction, imitation and variation) (Klug 2023: 206).

On one hand, memes are simple. The mutual integration of the sign modalities involved goes hand in hand with a reduction of information complexity, that is, the process relies on structural and content-related simplicity (Breitenbach 2015: 37). On the other hand, memes are sophisticated insofar as the integration of verbal and pictorial sign modalities generates an emergent meaning. In order for the intended significance to be derived despite these semiotic challenges, memes make use of interpretation patterns for the reception process on the semiotic surface. These have both a regulatory effect with regard to pragmatic (cognitive) usability and a selective effect with regard to the use of semiotic resources for the respective arrangements: memes establish common spheres of cultural knowledge, so that they can be decoded by web users who are familiar with the communication format (Breitenbach 2015: 45).[2] In other words, the production of a meme is structured by a functional matrix that provides a framework for the semantic organisation as well as the pragmatic usability of the text-image structures, but the cognitive processing of this matrix or framework also limits the meme. For, both the production and the reception of a meme are dependent on web users' knowledge of the world but also of the relations to other text-image structures of the same pattern. Hence, the constitution of meaning in a meme takes place through the family resemblance of the individual artefacts to each other. Consider the following examples:

---

2   Every form of communication, including memes, requires the mastery of certain cultural practices (reading, writing, speaking) that productively as well as receptively define a framework for the use of the respective communicative form.

Figure 6.1: One example of the "Galaxie Brain" meme, *Know Your Meme*, reproduced under fair dealing, https://knowyourmeme.com/photos/1217719-whomst.

Figure 6.2: A second example of the "Galaxie Brain" meme, *Know Your Meme*, reproduced under fair dealing, https://knowyourmeme.com/photos/1755097-galaxy-brain

The vertical arrangement of the pictorial and verbal elements in both Figure 6.1 and Figure 6.2 encourages a consecutive interpretation of the contents, which themselves depict an experiential intensification. This intensification is realised in the correlation of the (fictitious) syntactic expansion of the verbal expression "who" with the pictorial representations of increasingly illuminated brains. Figure 6.2 evokes this interpretation through corresponding (visual) ellipses. The linking patterns used between the verbal and pictorial sign acts in Figure 6.2 refer to the knowledge and communicative expectations of a web user with regards to the prototypical realisation possibilities of the meme in Figure 6.1. Accordingly, Figure 6.2 can also be interpreted as an intensification of Figure 6.1, although verbal and pictorial ellipses have been introduced. This example demonstrates that recurring composition or linking patterns both force and limit specific semiotic practices as well as communicative structures within memes.

The realisation of a meme is to be understood as an expression of discursive practices insofar as the compositional organisation of the semiotic elements in a text-image structure provide information about the discursive practice in which they occur: "At all points, design realizes and projects social organisation and is affected by social and technological change" (Kress 2010: 139). The placement of the individual sign modalities actualises communicative structures, constitutes social relations through composition patterns and realises communicative functionalities by means of the connection or separation of communicative elements (Kress and van Leeuwen 2006: 177). As web users employ a wide variety of memes to convey the most diverse contents, memes present themselves as a discursive practice of knowledge generation:

> First, memes may best be understood as pieces of cultural information that pass along from person to person, but gradually scale into a shared social phenomenon. Although they spread on a micro basis, their impact is on the macro level: memes shape the mindsets, forms of behaviour, and actions of social groups (Shifman 2014: 18).

Each meme can be characterised as the sedimentation of a discursive production process, which at the moment of its execution uses discursively conventionalised templates to satisfy the communicative needs of digital communication (Beißwenger 2007: 202). Hence, the constitution of meaning takes place as a process of double emergence: on the one hand, the text-image structure must be decoded as such and, on the other hand, the resulting patterns of interpretation must be placed in relation to the framework structure of the communication format. The individual meme is actualised as a punctual event, which—as a text-image structure with a communicative function—carries meaning in itself, but it also reveals a discourse-semantic network structure in the process of reception or identification as a communication format. The condition of its constitution is therefore based on the relation of a meme to other memes of the same pattern.[3]

5. From conceptual metaphors to blending

According to conceptual metaphor theory, metaphorical mappings can be defined at the physical level as neural networks that link sensorimotor information to more abstract concepts (Tendahl 2015: 28). A useful way to think about this is that "[m]etaphors provide sets of mappings between a more concrete or physical source domain and a more abstract target domain. For example, since we all feel hot as a result of physical exertion or excitement, metaphors that are rooted in the concept of *Intensity is heat* seem entirely natural to us" (El Rafaie 2015: 14).[4]

Therefore, an entity—however abstract—is made cognitively available through conceptual metaphors by relating it to a sensory realm of experience. In this way, metaphors serve as elementary structures of order by means of simplification. The anchoring of abstract conceptual domains in experience enables a cognitive orientation in the world because the metaphorical concepts are able to partially structure an experience in terms of another experience (Rolf 2005: 235).

Within such an understanding, the semiotic formations of these structures function merely as a reflex of the underlying conceptual representation (Stöckl 2004: 202). However, since sign resources are to be understood not only as a medium for conveying reality but also as a means of constituting it, cognitive structures cannot be granted primacy over their semiotic manifestations (Spitzmüller and Warnke 2011: 46). Sensory impressions do not present themselves in consciousness as

---

3   There are possibilities for variation, individualisation and hybridisation of individual memes in relation to the basic pattern, since reproduction of an artefact without variation of the same does not necessarily establish meme character: patterns in relation to memes must be determined in the sense of family resemblance.

4   Conceptual metaphors comprise a systematic connection between two conceptual domains, one of which functions as the target domain and the other as the source domain of metaphorical mapping (Jäkel 2003: 23). The metaphorical transfer from the source domain to the target domain takes place non-directionally, so that there is no conceptual loopback from the latter to the former (Drewer 2003: 6), https://doi.org/10.1515/zrs.2009.037

they are but as they appear conditionally; that is, they are shaped by the fact that referential access to them can only take place via actualised sign resources in their communicative contexts of use. However, since every sign belongs to a cognitive category as a sign of a certain type, these sensory impressions are categorically grasped in the act of their referential access. These categories of conceptualization, in turn, determine which aspects of an entity one is interested in and which not, so that conceptual structures and their semiotic manifestations are mutually dependent (Köller 2004: 330): cognitive structures are materialised by means of various sign resources and, at the same time, semiotic units model cognitive structures. An absolute epistemological claim of metaphorical mapping must therefore be contradicted in favour of an epistemic relation between abstract cognitive operations and semiotic acts corresponding to these operations, so as not to fall prey to logical cognitivism.

Blending theory arises because of this criticism, since it is mindful of the fact that metaphorical mapping is always bound to the prototypically expected contextualisation and reveals itself as a reciprocal process. Blending theory takes the form of a network model that replaces the two-domain model of conceptual metaphor theory with a fourfold concept consisting of two inputs: one, a generic space that controls relations and units common to the inputs as a kind of template, and two, the result of this process—the blend (Schröder 2012: 83). "In blending, structure from two input mental spaces is projected to a new space, the blend. Generic spaces and blended spaces are related: blends contain generic structure captured in the generic space but also contain more specific structure, and they contain structure that is impossible for the inputs" (Fauconnier and Turner 2002: 47).

Hence, the process of blending takes place through the partial projection of certain elements in the blend that are assigned to the input spaces based on cultural knowledge or frames. Within the blend, these elements are integrated into each other, and the structure that emerges cannot be found in the individual input spaces but exclusively as the result of the blend (Fauconnier and Turner 2002: 48).[5] An example of a

---

5   From the perspective of blending theory, the source domain and the target domain do not differ: both are equally involved in the meaning making of a metaphorical utterance, since both provide structures to generate the blend.

metaphorical utterance such as "The surgeon is a butcher" is illustrative. Conceptual metaphor theory is not able to explain the negative connotation carried by this metaphor because it cannot make its emergent structure comprehensible. The negative evaluation of a "surgeon" when likened to a "butcher" results, by means of a functional linkage of the two, from the discrepancy of their predications as emergence, not from the unidirectional transfer of certain qualities of the expression "butcher" to the expression "surgeon". Consequently, the metaphor can only be experienced in the juxtaposition of the two professions against the background of a cultural knowledge frame. The contrast between them is realised by referring the blend back to the two input spaces and the generic space (Evans and Green 2006: 410). Accordingly, metaphorical structures must be understood as semiotically bound constructions that generate a specific extension of meaning of the sign modalities used in the overall communicative process. They generate a horizon of meaning situationally, not simply a selective projection of a specific conceptual excerpt.

6. Utilising antisemitic memes for blending

"If text and images were more or less the same, then combining them also would not lead to anything substantially new. [...] If text and images were completely different, totally incommensurate, then combining them would not produce anything sensible either" (Bateman 2014: 7). The negation of these two extreme positions, that is, the fact that a combination of verbal and pictorial signs exists, legitimates the analysis of memes by means of the blending theory. For, multimodal units—which include antisemitic memes—by their very nature consist of a cognitive integration in terms of the blending of different sign modalities. In "The surgeon is a butcher", for example, the concepts to be integrated from Input Space I ("surgeon") and Input Space II ("butcher") are both of a single sign modality (verbal text). However, in an antisemitic meme, different sign modalities are used and must be integrated into one another. The difference between the sign systems now has a functional effect on the transfer process. An image cannot transfer the same values as the verbal text and vice versa, because both have prototypically different functions: while images visualise or intensify the content of the message, verbal signs can express illocutions and realise negations (Meier 2014: 125). Without a divergence in the prototypical predication structure of the two sign modalities in their cognitive anchoring, their combination could not take place.

At the same time, the relation between the relevant properties of the elements involved in the blending process are not inherent but originate in experience-based knowledge. This knowledge is drawn from a certain perspective of reality, and the blending is, therefore, subject to a context-bound expectability (Skirl 2008: 25). The reason for this is that the conceptualisation of a semiotic unit is realised via situational, textual and epistemic contexts and is subject to knowledge that has been negotiated in a social practice and that has emerged in a domain-specific manner (Wrede 2013: 183). Hence, the sign acts used in an antisemitic meme do not themselves determine the property dimensions that are correlated in the blend. They are, rather, based on knowledge of the conventionalised meanings of those concrete sign acts against the background of their contextual use (Bateman 2014: 176). In other words, the selected property dimensions in the process of blending are not only registered but, above all, interpreted against the background of existing knowledge and modified with regard to current communicative needs as well as antisemitic projections.

Certain aspects or property dimensions of a concrete (multimodal) communicative element are projected onto another element because these have prototypically communicative relevance in the given context. Their selection is not a determined or mechanical process that takes place continuously in the same way that the sign resources are correlated with each other in a relational structure. Rather, the process is a highly dynamic and flexible one: two people can receptively decode different meanings from one and the same multimodal unit due to their different experiences and knowledge (Evans and Green 2006: 409). This observation is especially relevant when considering antisemitic memes, since these usually contain components that a web user is not able to understand without contextual knowledge of the world. Analysis of antisemitic memes regarded as metaphorical structures, therefore, is an analysis of semiotically bound knowledge representation on a cognitive level in which the semiotic structures are an expression of the cognitive-processing mechanisms and these mechanisms are based on culturally anchored antisemitic projections.

7. Analysis: cognitive anchoring of antisemitic memes

Based on the previous explanations, the following list of questions forms the focus of the analysis to outline the production conditions and reception processes of antisemitic memes:

- Which textual elements and visual figures are used to convey which information?
- How does the web user navigate cognitively in the text and image space of the meme's communication format?
- What knowledge does the user need to have to understand the semiotic arrangement with respect to the antisemitic interpretation?
- How is the blend created?
- Which aspects of meaning are (selectively) projected or integrated into each other?
- What emergent antisemitic meaning results from this?

Consider the following examples:

Figure 6.3: One example of the "Everyone loses their minds over clothes" meme, *Know Your Meme*, https://knowyourmeme.com/photos/544777-everyone-loses-their-minds

Figure 6.4: An antisemitic example of the "Everyone loses their minds over Russia" meme, *Quick Meme*, http://www.quickmeme.com/p/3vtyqp

The microstructure of the antisemitic meme in Figure 6.4 already places demands of the most complex kind on the users. They must first identify the semiotic components of the text-image structure before they can integrate these and decode the emergent antisemitic meaning.

The realization users reach via the process of object recognition is that the memes in Figures 6.3 and 6.4 are constituted of several sign acts. This corresponds to their expectations regarding the communication format and the way it makes recourse to existing knowledge about the prototypical realisation possibilities of the same: memes are prototypically multimodal. In the selective sensory reception of information, focus is given first to the individual pictorial signs because these claim a higher relevance in the cognitive processing of a text-image relationship; only in a second step does the user turn to the verbal sign acts (Geise and Müller 2015: 97).[6] Yet, the verbal parts of the memes above generate a frame, within which their contents are arranged in a communicative logic of action and a linear-time axis, that is, they are localised in a situational reality. Accordingly, assumptions regarding material and other qualitative properties, such as the spatial-temporal location of the respective reference objects, must be already established so that it is possible to conceptualise them.[7] The semiotic

---

6   This is also one of the reasons why memes are popular for propagating antisemitic beliefs, as memes are grasped both sensory and cognitively faster than purely verbal units, since they are based on a sensory immediacy (Geise/Müller 2015: 109), https://doi.org/10.36198/9783838524146

7   In the act of referentialisation, a spatial-temporal existence is presupposed, which then takes the form of an implicit predication in Generic Space.

formations in question must necessarily exist as perceptible entities and in a way that allows predications to be attributed or denied to them on a representative level.

Figures 6.3 and 6.4 use the same pictorial elements. These intensify the messages displayed in the textual elements by emphasising the difference between them via conventionally established visual patterns. The open mouth as well as the forward posture of the person depicted signal danger and aggression. In this way, the pictorial elements express a lack of understanding that is to be interpreted as a reaction to the verbal elements: the (seemingly) identical course of action of the Israeli expansionist policy is given a different representation than the Russian one, although both of them deserve the same evaluation. While Israel's actions do not cause a disturbance ("Israel occupies Palestine for 47 years and no one bats an eye"), the Russian actions cause an outrage ("Russia does it for a week and everybody loses their minds", Figure 6.4). The fact that the two states and their respective military actions are placed in relation to each other at all, or that this relation is not questioned, presupposes the possibility of comparability; this is a fundamental element of the antisemitic construction of meaning within the meme. "Russia does it for a week" refers to Russia's violation of international law by deliberately and unjustifiably attacked a sovereign state, while the duration "47 years" is a reference to the Six-Day War and Israel's territorial gains afterwards—knowledge that users must possess and must have implicitly activated in order to decode the meaning of the meme: although they are legally, historically and morally different circumstances, Russia's actions in violation of international law are equated with Israel's historical developments. The meme thus activates and articulates a reductionist scheme or antisemitic concept within which only negative characteristics are attributed to Israel. It does so by both equating Israel's history with Russia's (morally objectionable) actions and by distortedly simplifying these historical circumstances to 47 years of occupation.

The meme's antisemitic meaning is realized, therefore, through the expressed indignation of the (supposed) contradiction that Israel is assessed differently to Russia despite its actions being just as reprehensible. If the person depicted is now recognised as the figure of the Joker, the pictorial part of the meme allows this contradiction to be directly experienced in its disproportionality and, consequently, amplifies the antisemitic meaning.[8] This figure, profiled as an antitype, has the property of expressing (seemingly) uncomfortable truths in the form of a contradiction. By drawing attention to such contradictions, the Joker—in the ironic doubling of the function of a 'joker' and, in the referenced film scene, the only one who can proclaim the truth because he does not have to fear any negative consequences—legitimises the comparison and makes it a fact: the antisemitic meaning of the meme constitutes a negative conceptual structure of Israel.

Figure 6.4 also realises the multi-phrase compound "and no one bats an eye / and everyone loses their minds", which is a necessary condition for the meme: every text-image structure that uses precisely this image must include this text for the meme to be recognised and interpreted as such, with its specific meaning potential and affordances. Web users who are familiar with the communication format base their interpretation on the expectation that these multi-phrase compounds will be present as soon as the image of the Joker is used.[9] The semantic restrictions of the communication format thus give rise to a patterned communicative structure that must correspond to user expectations if the intended (antisemitic) reception is to be guaranteed. The structure provides a framework that forces a certain reading of the meme in that the semantic relations of the verbal elements generate a global scope on the text-image structure. The consequence of such semantics determined by the structure is formulated as a lack of alternatives in the concrete meme, and the creative and cognitive limitations associated with it. Reception of the internal communicative organisation of the meme takes place when the pictorial signs are used to fill the gaps opened by the verbal sign acts. This takes the form of an antonymic juxtaposition

---

8   The meme *"Everyone loses their minds"* originates from a scene in the 2008 superhero film *The Dark Knight*, which shows a villainous character called the Joker, the protagonist's adversary. In the scene depicted, the Joker utters the following words: "If, tomorrow, I tell the press that, like, a gang banger will get shot, or a truckload of soldiers will be blown up, nobody panics, because it's all part of the plan. But when I say that one little old mayor will die, well then everyone loses their minds".

9   Nevertheless, familiarity with the Joker is not necessary to grasp the text-image structure at a basic level; the posture and facial expression of the person depicted already signal danger and aggression, characteristics that correlate with the assessment of reality with regard to an antisemitic perspective on Israeli actions.

that, then, is also manifested in the spatial arrangement of the verbal elements. The arrangement can be characterised as prototypical for the meme of this class and reveals a further semantic dimension: the spatial arrangement of verbal and pictorial signs follows the interpretative pattern in which elements positioned at the top are interpreted as positive (ideal) and units positioned at the bottom as negative (real) (Kress and van Leeuwen 2006: 186), and it correlates with the verbally executed contradiction. Placement of the statement "Russia does it for a week and everybody loses their minds" in the lower part of the meme portrays the Russian actions negatively and prompts criticism or questioning of Israeli actions. Indeed, the meme's ironically constructed and contradictory nature suggests that Israel's action is even worse than Russia's, thereby contributing to its antisemitic meaning.

This top-bottom reading of ideal and real categories should not be applied to all text-image structures, since, on the one hand, such a dichotomy is empirically untenable and, on the other, what assigns a corresponding value to the contribution element is not spatial organisation but the user (Bucher 2011: 133). Although this criticism is justified in principle, Kress and van Leeuwen's dichotomy is valid with regard to this meme. In its prototypical manifestation, the meme exhibits precisely those semiotic restrictions of placement and an accompanyingly limited framework of processing. Hence, the respective zones do not actually have any meaning *per se*, but users ascribe certain functions to them in a pattern-like manner due to their knowledge of the supra-individual interpretation patterns or the cognitive-realisation possibilities of the respective memes.

Even though the selection and structural composition of the sign resources used in this meme are limited, the conceptual representation of this text-image structure is an extremely complex process since the verbal parts of it already represent an independent blend.[10] Two blends are

---

10 Although the meme is understood even without knowledge of the person depicted, insofar as the gestures are interpreted as an expression of incomprehension within the framework of socially traditional patterns of interpretation, the pictorial part of this meme also already represents a blend. For within the text-image structure, it is not just any person who takes on the function of a nurse, but the figure of the Joker. The knowledge about the Joker provides input I and the knowledge about the activities of a nurse provides input II. In the context of the film *The Dark Knight*, from which the image originates, this character is now profiled as a person whose actions reveal themselves to be contrary to the

constructed via the necessary phrases "and no one bats an eye" and "and everyone loses their minds". In the cognitive processing of this meme, a correlation is then established between the blends and the metaphorical utterances, insofar as both the verbal utterances positioned above and those mounted below reveal themselves as single-scope networks.[11]

However, conceptualisation of the metaphorical utterances "no one bats an eye" and "everyone loses their minds" is determined in each case with the help of a different semantic dimension. While "everyone loses their minds" represents a relational link between a physical experience and an abstract entity, the conceptual projection in the utterance "no one bats an eye" only takes place within the conceptualisation of a physical process (Input Space I) against the background of the cultural interpretive framework (Generic Space) around the concept "eye" (Input Space II). The phrase "to bat" is, first, to be understood as a physical process within which the physical entity eye correlates with the function of making emotions visible or which has the function of generating emotional affects—be it through open or closed eyes or in the form of another bodily expressive movement. Consequently, the emergent structure of the phrase "no one bats an eye" results from the linking of its physical dimension of meaning, realised in the phrase "no one bats", and the conceptual frame around the expression "eye". Taken together, these structure the blend. Since Israel's actions do not evoke any physical reaction, the metaphorical statement "Israel occupies Palestine for 47 years and no one bats an eye" by itself, likewise, does not produce a strong emotional reaction. In contrast, the statement "everybody loses their minds" partially projects the physical experience of losing something onto the abstract entity "mind". See, in Figure 6.5, that Input Space I contains the structures around the syntagma "losing something" (a), while Input Space II has the abstract nomination "mind" (b). The Generic Space then provides the conceptual framework for the functional

---

expected activities of a nurse: Instead of helping or caring for other people, he harms them. The conceptual integration of these opposites results in the blend as the culmination of the contradictory nature of the Joker's character, in that he portrays a nurse.

11 Since a detailed presentation of the various possibilities of cognitive configurations of integral network structures would go beyond the scope of this chapter and only individual types of these are relevant for the analysis, the explanations have to remain brief. For more discussion, see Evans and Green 2006, 400–440.

integration of these two concepts. For, this is realised, on the one hand, by the knowledge that people can lose objects and that, furthermore, the loss of an object makes it impossible to carry out activities for which that object is intended (A). On the other hand, it contains the knowledge that the expression "mind" has a physical component (B), insofar as the mind is mostly located in the brain. Hence, the blend results from the functional linkage of the abstract nomination "mind" (b), which is identified as a physical entity (b^1), with the physical process of loss (a^1). By this mechanism, the absence of mind is interpreted as a dysfunction of mind. The blend is structured by the concept of loss, in that the construction uses the knowledge of the users to correlate the concepts involved in an integral conceptual structure:

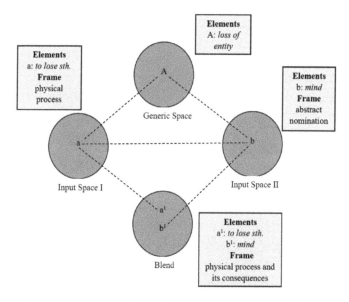

Figure 6.5: Conceptual Blend "Everyone loses their minds" [12]

At the same time, the loss of mind appears as an extreme reaction to Russia's actions in Ukraine insofar as the identical actions of Israel occupying Palestine do not evoke any emotional affects (which it should if they are equated—at least this is the antisemitic claim of the meme).

---

12   Mental spaces are represented as circles, their conceptualisations as rectangles and the individual elements as letters. The cross-mapping between the elements is visualised as a dashed line.

The meme's pictorial part can amplify this contradiction by materialising the disproportion that arises in the antonymic juxtaposition of the verbal utterances. Therefore, the functional complementarity of pictorial and verbal sign modalities gives rise to a cognitive-semantic interplay, by means of which the meme is always conceptualised in this way at a semiotic level and functions as a communicative template to carry the antisemitic meaning. In the two-dimensional compositionality of the meme, the temporal-sequential arrangement of verbal sign modalities in each exemplar of the same pattern is modified in favour of a spatial-visual organisation; however, the antisemitic meaning is evoked dynamically and discourse-sensitively insofar as the most diverse antisemitic concepts can be utilised for the same meme within the framework of its cognitive-semantic and discursive-medial realisation possibilities. Figure 6.6 illustrates this template character, which applies to all antisemitic memes:

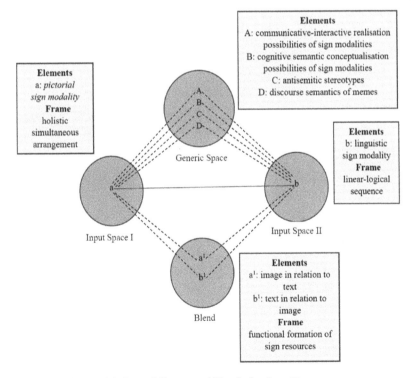

Figure 6.6: General Conceptual Blend of antisemitic memes

The fact that the antisemitic conceptual structure in memes is metaphorically structured or can be grasped with the blending theory is also evident in the next example. The meme in Figure 6.7 comprises a semiotically complex arrangement of four different memes and, in this way, further demonstrates what discursive knowledge is needed to decode and process antisemitic memes.

So, it was the Jews?   Always has been.

Figure 6.7: An antisemitic meme "Always has been Jews", *9 Gag*, https://comment-cdn.9gag.com/image?ref=9gag.com#https://img-comment-fun.9cache.com/media/aerRRp/adRKBKAE_700w_0.jpg

As we have seen in previous examples, the pictorial patterns here are highly conventionalised. The semiotic restrictions of the format give rise to a communicative structure that corresponds to web users' expectations and ensures the intended antisemitic reception of the meme. For, recognition of the pictorial components is sufficient to activate the prototypical mental representation of the meme in memory, that is, the visual organisation refers to already-existing and familiar structures of the same pattern and is then contextualised by the verbal component.

In the upper part of Figure 6.7, the pictorial sign actions of the illustrated figures, which refer to the "Boys vs. Girls" meme, are accompanied by text that expresses agreement within the in-group comprised of the person of colour and the white person. In the lower part of the meme, this agreement is amplified in the visual form of an arm-wrestle handshake, generating an intrapictorial coherence. The relationship between the pictures functions as a *pars pro toto* for overcoming racism in that the handshake both refers to the "Epic Handshake" meme and activates the socially traditional interpretation of this gesture as a realisation of approval.

The person of colour and the white person are in agreement about their evaluation of a figure who is shown in the lower part of the meme behind the handshake. This is the Happy Merchant, from the eponymous meme, that relies on antisemitically charged conceptual elements. The figure's appearance—including curved nose, bulging lips, and crooked posture recalls physical attributes associated with Jews in antisemitic readings. Likewise, his identification as a "merchant" aligns with the antisemitic stereotype that Jews enjoy harming non-Jewish people through financial and other activities (Scheiber, Troschke and Krasni forthcoming). In bringing together these pictorial sign actions and activating this knowledge, the meme calls upon the blend available in an antisemitic reality: in the face of the Jewish threat—personified in the Happy Merchant—white people and people of colour overcome their differences to oppose this threat. This agreement worries the Happy Merchant to the extent that beads of sweat run down his face. These are not part of the prototypical portrayal of the meme-figure, and their addition here implies a demand for action from the user. The suggestion is that cooperation between a white person and a person of colour produces a negative effect on the Happy Merchant and, as their stereotypical representative, all Jews.

On the verbal level, the meme realises the pair sequence of a question "So, it was the Jews?" followed by an answer "Always has been". This refers to another meme, the "Always has been" meme, but gives it a specific antisemitic dimension by generating a coherent interrelation between the individual pictorial and verbal components of the sequential text-image structure. The "Always has been" meme expresses a moment of realisation in which a controversial issue is recognised as an absolute truth. By recontextualising the verbal part of the "Always has been" meme (transposing its semantic structure to this context), the meme in Figure 6.7 essentialises Jews and identifies them as (despicable) Happy Merchants. This characterisation is presented as an absolute and inescapable truth, provided that the phrase is recognised as a meme in its own right.[13]

Each component within Figure 6.7 that is borrowed from another meme represents an input space that reveals itself as a separate blend, so that the cognitive processing of the meme can be described as a multiple blend (Evans and Green 2006: 431). The blend of meaning from the input spaces gives rise to a complex consecutive text-image structure, and realisation of the pair sequence does not take place exclusively through the verbal sign actions but is also expressed in the relationship of the individual pictorial sign actions to each other against the background of an antisemitic contextualisation. At the same time, it should be emphasized, once again, that what is interacting is not the semiotic elements of the antisemitic meme but, rather, the users who read these elements with a particular knowledge of the world and who have certain media competencies in relation to the communication format of the meme. Which antisemitic concept is attributed to a meme depends on the normativity of discursive practices. Hence, once a blend and its cognitive mechanisms have been activated, the users perform semantic construction work in the course of meaning constitution by independently filling the antisemitic conceptual structure with textual, world or situational knowledge within an antisemitic belief system and decoding the antisemitic meaning in this way.

8. Conclusion

Memes have become part of our everyday communication. This chapter explored the patterns of cognitive anchoring in antisemitic memes to find out how memes are utilised on a cognitive level to disseminate antisemitic content. It became apparent that the cognitive anchoring of antisemitic concepts in memes can be described through multistage processes of blending. The understanding of an antisemitic meme takes place through several interlocking operations. On one hand, web users recognise and categorise the participating sign actions and their

---

13   If the phrase is not recognised as a meme in its own right, then this layer of
      meaning is lost. However, the meme is still interpreted as antisemitic because
      the phrase implies a causal relationship between Jews and all imaginable (EVIL)
      actions.

prototypical functions; on the other, their focus oscillates back and forth between the different sign actions, since it is only in their interdependent interaction that the meaning is constituted. Furthermore, users qualify this interaction with regard to the (discourse-)semantic properties of the prototypical reference pattern of the meme. Finally, they contextualise the meme within an antisemitic belief system. A multimodal understanding of an antisemitic meme results, therefore, from the recognition of the functional linking patterns and their respective communicative implications, which generate synergetic action between the prototypical modalities and an antisemitic conceptual structure.

References

Bateman, John A., 2014. *Text and Image. A critical introduction to the visual/verbal divide*. Abingdon: Routledge, https://doi.org/10.1080/14725 86X.2016.1260358

Beißwenger, Michael, 2007. *Sprachhandlungskoordination in der Chat-Kommunikation*. Berlin: De Gruyter, https://doi.org/10.1515/9783110953121

Bolton, Matthew, 2024. "Evil/The Devil". In: Matthias J., Becker, Hagen, Troschke, Matthew, Bolton and Alexis, Chapelan (eds). *A Guide to Identifying Antisemitism Online*. London: Palgrave Macmillan

Breitenbach, Patrick, 2015. "Memes. Das Web als kultureller Nährboden". In: Patrick, Breitenbach, Christian, Stiegler and Thomas, Zorbach (eds). *New Media Culture. Mediale Phänomene der Netzkultur*. Bielefeld: transcript, 29–49, https://doi.org/10.14361/9783839429075-002

Bucher, Hans-Jürgen, 2011. "Multimodales Verstehen oder Rezeption als Interaktion. Theoretische und empirische Grundlagen einer systematischen Analyse der Multimodalität". In: Hajo, Diekmannshenke, Michael, Klemm and Hartmut, Stöckl (eds). *Bildlinguistik. Theorien. Methoden. Fallbeispiele*. Berlin: Erich Schmidt, 123–156, https://doi.org/10.3730 7/b.978-3-503-12264-6

Drewer, Petra, 2003. *Die kognitive Metapher als Werkzeug des Denkens. Zur Rolle der Analogie bei der Gewinnung und Vermittlung wissenschaftlicher Erkenntnisse*. Tübingen: Narr, https://doi.org/10.1515/zrs.2009.037

El Refaie, Elisabeth, 2015. "Cross-modal resonances in creative multimodal metaphors. Breaking out of conceptual prisons". In: María Jesús Pinar, Sanz (ed). *Multimodality and Cognitive Linguistics*. Amsterdam: Benjamins, 13–26, https://doi.org/10.1075/rcl.11.2.02elr

Evans, Vyvyan and Melanie, Green, 2006. *Cognitive Linguistics. An Introduction*. Edinburgh: Edinburgh University Press

Fauconnier, Giles and Mark, Turner, 2002. *The Way We Think. Conceptual Blending and the Mind's Hidden Complexities.* New York: Basic Books, https://doi.org/10.1086/378014

Geise, Stephanie and Marion G., Müller, 2015. *Grundlagen der visuellen Kommunikation.* UVK Verlagsgesellschaft, https://doi.org/10.36198/9783838524146

Iedema, Rick, 2003. "Multimodality, resemiotization: extending the analysis of discourse as multi-semiotic practice". *Visual Communication* 2 (1), 29–57, https://doi.org/10.1177/1470357203002001751

Jäkel, Olaf, 2003. *Wie Metaphern Wissen schaffen. Die kognitive Metapherntheorie und ihre Anwendung in Modell-Analysen der Diskursbereiche Geistestätigkeit, Wirtschaft. Wissenschaft und Religion.* Hamburg: Dr. Kovač

Klug, Nina-Maria, 2023. "Verstehen auf den ersten Blick – oder doch nicht? Zur (vermeintlichen) Einfachheit kleiner Texte am Beispiel von Internet-Memes". In: Angela, Schrott, Johanna, Wolf, Christine, Pflüger (eds). *Textkomplexität und Textverstehen.* Berlin: De Gruyter, 195–230, https://doi.org/10.1515/9783111041551-008

Köller, Wilhelm, 2004. *Perspektivität und Sprache. Zur Struktur von Objektivierungsformen in Bildern, im Denken und in der Sprache.* Berlin: De Gruyter, https://doi.org/10.1515/9783110919547

Kress, Gunther and Theo, van Leeuwen, 2006. *Reading Images. The Grammar of Visual Design.* Abingdon: Routledge, https://doi.org/10.1075/fol.3.2.15vel

Kress, Gunther, 2010. *Multimodality. A social semiotic approach to contemporary communication.* Abingdon: Routledge, https://doi.org/10.1080/10572252.2011.551502

Meier, Stefan, 2014. *(Bild-) Diskurs im Netz. Konzept und Methode für eine semiotische Diskursanalyse im World Wide Web.* Köln: Halem

Quasthoff, Uta M., 1973. *Soziales Vorurteil und Kommunikation. eine sprachwissenschaftliche Analyse des Stereotyps. Ein interdisziplinärer Versuch im Bereich von Linguistik, Sozialwissenschaft und Psychologie.* Athenäum

Rolf, Eckard, 2005. Metapherntheorien. *Typologie. Darstellung. Bibliographie.* Berlin: De Gruyter, https://doi.org/10.1515/arb-2013-0086

Sachs-Hombach, Klaus, 2003. *Das Bild als kommunikatives Medium. Elemente einer allgemeinen Bildwissenschaft.* Köln: Herbert von Halem

Salzborn, Samuel, 2011. "Antisemitismus". In: *Europäische Geschichte Online* (EGO), http://www.ieg-ego.eu/salzborns-2011-de

Scheiber, Marcus, 2019. "Perspektivistische Setzungen von Wirklichkeit vermittels Memes. Strategien der Verwendung von Bild-Sprache-Gefügen in der politischen Kommunikation". In: Lars, Bülow and Michael, Johann (eds). *Politische Internet-Memes – Theoretische Herausforderungen und empirische Befunde.* Berlin: Frank & Timme, 145–168

Scheiber, Marcus, Hagen, Troschke and Jan, Krasni, forthcoming. "Vom kommunikativen Phänomen zum gesellschaftlichen Problem: Wie Antisemitismus durch Memes viral wird". In: Susanne, Kabatnik, Lars, Bülow, Marie-Luis, Merten and Robert, Mroczynski (eds). *Pragmatik multimodal*. Tübingen: Narr

Schröder, Ulrike, 2012. *Kommunikationstheoretische Fragestellungen in der kognitiven Metaphernforschung. Eine Betrachtung von ihren Anfängen bis zur Gegenwart*. Tübingen: Narr

Schwarz-Friesel, Monika and Jehuda, Reinharz, 2017. *Inside the antisemitic mind. The language of Jew-Hatred in contemporary Germany*. Waltham, MA: Brandeis University Press, https://doi.org/10.26530/oapen_625675

Shifman, Limor, 2013. *Memes in Digital Culture*. Cambridge, MA: MIT Press, https://doi.org/10.1080/01972243.2016.1130504

Skirl, Helge, 2008. "Zur Schnittstelle von Semantik und Pragmatik. Innovative Metaphern als Fallbeispiel". In: Inge, Pohl (ed). *Semantik und Pragmatik – Schnittstellen*. Berlin: Lang, 17–40

Spitzmüller, Jürgen and Ingo, Warnke, 2011. *Diskurslinguistik. Eine Einführung in Theorien und Methoden der transtextuellen Sprachanalyse*. Berlin: De Gruyter

Tendahl, Markus, 2015. "Relevanztheorie und kognitive Linguistik vereint in einer hybriden Metapherntheorie". In: Klaus-Michael, Köpcke and Constanze, Spieß (eds). *Metonymie und Metapher – Theoretische, methodische und empirische Zugänge*. Berlin: De Gruyter, 25–50, https://doi.org/10.1515/9783110369120.25

Wrede, Julia, 2013. *Bedingungen, Prozesse und Effekte der Bedeutungskonstruktion. Der sprachliche Ausdruck in der Kotextualisierung*. Rhein-Ruhr Press

7. Discussion Trees on Social Media

A New Approach to Detecting Antisemitism Online

Chloé Vincent

Antisemitism often takes implicit forms on social media, therefore making it difficult to detect. In many cases, context is essential to recognise and understand the antisemitic meaning of an utterance (Becker et al. 2021, Becker and Troschke 2023, Jikeli et al. 2022a). Previous quantitative work on antisemitism online has focused on independent comments obtained through keyword search (e.g. Jikeli et al. 2019, Jikeli et al. 2022b), ignoring the discussions in which they occurred. Moreover, on social media, discussions are rarely linear. Web users have the possibility to comment on the original post and start a conversation or to reply to earlier web user comments. This chapter proposes to consider the structure of the comment trees constructed in the online discussion, instead of single comments individually, in an attempt to include context in the study of antisemitism online.

This analysis is based on a corpus of 25,412 trees, consisting of 76,075 *Facebook* comments. The corpus is built from web comments reacting to posts published by mainstream news outlets in three countries: France, Germany, and the UK. The posts are organised into 16 discourse events, which have a high potential for triggering antisemitic comments. The analysis of the data help verify whether (1) antisemitic comments come together (are grouped under the same trees), (2) the structure of trees

    https://doi.org/10.11647/OBP.0406.07

(lengths, number of branches) is significant in the emergence of antisemitism, (3) variations can be found as a function of the countries and the discourse events.

This study presents an original way to look at social media data, which has potential for helping identify and moderate antisemitism online. It specifically can advance research in machine learning by allowing to look at larger segments of text, which is essential for reliable results in artificial intelligence methodology. Finally, it enriches our understanding of social interactions online in general, and hate speech online in particular.

1. Introduction

While research on automatic detection of hate speech is a growing field, the focus on antisemitism is rarer in comparison to other hate ideologies. Unlike other forms of hate speech, antisemitism has always changed and adapted to conditions throughout its history (Wistrich 1992). In the awareness of the Holocaust, it is often expressed implicitly in mainstream public discourse and is therefore making it difficult to detect automatically. This is also the case in social media contexts of the political mainstream, where antisemitism is generally not accepted.

Previous quantitative work on antisemitism online has focused on independent comments obtained through keyword search (e.g. Jikeli et al. 2019, Jikeli et al. 2022b). These studies often ignored the discussions in which they participated; the comments were analysed independently of this context. This poses a problem because discussions on social media are rarely linear: web users have the possibility to comment on the original post and start a conversation or to reply to earlier web user comments.

In many cases, context is essential to recognise and understand the antisemitic meaning of an utterance (Jikeli et al. 2022). In our corpus, more than half of the comments that were annotated as antisemitic could be considered as such by taking the context into account, that is, by considering either the article to which the comment refers or the comments to which the web user is replying. For instance, a simple comment with only the word "who?" would not be considered antisemitic in most contexts. However, in the French context of the

2021 protests against the health pass during the Covid-19 pandemic, "who?" ["qui?"] can be understood as a dog whistle—an antisemitic coded phrase which implies that Jews are controlling the world and are responsible for the pandemic. Being able to refer to the article in order to evaluate the comments might help categorise the comment accordingly. Another example is the antecedents of pronouns. In a discussion, if one user mentions Jewish people then the next makes a reference to the previous comments using pronouns (for example, "They are evil"), the pronoun's meaning can only be understood using the contextual information provided by the previous comment. Therefore, within our corpus, more than half of antisemitic comments (56%) could not have been categorised as such if context had not been taken into account.

My contribution aims at exploring new ways of handling social media data with the goal of adding context to the short texts that constitute comments. Taking a data-based approach, it examines how antisemitic comments are distributed, how the online discussions are structured and how the patterns observed vary depending on discourse event and country.

In this chapter, I first present the dataset I studied by describing the collection and its processing. I then move on to answer the following three research questions: (1) are antisemitic comments more likely to be grouped under the same trees, (2) is the structure of trees (lengths, number of branches) significant in the emergence of antisemitism and (3) are there any variations depending on the countries and the discourse events? I consider the structure of the comment trees constructed in the online discussion, instead of single comments individually, in an attempt to include context in the study of antisemitism online. The results of the statistical models are presented, followed by a discussion.

2. Data collection

This study uses the data collected in the context of the ongoing project Decoding Antisemitism in the period between June 2021 and December 2022. The data was obtained by collecting comments reacting to news articles published in the context of specific discourse events. The discourse events are delimited by the research teams in preparation of the data collection. The discourse events are chosen according to whether the articles from the mainstream media reporting on them are potentially triggering antisemitism and whether they generate a large enough online discussion (at least one or two posts per news outlet, for which at least fifty comments were posted). The delimitation of which articles will be included in the analysis varies from one discourse event to the other. The articles must fit the topic, the period in time and in case the discourse event triggered large discussions we focus on articles that had more comments.

Some discourse events studied in this chapter are international, such as the Russian invasion of Ukraine, the Arab-Israeli conflict, the Covid-19 vaccination campaign in Israel, the terrorist attacks perpetrated in Israel in the spring of 2022 and the company Ben & Jerry's decision not to sell their products in Israeli settlements. Others are country specific, for instance the reactions to the emergence of antisemitic slogans in the demonstrations against the health pass, the use of the Pegasus spyware (developed by the Israeli cyber-arms company NSO Group) to spy on various French politicians, the ban of both the comedian Dieudonné M'bala M'bala's and the political essayist Alain Soral's *Facebook* and *YouTube* accounts in France, the trials of the concentration camps guards, the Gil Ofarim and Maaßen controversy in Germany, the case of the Irish novelist Sally Rooney who refused permission for an Israeli publishing company to translate her best-selling novel *Beautiful World, Where Are You* into Hebrew as part of a cultural boycott of Israel and the claims made by Professor David Miller, who alleged that the students from the University of Bristol's Jewish Society were "political pawns by a violent, racist foreign regime engaged in ethnic cleansing" in the United Kingdom (Liphshiz 2021). Once the discourse event is clearly delimited, all articles and social media posts that meet the selected criteria are crawled (that is, collected and downloaded from their source website) to gather all comments reacting to them, in the order they appear online.

For each discourse event, the research team from Decoding Antisemitism annotated the comments using the software MAXQDA, following a guidebook. The comments are annotated not only for ideation—that is, whether the comment is (contextually) antisemitic, countering antisemitic speech, or not antisemitic—but also for linguistic characteristics, antisemitic tropes and mentions of Jewish people, Jewishness or Israel.

2.1 Contextual antisemitism and mentions

Previous studies examining antisemitism online have used keyword search, ignoring most of the contextual antisemitism. Figure 7.1 shows that, in our corpus, while antisemitic comments are found most often when Jewish people, Jewishness or Israel is mentioned, context is still essential to understand the antisemitic meaning of the comment in 26% of cases. More importantly, even though our corpus is built by focusing on discourse events likely to trigger antisemitism, the vast majority of comments do not explicitly mention Jewish people, Jewishness, Israel or related words and phrases (40,547 comments, compared to 6,384 that include such mentions), and therefore would not be found by keyword search. Context is essential to understand the antisemitic meaning in 67% of these cases.

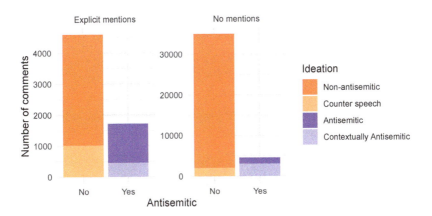

Figure 7.1: Distribution of comments in the Decoding Antisemitism dataset, depending on their ideation and on the presence of specific mentions. Note that the scale varies between mentions and no mentions

3. Data processing

The annotated data is exported from the MAXQDA content analysis software to the CSV (comma-separated values) file format and then processed in the statistical analysis programme R. The complete dataset consists of 76,075 comments. This chapter focuses on *Facebook* data, which represents 54,215 comments taken from 371 posts. In order to avoid outlier skews, I eliminated the 5% shortest and 5% longest threads; a thread is defined, for the purpose of this study, as the totality of comments annotated under a specific post, regardless of the structure of the conversation. This elimination resulted in a dataset of 333 threads containing from 71 to 256 comments (with the mean of 141 and a median of 117). In total, the threads comprised 46,931 web comments, out of which 6,484 were considered antisemitic (either explicitly or contextually).

In general, the threads below the posts are constituted of *trees of comments*. Some trees are very short; these might contain only one comment to which no other web user replied. Others are composed of multiple comments, organised in branches. On *Facebook*, web users wishing to comment under a post have two options. They can either post their comment directly in reply to the initial post, or they can reply to another comment. The direct-response comments form the trunk of the trees, while the replies are their branches. Replies are restricted to a depth of two levels—the first level being a user's reply to the initial comment (the trunk) and the second level a user's reply to another reply.

In order to analyse the data, the comments were grouped together by trees. Within each tree, the proportion of antisemitic comments is computed as well as the length of the tree—single comments that received no replies are of length 1—and the number of branches or replies to the initial 'trunk' comment. For the purpose of this chapter, I use the term 'discussion' to refer to a succession of comments responding directly to one another, as opposed to responding directly to the post published by the news outlet on their social account; a discussion is a tree of length greater than 1.

For our three research questions, I formulate the following hypotheses:

1. Antisemitic comments are grouped together:

    a. The proportion of antisemitic comments is higher in discussions than in single comments (H1)

    b. Replies to comments are more likely to be antisemitic than replies to media posts (H2)

    c. Discussion starting with antisemitic comments are more likely to trigger antisemitism (H3).

2. The structure of trees is related to the emergence of antisemitism:

   a. The longer the trees, the higher the proportion of antisemitism (H4)

   b. The larger the trees, that is to say, the more branches there are, the higher the proportion of antisemitism (H5).

3. There is variation depending on the countries and the discourse events (H6).

4. Statistical analysis

In order to answer the three research questions laid out in the introduction, I build statistical models using the ideation of the comment, simplified to antisemitic versus not antisemitic, as the dependent variable. The independent variables differ depending on the research question I try to answer. Given that the dependent variable can only take two values (either antisemitic or not), I run a generalised linear model in R with a binomial family.

4.1 RQ1: Are antisemitic comments grouped together?

The first research question deals with whether more antisemitic comments can be found in a conversation about the topic that has been identified as a potential trigger for antisemitic reactions, as opposed to stand-alone comments. Three hypotheses were made in this regard: (H1) there are more antisemitic comments in discussions than in single comments, (H2) initial comments are less likely to be antisemitic than replies to comments and (H3) in case an antisemitic comment triggers the discussion, antisemitic comments are more likely to be found in the corresponding discussion.

H1: In order to verify whether the proportion of antisemitic comments is higher in the discussions than in the single comments, I built a linear model using the simplified ideation of the comment ('antisemitic' versus 'not antisemitic') as the *dependent* variable, and the type of tree the comment is in as *independent* variable. The type of tree determines whether the tree comprises a single comment or a discussion (that is, at least one reply to the initial comment).

Table 7.1 shows the results of the statistical analysis. The p-value ($<2e-16$) stands for the probability of observing this result due to chance. A p-value lower than 0.05 is widely taken as threshold for significance. The type of tree is thus a significant variable in determining if a comment is more likely to be antisemitic. The estimate corresponds to the log odds of a comment being antisemitic. The intercept is the basis (here a single comment), and the value for the discussion is the estimated difference for the log odds in case the tree is a discussion. The odds of a comment being antisemitic decrease when in a discussion in comparison to single comments: Figure 7.2 shows that, contrary to my first hypothesis (H1), comments in a discussion are less likely to be antisemitic than single comments (note that the scales on the y axis differ: there are three times as many comments in the discussion than there are single comments). In discussions, 13% of the comments are antisemitic, whereas 17% out of the individual comments are antisemitic.

	Estimate	Standard error	P-value
(Intercept)	−1.59	0.02	$<2e-16$ ***
Type of tree (discussion)	−0.32	0.03	$<2e-16$ ***

Table 7.1: Results of the statistical analysis modelling the ideation as a function of the type of comment. The three stars indicate the high significance of this relation.

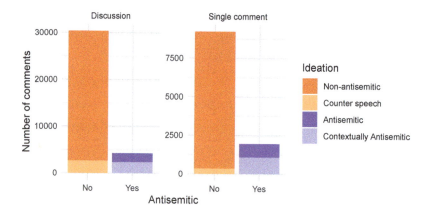

Figure 7.2: Ideation of comments from the Decoding Antisemitism dataset depending on whether the comment is an individual comment, or taken from a discussion. Note that the scale varies between Discussion and Single comment.

H2: Another possible approach to this question is to regard comments as sequential, in opposition to the end results that were crawled. We can understand all heads of trees to be single comments, and assume that trees only start with the replies to the initial comments, instead of considering the trees *a posteriori*.

Figure 7.3 shows a coherent result with reply to comments being significantly less likely to be antisemitic than initial comments: thus, the second hypothesis (H2) is also invalidated. Of the initial comments, 18% are antisemitic (Level 0) compared to 12% and 11% for the direct and indirect replies (Level 1 and 2 respectively), which are not significantly distinct. Table 7.2 shows the estimate of the statistical analysis, together with the p-value. The diagonal corresponds to the log odds for a comment being antisemitic for each level. The rest of the table indicates the estimated difference for the log odds between the different level of comments. The odds of a comment being antisemitic decrease when the level increase, but the difference between level 1 and 2 is not significant.

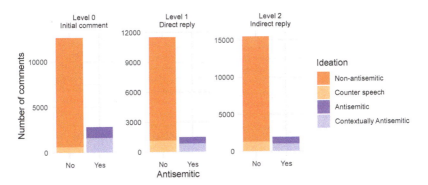

Figure 7.3: Distribution of comments depending on the levels. Note that the scale varies between the different levels.

Estimate (p-value)	Level 0	Level 1	Level 2
Level 0	−1.50 (<2e−16 ***)		
Level 1	−0.54 (<2e−16 ***)	−2.04 (<2e−16 ***)	
Level 2	−0.59 (<2e−16 ***)	−0.05 (0.198)	−2.09 (<2e−16 ***)

Table 7.2: Results of the statistical analysis modelling the ideation as a function of the level of the comment.

H3: To evaluate the hypothesis that discussions beginning with an antisemitic comment are more likely to trigger antisemitism, I ignored the single comments since their ideation automatically matches the initial comment of the tree, which, in this situation, is of length 1.

As shown in Figure 7.4, antisemitic comments are more likely to be found in a discussion that started with an antisemitic comment. In such discussions, 28% of comments in the dataset are antisemitic, compared to 9% for discussions starting with a non-antisemitic comment. Table 7.3 presents the results of the statistical model, showing that the ideation of the initial comment of a discussion is significant in explaining the variation of the comments' ideation and that the odds of a comment being antisemitic increase when the initial comment of the tree is antisemitic.

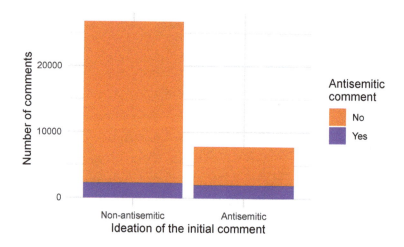

Figure 7.4: Distribution of ideation of comments in discussions, depending on the ideation of the first comment of the tree

	Estimate	Standard error	P−value
(Intercept)	−2.36	0.02	<2e−16 ***
Ideation of the initial comment (antisemitic)	1.39	0.03	<2e−16 ***

Table 7.3: Results of the statistical analysis modelling the ideation of a comment as a function of the ideation of the initial comment of the tree.

To conclude, I invalidated the first two hypotheses, both of which claim that antisemitic comments are more likely to appear in discussions. However, the analysis revealed a new correlation: when a discussion starts off with an antisemitic comment, it is more likely that more antisemitic comments will follow. I review this result further in the discussion section.

4.2 RQ2: Does the structure of trees reflect the proportion of antisemitism?

For the second research question, I focused on the discussions in the corpus and ignored single comments; that is to say, I concentrated on trees that contain at least two comments. Two hypotheses were formulated regarding the structure of the trees: that the proportion of antisemitic comments increases as the conversation grows in length (H1), and in width (H2). The width refers to the number of branches started by replies (Level 1) to the initial comment (Level 0), while the length is the overall number of replies (Level 1 and 2) to the initial comment (Level 0).

H4: Aligned with the results from the previous research question, I found that the proportion of antisemitism decreases with the length of the discussion. These results show that the discussion does not trigger more antisemitism as it develops.

The fourth hypothesis (H4) was, therefore, invalidated. On the contrary, the median of tree lengths for antisemitic comments is 7, while it is 9 for non-antisemitic comments. Given the variation in the length of comment trees, as shown in Figure 7.5, it is not the best indicator of the variation between antisemitic and non-antisemitic comments. Table 7.4 shows that, while the length of the tree is not significant (p value 0.856) in explaining the variation of the odds, the estimated variation is very small in any case (0.0001 per additional comment in the tree).

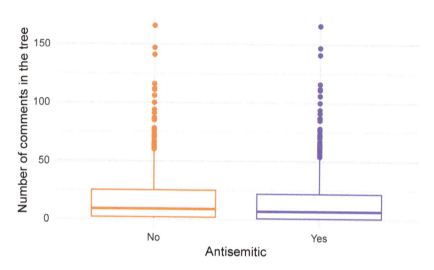

Figure 7.5: Distribution of the length of trees for antisemitic and non-antisemitic comments.

	Estimate	Standard error	P−value
(Intercept)	−1.96	0.02	<2e−16 ***
Length of tree	0.0001	0.0005	0.856

Table 7.4: Results of the statistical analysis modelling the ideation of a comment as a function of the length of the tree.

H5: Regarding another element of the structure of trees, I studied the potential effect of the number of branches of a discussion tree on the probability of finding antisemitic comments. When focusing only on comments that are part of a discussion, that is to say where there is at least one branch of replies, I found that (1) the relationship is significant in explaining the variation in the data and (2) the more branches there are, the more likely it is to find antisemitic comments (cf. Table 7.5).

	Estimate	Standard error	P−value
(Intercept)	−2.01	0.02	<2e−16 ***
Length of tree	0.007	0.001	1.2e−05 ***

Table 7.5: Results of the statistical analysis modelling the ideation of a comment as a function of the number of branches in the tree

The variation is so small, however, in comparison to the variation in the data (cf. Figure 7.6), that I could disregard its use in distinguishing between these parameters. The median of branch numbers in both cases is 4.

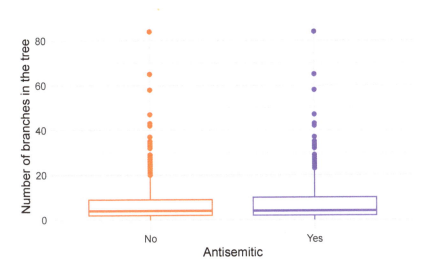

Figure 7.6: Distribution of the number of branches in a discussion tree for antisemitic and non-antisemitic comments

To conclude, I found that the elements of the structure of the trees that I examined are not significant in representing the proportion of antisemitism in the discussion. The length of the discussion in not significant, while the number of branches is significant in showing there is no evolution depending on the width of the conversation.

4.3 RQ3: Is there variation depending on the countries and the discourse events?

Finally, the question remains whether the structure of the conversation varies between the three language communities under analysis. I found that there are slightly more discussions in the UK (26%) and France (24%) compared to Germany (22%), as shown in Figure 7.7 and Table 7.6.

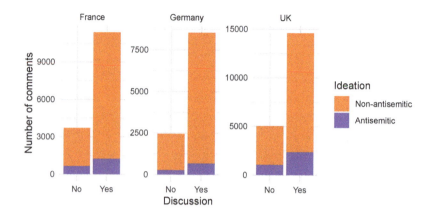

Figure 7.7: Discussions and single comments depending on the country. Germany differs significantly from France and the UK. The variation between France and the UK is less significant. Note that the scale varies between the countries.

Estimate (p–value)	Germany	UK	France
Germany	1.26 (<2e−16 ***)		
UK	−0.19 (3.4e−11 ***)	1.07 (<2e−16 ***)	
France	−0.13 (1.5e−05 ***)	0.06 (0.02 *)	1.13 (<2e−16 ***)

Table 7.6: Results of the statistical analysis modelling the odds of a comment being in a discussion as a function of the speech community

The lengths of the trees across the three country datasets are similar (median are 8, 9 and 10 for Germany, the UK and France respectively) and do not vary significantly.

Regarding the effect of the initial comment on the rest of tree, the statistical analysis shows that both variables (the country and the initial comment), and their interactions are significant, as shown in Figure 7.8 and Table 7.7. The effect of the initial comment is most important in the German corpora and least important in the British corpora.

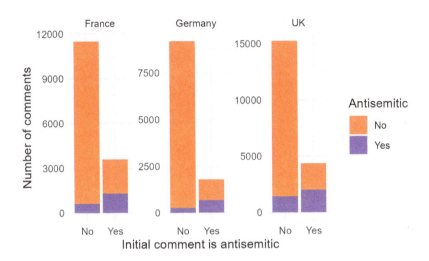

Figure 7.8: Interaction between the country and the initial comment ideation in determining the ideation of a comment. Note that the scale varies between the countries.

Estimate (p–value)	Germany	UK	France
Germany	−3.48 (<2e−16 ***)		
UK	1.21 (<2e−16 ***)	−2.27 (<2e−16 ***)	
France	0.61 (<2e−16 ***)	−0.60 (<2e−16 ***)	−2.87 (<2e−16 ***)
Ideation of the initial comment (antisemitic)	3.05 (<2e−16 ***)	2.13 (<2e−16 ***)	2.25 (<2e−16 ***)
Interaction between initial comment and Germany		0.92 (<2e−16 ***)	0.70 (8.1e−14 ***)
Interaction between initial comment and UK			−0.22 (0.001 **)

Table 7.7: Results of the statistical analysis modelling the odds of a comment being antisemitic as a function of the interaction between the speech community and whether the initial comment of the tree is antisemitic

Overall, the proportion of antisemitic comments varies significantly from one country to the other: 18 % in the UK, 13 % in France and 9 % in Germany as shown in Figure 7.9 and Table 7.8. I also observed that there are many more non-contextual antisemitic comments in the UK corpus than were found in the French and German corpora.

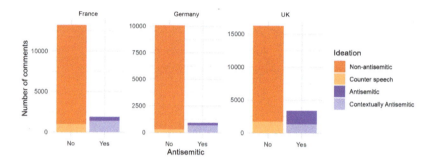

Figure 7.9: Overall distribution of comments in the three countries. The three countries differ significantly from one another (p value is <2e−16 for all relations). Note that the scale varies between the countries.

Estimate (p−value)	Germany	UK	France
Germany	−2.31 (<2e−16 ***)		
UK	0.77 (<2e−16 ***)	−1.54 (<2e−16 ***)	
France	0.41 (<2e−16 ***)	−0.36 (<2e−16 ***)	−1.90 (<2e−16 ***)

Table 7.8: Results of the statistical analysis modelling the odds of a comment being antisemitic as a function of the speech community

5. Discussion

The statistical analysis shows that antisemitic comments are not distributed in a specific pattern in the examined corpus. Whether or not antisemitism is present in a discussion is not reflected in the structure of the trees of the online conversation. Contrary to our hypotheses, the longer a discussion continues, finding antisemitic comments does not become more likely and replies to the initial comments are less likely to be antisemitic. Antisemitic comments are more numerous in single comments than in the discussions.

This result shows that conversations around potentially triggering topics do not necessarily lead to antisemitism in higher proportions as discussion develops. However, in the process of analysis, I found that replies in discussions with an antisemitic starting point—ones in which the initial post in a comment tree is antisemitic—are more likely to contain antisemitism than those in discussions that start with a non-antisemitic statement. This could be due to the fact the web user who opens the discussion is more likely to comment further in the discussion, continuing to express either the same or new antisemitic tropes, which will then lead to increased probability of finding an antisemitic comment in that discussion. Moreover, comments on public posts—such as the ones under scrutiny in the Decoding Antisemitism project—are visible not only to any *Facebook* user exploring the thread but also on timelines of *Facebook* friends of that user (depending on their privacy settings). This visibility may trigger response from a specific social group influenced, in the same way as the initial user, by antisemitism.

Thus, while it seems that conversation on social media in itself does not trigger greater antisemitism, these platforms are conceived and built in a way that will lead to the comments attracting web users who hold similar world views and, thus, amplifies antisemitism online.

Another finding of this study is the variation between the speech communities both in terms of the structure of the discussion and in terms of antisemitic content. I found that the overall proportion of antisemitism is much higher in the data collected from the comment sections of news outlets in France and the United Kingdom compared to those in Germany.

I can only speculate on the reasons for the variation between the three countries. One potential explanation is that there is less antisemitism in German society than in France and the UK. One can suppose that, contrary to France and the UK, the memory work done by the German society in the past decades has led its web users to understand better what constitutes antisemitic statements, to recognise antisemitic stereotypes and concepts and to grasp why they are harmful. There is, of course, no denying that there is still antisemitic hate speech in Germany, but the findings here might be an invitation to educate society at large.

Another reason, related to the above, may be a difference in the countries' moderation policies: these might be stricter in Germany and more permissive in the UK and in France.

The third potential reason is that French and English, unlike German, are global languages. Both are spoken by hundreds of millions of people around the world. The proportion of antisemitism in the comments does not represent only the British and French society respectively but, rather, the language communities linked to, or under the sphere of influence of, the two countries.

In the UK data, I found that many more discussions starting with non-antisemitic statements still triggered a considerable amount of antisemitic content, and discussions from that corpora that do start with antisemitic statements (which are proportionally less contextual than in France or Germany) do not trigger as much antisemitism as those in the German or French corpora. The reasons for this finding are still to be uncovered and could form the topic of future study.

6. Conclusion

In this chapter, I explored several hypotheses regarding the structure of online conversations on the social media platform *Facebook* in comment threads posted by web users on the official pages of mainstream news outlets. The analysis found that the structure of the conversation does not determine and, therefore, does not offer insight into the patterns of antisemitism online. Nevertheless, some structural parameters can be very useful in predicting antisemitic hate speech content in online debates.

More importantly, these findings point towards a new way of organising data to provide machine-learning models with more context for the evaluation of comments, with the goal of categorising them as antisemitic or not antisemitic with greater accuracy.

6.1 Potential applications: Providing context to the evaluation of single comments

The study presented in this chapter did not provide evidence that some types of structures in an online conversation are more likely to contain antisemitic comments. It cannot be used to inform or streamline moderation guidelines and processes, as we have seen that the activity on one particular tree does not mean that the proportion of antisemitic comments is likely to increase. All comments, therefore, must be evaluated however different their structure (whether they appear singly or in trees).

The results regarding the initial comment on the tree are particularly interesting from the point of view of online content moderation, as one could imagine focusing initially on comments replying directly to the post (first level), then moving on to the discussions triggered by the comments categorised as antisemitic. However, while discussions starting with antisemitic comments should be given priority, discussion starting with a non-antisemitic statements should not be ignored as they still contain many antisemitic comments. This way of processing could be helpful for assisting in the identification and prioritisation of discussions in need of moderation.

This way of processing is also very beneficial because the context needed to understand the meaning of the comments might differ depending on the level of the comment. The introduction presented the two types of context needed to understand the meaning of a comment. The discourse event context (the abovementioned "who/qui" example) is found in the article or initial media post. For the initial categorisation focusing on the first level comments, context can only be the media article posts or current events, since at this level web users do not refer (yet) to each other. To understand the replies to the initial (trunk) comment, however, further context is required from surrounding (branch) comments. The context for the deeper levels can then be understood as the entirety of the tree in which the comment is placed. In other words, a second categorisation of comments can then take place at the tree level.

Machine-learning models require context for a better categorisation of small pieces of text (see Chapter 8). Distinguishing between the initial comments that reply directly to a post or article and replies to this initial comment provides context to aid in categorising comments for antisemitic ideation.

References

Becker, Matthias J., Daniel Allington, Laura Ascone, Matthew Bolton, Alexis Chapelan, Jan Krasni, Karolina Placzynta, Marcus Scheiber, Hagen Troschke and Chloé Vincent, 2021. *Decoding Antisemitism: An AI-driven Study on Hate Speech and Imagery Online. Discourse Report 2.* Technische Universität Berlin. Centre for Research on Antisemitism, https://doi.org/10.14279/depositonce-15310

Becker, Matthias J., and Hagen Troschke, 2023. "Decoding implicit hate speech: The example of antisemitism". In: Christian Strippel, Sünje Paasch-Colberg, Martin Emmer and Joachim Trebbe (eds). *Challenges and Perspectives of Hate Speech Research.* Digital Communication Research, 335-352, https://doi.org/10.48541/dcr.v12.0

Jikeli, Günther, Damir Cavar and Daniel Miehling, 2019. *Annotating Antisemitic Online Content. Towards an applicable definition of antisemitism,* https://arxiv.org/pdf/1910.01214, https://doi.org/10.5967/3r3m-na89

Jikeli, Günther, Damir Cavar, Weejeong Jeong, Daniel Miehling, Pauravi Wagh, Denizhan Pak, 2022a. "Toward an AI Definition of Antisemitism?" In: Monika Hübscher and Sabine von Mering (eds). *Antisemitism on Social Media.* Abingdon: Routledge, 193–212, https://doi.org/10.4324/9781003200499

Jikeli, Günther, David Axelrod, Rhonda K. Fischer, Elham Forouzesh, Weejeong Jeong, Daniel Miehling and Katharina Soemer, 2022b. "Differences between antisemitic and non-antisemitic English language tweets". *Computational and Mathematical Organization Theory,* 1-35, https://doi.org/10.1007/s10588-022-09363-2

Liphshiz, Cnaan, 27 February 2021. "Nearly 200 scholars back UK lecturer who called Jewish students Israel 'pawns'" *The Times of Israel,* https://www.timesofisrael.com/nearly-200-scholars-back-uk-lecturer-who-called-jewish-students-israel-pawns/

Steffen, Elisabeth, Milena Pustet and Helena Mihaljević. "Algorithms against antisemitism? Towards the automated detection of antisemitic content online". In this volume.

Wistrich, Robert, 1992. *Antisemitism: The Longest Hatred.* New York: Pantheon

8. Algorithms Against Antisemitism?

Towards The Automated Detection of Antisemitic Content Online

Elisabeth Steffen, Milena Pustet,
Helena Mihaljević

The proliferation of hateful and violent speech in online media underscores the need for technological support to combat such discourse, create safer and more inclusive online environments, support content moderation and study political-discourse dynamics online. Automated detection of antisemitic content has been little explored compared to other forms of hate-speech.

This chapter examines the automated detection of antisemitic speech in online and social media using a corpus of online comments sourced from various online and social media platforms. The corpus spans a three-year period and encompasses diverse discourse events that were deemed likely to provoke antisemitic reactions. We adopt two approaches. First, we explore the efficacy of Perspective API, a popular content-moderation tool that rates texts in terms of, e.g., toxicity or identity-related attacks, in scoring antisemitic content as toxic. We find that the tool rates a high proportion of antisemitic texts with very low toxicity scores, indicating a potential blind spot for such content. Additionally, Perspective API demonstrates a keyword bias towards words

https://doi.org/10.11647/OBP.0406.08

related to Jewish identities, which could result in texts being falsely flagged and removed from platforms.

Second, we fine-tune deep learning models to detect antisemitic texts. We show that OpenAI's GPT-3.5 can be fine-tuned to effectively detect antisemitic speech in our corpus and beyond, with F1 scores above 0.7. We discuss current achievements in this area and point out directions for future work, such as the utilisation of prompt-based models.

1. Introduction

In the third quarter of 2022, the US technology giant Meta reported that it had taken action on 10.6 million pieces of *Facebook* content considered to be hate speech. Of these posts, over 90% were found and acted on proactively, that is, prior to users reporting them (Meta 2022). Given the sheer volume of content published on social media, automatic detection of hate speech and other offensive content has become a key task for mainstream social media platforms. Similar challenges arise in the research based on empirical data and in the monitoring work of NGOs or journalists who analyse political discourses.

The technical foundation of this task is text classification, which is the process of automatically assigning categories (or classes) to a text. In the realm of political online communication, examples of such categories include various forms of hate speech, devaluation and exclusion related, for example, to misogyny, racism and antisemitism. Historically, individually formulated rules targeting particular textual aspects were used to perform text classification; however, modern approaches leverage machine learning and deep learning for superior results. This entails feeding large datasets into, for example, deep neural networks from which they learn patterns in the texts that allow them to more accurately predict classes for new, unseen data.

So far, classification of texts is usually done in a supervised manner, whereby an algorithm is trained using human-labelled data to make accurate predictions. The human annotations serve as a 'gold standard' and are used to 'teach' the algorithm. Labelled examples are also utilised to evaluate the learned model's predictions based on standard metrics. Often, so-called benchmark datasets are used to compare the performance of different machine learning models for a specific task on a common set of data, using task-specific metrics. Efforts to generate benchmark datasets for the automated detection of antisemitism have been conducted so far by only a handful of researchers (Chandra et al. 2021, Jikeli et al. 2022, Steffen et al. 2022, Jikeli et al. 2023), and have not yet resulted in datasets comparable to available scientific corpora for related phenomena, such as offensive language, toxic language and other forms of hate speech.

For the recognition of broader linguistic phenomena intersecting with antisemitism, such as hate speech and toxic language, openly accessible production-ready web services have been established. A prominent example is Perspective API, a free service created by Jigsaw and Google's Counter Abuse Technology team, which is widely applied for content moderation and research. For example, it has been used for analyses of moderation measures on *Reddit* (Horta Ribeiro et al. 2021), for investigations of political online communities on *Reddit* (Rajadesingan, Resnick and Budak 2020) and *Telegram* (Hoseini et al. 2021) and for identifying antisemitic and Islamophobic texts on *4chan* (González-Pizarro and Zannettou 2022). The service allows for the detection of abusive content by providing scores (between 0 and 1) for different attributes such as toxicity, insult or identity attack. The definition of what constitutes (severely) toxic or identity attacking comments in Perspective API suggests that antisemitic speech should be detectable through the service, thus offering an easily accessible approach to recognising certain forms of antisemitic speech. However, recent work on German-language communication on *Telegram* and *Twitter* (now X) indicates an oversensitivity to identity-related keywords such as 'jew' or 'israel', which makes the service prone to falsely classifying texts as antisemitic simply for addressing Jewishness or mentioning Israel (Mihaljević and Steffen 2022). It has been found, furthermore, that the service performs rather poorly on more subtle or encoded forms of antisemitism, often failing to recognise them as toxic (ibid.).

In this chapter, we evaluate Perspective API on a multilingual dataset comprising more than 55,000 comments from online platforms that were manually annotated by experts working on the international project Decoding Antisemitism. In our experiments, the service shows a bias towards identity-related keywords and tends to penalise expressions of counter speech. We therefore argue that the Perspective API is only of very limited use for tackling antisemitism online and is likely to produce a high number of false positives when applied in contexts with a frequent occurrence of counter speech.

With the advancement of machine learning, particularly deep learning, non-profit anti-hate organizations have expanded their focus to include large-scale analyses of online content that often entail the development of machine learning-based text classifiers. Several organisations have reported successfully establishing models for the detection of antisemitic speech. For instance, the Anti-Defamation League (ADL) has developed a model for detecting antisemitic speech across various social media platforms as part of their Online Hate Index (OHI).[1] The tool is being developed by experts in antisemitism and volunteers from the targeted community. The Institute for Strategic Dialogue (ISD) has also conducted various analyses of large social media datasets requiring automated detection of antisemitic content,[2] while Fighting Online Antisemitism (FOA) reports to have begun using an antisemitism detection model recently developed through collaboration with Code for Israel, a tech-for-good volunteer organisation, and an Israeli tech company.[3] However, these tools, while presumably offering superior effectiveness in detecting antisemitic speech compared to the generalistic Perspective API, are not readily accessible to the broader research community and are primarily utilised within the respective organisations for research and monitoring purposes. This limitation makes it challenging to employ them for custom analyses or to evaluate their performance on other datasets. For instance, the antisemitism classifier for German-language *YouTube* comments developed by the ISD and the Centre for Analysis of Social Media (CASM) involves filtering the corpus by keywords related to Judaism, Jewish people or the state of Israel, as well as other keywords derived from previously developed

---

1   The Anti-Defamation League, 2022. "How Platforms Rate on Hate: Measuring Antisemitism and Adequacy of Enforcement Across Reddit and Twitter", https://www.adl.org/sites/default/files/pdfs/2022-05/How%20Platforms%20Rate%20on%20Hate%202022_OHI_V10.pdf

2   Institute for Strategic Dialogue, 2020. "Das Online-Ökosystem Rechtsextremer Akteure", https://www.isdglobal.org/isd-publications/das-online-okosystem-rechtsextremer-akteure/ and "Mapping hate in France: A panoramic view of online discourse", https://www.isdglobal.org/isd-publications/mapping-hate-in-france-a-panoramic-view-of-online-discourse-2/

3   The Jerusalem Post, 2023. "Israeli tech warriors code a solution to fight online antisemitism", https://www.jpost.com/diaspora/antisemitism/article-749349

classifiers.[4] These restrictions result in a higher proportion of relevant content and enable the labelling of a sufficient number of texts from all classes, particularly antisemitic ones, within a reasonable timeframe. However, classifiers trained on such datasets, which are more balanced regarding the class distribution, may not generalise well to more realistic corpora representing discourses that were not pre-filtered.

We thus trained custom classification models using the corpus of the Decoding Antisemitism project. The dataset comprises online comments in English, German and French from various sources such as news portals, *Twitter* or *Facebook*, annotated regarding a plethora of additional attributes, including rhetoric and linguistic aspects of antisemitic speech. Our experiments are focused solely on English-language data and aim to distinguish between antisemitic and non-antisemitic posts. The results demonstrate that effective models can be trained even in the more challenging scenario of a corpus that has not been pre-filtered by selected keywords related to Jewishness or Israel, where implicit expressions of antisemitism are frequent and the class of antisemitic posts is significantly underrepresented. We show that fine-tuning an openly available BERT-like model achieves satisfactory results on test data but is significantly outperformed by a fine-tuned GPT-3.5 model not only on the test data but also in discourse and domain transfer. We discuss the practical implications of these findings, potential future directions and plans for research using prompt-based approaches.

2. Dataset

The team of the project Decoding Antisemitism has annotated online comments in English, French and German from various leading media sources, including a range of news portals and social media platforms such as *Twitter* or *Facebook*, using a self-developed code schema based on the IHRA definition.[5] The resulting corpus spans a three-year period

---

4 Institute for Strategic Dialogue, 2020. "Using a German-language classifier to detect antisemitism on YouTube", https://www.isdglobal.org/digital_dispatches/using-a-german-language-classifier-to-detect-antisemitism-on-youtube-background-and-methodology/

5 The International Holocaust Remembrance Alliance (IHRA), 2024. "Working definition of antisemitism", https://holocaustremembrance.com/resources/working-definition-antisemitism

and encompasses diverse discourses that were deemed likely to provoke antisemitic reactions. The focus on mainstream political milieus while dispensing keyword filters in the corpus creation yields a broad set of covered topics as well as represented antisemitic narratives, often expressed in a rather implicit way resorting to puns, allusions or irony.

The ideation level is annotated on a comment-by-comment basis, and it comprises the classes 'not antisemitic', 'counter speech', 'antisemitic', 'contextually antisemitic', 'confirmation of antisemitism' and 'unclear ideation'. The scheme contains a plethora of additional codes; some of these are applied at the level of entire comments, while others refer to specific segments within the text in order to describe, for example, the conceptual or linguistic layer of the antisemitic statement. It should be noted that comments responding to a post or news article are organised in a tree-like manner (depending on the platform) as users can respond directly to either preceding comments or the original posts (see Chapter 7).

Nevertheless, for the experiments presented in this chapter, we consider the texts as independent units and restrict modelling to those comments that could clearly be labelled as antisemitic ('AS') or not antisemitic ('not AS') on the level of ideation. In particular, this excludes texts labelled as contextually antisemitic, wherein antisemitic content cannot be detected without further information such as the content behind a linked URL, information from the article itself, previous comments or the reader's world knowledge. For instance, the comment 'I think you have been told to do this' might be antisemitic when taking into account previous comments that make clear to what 'this' and 'you' refer. While a human annotator (or a content moderator) can usually fully resolve such ambiguities—marking this case 'AS' if the user claims that a previous commenter is expressing themselves in a certain way due to an imagined Jewish influence—this poses a significant challenge when attempting to automate the task in practice. However, as a machine learning model or a service like Perspective API would need this information in order to make a correct inference, we proceed with the described setting only.

We ran the experiments with Perspective API on a part of the multilingual data from the Decoding Antisemitism project—a subset consisting of around 3,500 comments manually labelled as antisemitic and around 53,500 texts labelled as not antisemitic. Our custom models for the detection of texts labelled as antisemitic were trained on the English sub-corpus comprising around 23,000 examples for model training and evaluation.

3. Antisemitism and toxicity: potentials and limitations of Perspective API

Currently, Perspective API provides scores for six attributes of textual content: *toxicity*, *severe toxicity*, *threat*, *insult*, *identity attack* and *profanity*. The most relevant of these for our study, because they are defined in a way that suggests they are capable of detecting certain forms of antisemitic speech, are *toxicity*, *severe toxicity* and *identity attack*. Content is designated *toxic* if it is considered "rude, disrespectful, or unreasonable [...], likely to make people leave a discussion", while the related attribute of *severe toxicity* is supposed to be "much less sensitive to more mild forms of toxicity, such as comments that include positive uses of curse words". *Identity attack* refers to "negative or hateful comments targeting someone because of their identity" (Thain, Dixon and Wulczyn 2017; Google 2022).

Perspective API scores are computed by machine learning models (Lees et al. 2022) trained on crowd-labelled data. The underlying strategy is to create large sets of (diversely) labelled data by using simple definitions that can be understood and applied by non-experts. To counteract the subjectivity and vagueness of the definition, texts are annotated by multiple individuals and their assessments are aggregated before they are used to train the models.

We evaluated the scores for the attributes *identity attack*, *toxicity* and *severe toxicity*. Specifically, we looked at how many texts labelled as antisemitic by the human annotators were scored above 0.5 by the service, and investigated if certain keywords affected the API's performance.

3.1. Perspective API often scores antisemitic texts as little *toxic*

The distributions of all three attribute scores differ significantly between the two groups of antisemitic and non-antisemitic texts, as identified by the human annotators, with clearly higher scores for antisemitic texts (see Figure 8.1). However, 75% of antisemitic texts were scored with respect to *toxicity* or *severe toxicity* below 0.5, which is a typical threshold for assigning texts to one of two groups. This means that a high proportion of antisemitic texts would not be considered as toxic based on the assessment through Perspective API. Considering that the service currently recommends using 0.7 as a threshold, and that various existing studies even chose a threshold of 0.8, this would mean an even larger number of false negatives. The scores for the group of antisemitic comments are highest with regard to *identity attack*. However, even here, around 70% of antisemitic comments fall below 0.7 and would have been missed if one was to follow the official recommendation.

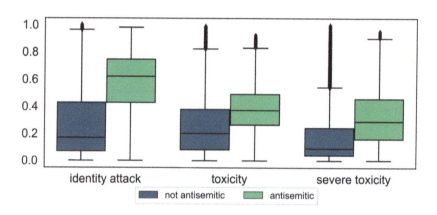

Figure 8.1: Distributions of scores for *identity attack*, *toxicity*, and *severe toxicity*, split according to the antisemitic/not antisemitic data labels. The horizontal lines of the boxes indicate the lower quartile (25%), the median (50%) and the upper quartile (75%) of the scores.

The higher scores for *identity attack* are not surprising, given the fact that antisemitism is an identity-related form of hate which involves prejudice and discrimination against Jewish people based on their perceived identity as a group. However, the high scores for this attribute might also indicate that the service is overly sensitive to certain identity-related keywords such as 'Jew(ish)' or 'Israel'. This 'false positive bias'—the system's tendency to overestimate the level of toxicity if 'minorities' are mentioned regardless of the stance expressed towards them—has been discussed by the developers of the API (Dixon et al. 2018) and confirmed by other research (Hutchinson et al. 2020, Röttger et al. 2021).

3.2. Texts containing identity-related keywords get higher scores

To explore the potential effect of identity-related keywords on *identity attack* scores, we tagged all texts that contained some variations of the keywords 'jew' and 'israel', depending on the corpus language. Figure 8.2 visualises how the scores are distributed when taking this additional information into account: comments containing identity-related keywords (green dots) tend to have higher *identity attack* scores, and this holds for the texts labelled as both antisemitic and not antisemitic. This suggests that texts with references to Jews, Jewishness or Israel, even if they do not express antisemitism, are likely to be flagged as an identity attack. Although the presence of respective keywords alone does not account for a high *identity attack* score[6] (see, for example, the first column in Table 8.1), it still shows a high positive correlation. More precisely, the median identity attack score for comments labelled as not antisemitic is 0.43 higher if the text contains one of the identity-related keywords. For antisemitic texts, the difference is less pronounced (0.15). Similar effects can be observed for the other two Perspective API attributes.

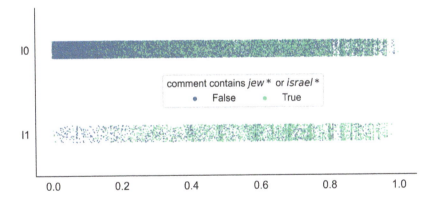

Figure 8.2: *Identity attack* scores broken down by text label and presence of identity-related keywords.

---

6   This is also not to be expected as the Perspective API models utilise far more information from text than the frequencies of certain words.

	median *identity attack* score		
	texts without identity-related keywords	texts with identity-related keywords	difference
texts labelled as not antisemitic	0.15 (N=45,761)	0.59 (N=7,769)	**+0.43**
texts labelled as antisemitic	0.49 (N=969)	0.64 (N=2,522)	**+0.15**
difference	**+0.34**	**+0.07**	

Table 8.1: Median *identity attack* scores per class label and presence of identity-related keywords, rounded to 2 decimal places. Group sizes are indicated in brackets. All four differences are statistically significant (Mann-Whitney-U test, p<0.01).

This analysis does not provide a causal relation between the occurrence of keywords related to Jewishness and the state of Israel and higher scores. However, prior research for German language data has shown that adding these keywords significantly increases the scores of texts (Mihaljević and Steffen 2022), which confirms the keyword bias. Other research indicates a similar identity-related keyword bias, showing that texts using standard group labels are assigned even higher scores compared to texts using slurs for referring to different communities (Mendelsohn et al. 2023).

3.3. A (partially) shared vocabulary: varying degrees of intersection between antisemitic texts, identity attacks, and toxic statements

To further investigate the relation between the phenomenon of antisemitism and the attributes *identity attack* and *toxicity*, we determined the 100 most significant terms using a chi-squared test in the English-language sub-corpus for the following categories:

1. texts labelled as antisemitic (or not)
2. texts with an *identity attack* score above 0.7 (or below 0.3)
3. texts with a *toxicity* score above 0.7 (or below 0.3)

The word cloud in Figure 8.3 reveals that words associated with Jewishness and Israel hold considerable significance in texts that were manually labelled by experts as antisemitic. Terms related to Palestinian identity are also prominent. Negatively connotated terms such as 'apartheid', 'terrorist', 'cleansing', 'occupy' or 'force' likely stem from text passages containing accusations against and demonisations of Israel within the context of the Arab-Israeli conflict.

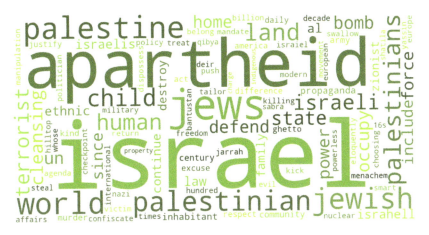

Figure 8.3: 100 most significant terms in texts manually labelled as antisemitic

There is a noticeable overlap between these terms and those found significantly often in text with high *identity attack* scores, particularly in relation to Jewishness. Interestingly, the significance of references to Palestinian identity is considerably reduced in this context. Instead, we observe a strong presence of terms relating to Muslim identities.

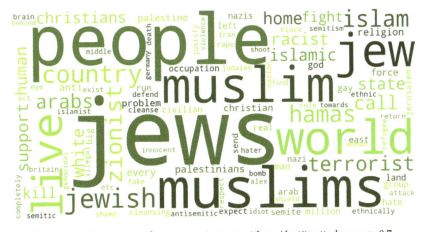

Figure 8.4: 100 most significant terms in texts with an *identity attack* score > 0.7

On the other hand, the 100 most significant terms in texts with a *toxicity* score above 0.7 overlap rather little with antisemitic texts, as shown in Figure 8.5. Note that the strong significance of terms like 'child' and 'kill' might be indicative of narratives surrounding the 'child murderer Israel' references, which are likely to appear in our corpus due to its topical focus.

Figure 8.5: 100 most significant terms in texts with a *toxicity* score > 0.7

3.4. From comment to sentence level: exploring the API's span score feature

While it is reasonable to observe a significant presence of identity-related keywords when utilising the attribute of *identity attack*, we believe that it is crucial to conduct further examination of the API's results before employing them for content moderation or research purposes related to antisemitism. A more thorough analysis would benefit from investigation into which parts of a text are responsible for a high score. In addition to the thus-far discussed summary scores, which represent the overall score of an attribute for the entire comment, Perspective API also offers individual scores for each sentence in a comment. These so-called 'span scores' are supposed to assist moderators in identifying the exact section of a longer comment that is, for example, particularly *toxic*. It is important to note that the relation between a comment's summary score and its span scores is neither documented nor easily observable from examples. In particular, the summary score is neither the average nor the maximum or some other obvious statistic based on the span scores.

We believe that exploring this feature is valuable not only for assessing the API's performance but also because the span scores could aid in conducting text analyses at a more granular level. Understanding which specific parts of a text contribute most to its *toxicity, identity attack,* or similar aspects is beneficial for in-depth investigations of respective corpora.[7]

To examine the API's capabilities in this aspect, we conducted a qualitative exploration of the summary scores versus the span scores in the English-language subcorpus, focusing on the attribute *identity attack.* In the following paragraphs, we will present noteworthy examples from our findings, providing the summary score of a given comment, as well as the span scores for each sentence in square brackets. Sentences with a score > 0.7 are coloured red.

Overall, our observations support previous indications of a keyword bias, particularly towards identity-related keywords and terms indicating violence, even when used to oppose violence. The following text provides an example:

Israel has shown itself as terrorists. [0.74] All for a land grab and power. [0.04] Stop evicting and killing Palestinians. [0.88]	summary score: 0.86

The last sentence in this comment, when considered independently, can be interpreted as a call to halt acts of violence against Palestinians. It is unclear why this has been assigned such a high score. We speculate that it may be due to the presence of the term "killing", possibly in conjunction with "Palestinians", within the sentence.

The following comment can be interpreted as advocating for tolerance, acceptance and the equality of all human beings regardless of "caste, creed, and religion". Given this, the high summary score is perplexing. It is likely driven by the term "Jews", as the segment containing the term "Jews" is, in fact, assigned a significantly higher span score than all other sentences:

---

7   Based on our experience as annotators, we would consider it useful if annotators would specify the parts of a text that guided their classifications, as this approach would help to avoid unintentionally calling upon contextual knowledge.

| There's nothing in caste, creed, and religion. [0.56] Does the blood color change? [0.15] Does the Jews come from another planet? [0.81] After all, we stay on the same planet, and we breathe the same air. [0.14] We are all humans [0.09] | summary score: 0.78 |

This highlights the API's sensitivity to identity-related keywords, which can lead to unintended consequences in scoring such comments, namely incorrectly flagging counter speech.

We observe a similar pattern in the following comment, which emphasises the importance of a state for Jewish people.

| USERNAME, that is why Jews need their own state. [0.80] | summary score: 0.80 |

The following comment presents a defence of Israel's rocket defence system, the "Iron Dome":

| USERNAME, Hamas is also attacking civilians. [0.23] If it wasn't for Israel's Iron Dome, more Israeli civilians would be killed. [0.84] | summary score: 0.74 |

One might expect that the first sentence would yield a relatively high score due to its mention of Hamas attacking civilians, but the assigned span scores provide a different perspective. Interestingly, the second sentence receives a significantly higher span score, which might result from the occurrence of the word "killed" in the text. Such a high *identity attack* score is not plausible, though, since the actual meaning of the sentence implies that the killing of Israeli civilians should be prevented.

We encounter a further case of counter speech that is assigned unreasonably high scores in the following comment against anti-Muslim racism:

| USERNAME, you clearly have no idea how many Muslims there are in the world if you believe most of them are violent would-be terrorists. [0.80] The vast majority of them want to live in peace and harmony with a roof over their head, just like the vast majority of human beings in general. [0.13] | summary score: 0.71 |

Once again, we believe that the API's sensitivity to identity-related keywords is at play here. The segment containing the reference to Muslims receives an unreasonably high score, despite the overall comment countering negative stereotypes. This highlights the limitations of the API's scoring system in accurately capturing the nuances and intentions behind certain comments. One could state that the Perspective API is almost incapable of correctly understanding the stance or sentiment of a text, being rather strongly guided by certain keywords.

It is important to note that our findings are exploratory in nature and should be further supported by systematic assessments of the API's span scores, which we consider an open task for future research.

3.5. Concluding remarks on usage of Perspective API for antisemitic speech detection

In summary, our findings suggest that the Perspective API could be useful for conducting corpus analyses on a broad level, particularly when using the *identity attack* attribute to detect texts related to Jewishness. However, it cannot be automatically assumed that these texts express explicit antisemitism. It is crucial to recognise that the service may not be as helpful for content-moderation efforts that aim to address more complex forms of antisemitism encoded within texts. It provides the ground for actors who strategically utilise linguistic codes, emojis or irony and sarcasm in order to bypass keyword-based automated detection methods. Presumably, the overall labelling approach of Perspective API is not suitable for the incorporation of antisemitic types of *toxic* content, given the difficulty even for experts in labelling short texts typical of online and social media communication. Furthermore, through various experiments, we have observed that the API tends to be overly sensitive to certain identity-related keywords and counter speech, which may impact its accuracy and effectiveness in certain contexts.

Thus, automatic detection of antisemitic speech is still needed and requires careful modelling based on high-quality labelled data.

4. Training of custom models to detect antisemitic comments

In recent years, the so-called 'pre-training and fine-tuning' approach has substantially improved the training of classification models. Fine-tuning leverages language models that were pre-trained using massive amounts of diverse data from corpora such as *Wikipedia* or *Google Books* on generalistic language tasks, such as predicting the next word or a masked word in a sentence. The pre-trained large language models (LLMs) made available in the last years—such as BERT, RoBERTa, GPT-2 or XLM—have learned rich representations of language that capture a variety of linguistic phenomena such as word- and sentence-level semantics, syntactic structures, discourse-level phenomena, as well as subtleties of human language like sarcasm or slang. A pre-trained LLM is adapted in the fine-tuning step to a specific task such as tagging each token in a sentence with respect to a grammar scheme, or, as in our case, to classify texts regarding antisemitism.

A plethora of pre-trained language models are available for fine-tuning different downstream tasks, including text classification. They differ, for example, in terms of the data source used for training (e.g., *Wikipedia* vs. *Twitter*) and its language(s), architecture (e.g., the type and number of layers), training task (e.g., predicting a masked token or the next token), or pre-processing of the text (e.g., lowercasing all words). One of the most popular models (and architectures) employed is BERT, first published in 2018, which has achieved the state of the art for a range of NLP applications, especially classification-oriented tasks. BERT-like pre-trained language models are typically used in recent research to build text classifiers for various text classification tasks, including hate speech (Basile et al. 2019, Aluru et al. 2020, Mathew et al. 2022), offensive language (Wiegand, Siegel and Ruppenhofer 2018, Zampieri et al. 2019 and 2020, Mandl et al. 2021) or (pre-specified) conspiracy theories (Pogorelov et al. 2020, Moffitt, King and Carley 2021, Elroy and Yosipof 2022, Phillips, Ng and Carley 2022). The majority of these benchmark datasets are in the English language and were drawn primarily from *Twitter* (cf. Poletto et al. 2021), in part because of the platform's popularity but also because it offered easy technical access to the data for researchers. As already mentioned, antisemitism has, so far, only been addressed in a handful of efforts for text classification. In addition to BERT-like models, other, significantly larger, models that have been developed for auto-regressive text generation, such as GPT-3, are increasingly being used for classification tasks.

In essence, the fine-tuning step makes use of the rather domain-independent general knowledge encoded by the source model, while 'only' needing to learn the particulars of the target categories/classes. Technically, this can be thought of as extending the source model with a comparatively small set of application-specific parameters that must be learned from the target task data (and modifying the existing model parameters slightly). Fine-tuning allows for the production of efficient classification models with a relatively small number of labelled data samples, which is often all that is available for texts in the political sphere. The approach also better handles out-of-distribution data (that is, data examples that differ from those in the training set) and, in general, provides higher level of generalisation.

However, the amount of text examples required to successfully train a classification model depends on several factors, including the complexity of the classification task, the variability of the text data and the algorithm used to train the model. Although data quality and relevance play a crucial role and can make up for a smaller size of a dataset, it generally makes sense to include as much training data as possible. As a rule of thumb, it is often recommended to provide at least 1,000 labelled examples per class during training.

4.1. Experimental results for English-language comments

In our experiments, we fine-tune BERT-like models as well as GPT-3.5. There are various differences between these two model families. Firstly, BERT, RoBERTa, etc., are open models, while GPT-3.5 is a closed model owned by OpenAI. Because the latter incurs monetary costs that can become substantial when applied on a large scale, many stakeholders might not be able to afford to use GPT-3.5 (or its successor GPT-4) for monitoring, content moderation and analyses. However, GPT-3.5 has been trained on a substantially larger dataset, yielding a model that is orders of magnitude larger than BERT. As such, it is expected to provide superior performance in many tasks and serves in this study as an 'upper bound' for what can be achieved in such a scenario if monetary constraints are not considered.

When fine-tuning BERT-like models, we explore the influence of aspects such as the choice of the pretrained language model, standard architecture-related hyperparameters (e.g., learning rate and attention dropout) and data-related settings (e.g., handling of particularly short texts). These hyperparameters determine the overall capabilities of a machine learning model, so combinations of different values are evaluated to find the optimal one.[8] However, since the hyperparameter space can be quite large, there is a need to balance exploration and exploitation for efficient hyperparameter tuning. To address this, we employ Bayesian optimisation, which maintains a probabilistic model that predicts the performance of different hyperparameter configurations. This allows us to exploit the best parameters while still exploring new options to make sure the best parameters are found. As fine-tuning GPT-3.5 is costly, we limited our fine-tuning experiments to using only the standard hyperparameters and fine-tuned the model for up to 2 epochs.[9]

We make use of around 23,000 English-language comments classified as either 'AS' or 'not AS'. It is typical for many text classification tasks, in particular when attempting to classify with respect to different political ideologies or stances, to be confronted with imbalanced data, for which one class is significantly more prevalent than the other(s). In our case, almost 90% of the comments were labelled as not antisemitic (class 'not AS'), leaving us with only about 10% of texts annotated as antisemitic (class 'AS'). After cleaning the data, including deduplicating texts and removing empty messages, we ended up with 2,410 samples in class 'AS' and 20,684 in class 'not AS'. We used 80% of data for training (16,539 records in class 'not AS' and 1,936 in class 'AS'), 10% for validation—which serves the identification of the best-performing hyperparameters—and 10% for testing the model yielding the lowest errors on the validation set.

---

8   The following hyperparameters were considered: model (roberta-base, bert-base-uncased), number of epochs, downsampling of the negative class, learning rate, batch size, weight decay, attention_probs_dropout_prob and hidden_dropout_prob.

9   The number of epochs refers to the number of times the model is presented with all of its training data in order to update its parameters based on the value of the loss function, which is being minimised during training.

Class	Records	Precision	Recall	F1-score	Accuracy
AS	225	0.75 / **0.76**	0.65 / **0.79**	0.7 / **0.77**	0.94 / **0.95**
not AS	2,084	0.96 / **0.98**	**0.98** / 0.97	0.97 / 0.97	

Table 8.2: Evaluation of the best performing fine-tuned BERT-like model and the fine-tuned GPT-3.5 model, separated by /, on the test data. The best score is highlighted in bold.

The performance metrics of both the best-performing fine-tuned BERT-like model and GPT-3.5 on the test set are displayed in Table 8.2. The scores for the best BERT-like model (represented by the first number per table cell) can be interpreted as follows: 96% of all texts predicted by the model as not being antisemitic were indeed labelled by the human annotators as such (precision class 'not AS'), and the model finds 98% of texts in this class (recall class 'not AS'). On the other hand, among the texts predicted as antisemitic, 75% were labelled as such (precision for class 'not AS'), while the model managed to find 65% of texts labelled as antisemitic by the annotators. To make this easier to grasp: if a content moderator was to apply this model to 1,000 comments, where 100 are assumed to be antisemitic, the model would find 65 of the 100 antisemitic texts and miss 35 of them. This could be seen as a low rate from the perspective of keeping the comments section free of antisemitic speech. However, the number of false alarms would be low, at 22, limiting the manual efforts required. This example highlights the trade-off between two types of errors: while one would want to increase the recall of class 'AS', it would also be desirable to keep the number of false alarms low. Thus, from an application perspective, one needs to decide which kind of error (false positives vs. false negatives) should be prioritised, and, for example, what minimum recall needs to be achieved for class 'AS' and what precision could be accepted in return.[10]

---

10 To illustrate this, let us assume that we want to achieve a recall of at least 0.8 while keeping the precision as high as possible. One simple option would be to adjust the probability threshold for assigning a prediction to a class label. The classifiers we train are probabilistic, thus for each text they produce probabilities of belonging to either of these classes. By default, the threshold for binary classification is set to 0.5, meaning the class with higher probability wins. However, the threshold can be changed in order to increase the value of a desired metric. By using the validation set to find out which threshold satisfies a recall of at least 0.8 while maximising the precision, we can identify a threshold that achieves a recall of 0.81 and a precision of 0.52 on the validation set. Thus, we would capture nearly 80% of all antisemitic texts, albeit with almost every second flag being a false alarm.

As presented in Table 8.2, the fine-tuned GPT-3.5 model outperforms the BERT model in terms of the F1 score, defined as the harmonic mean of precision and recall, on the class 'AS', primarily due to its higher recall of antisemitic texts. In the hypothetical scenario described above, the model would only miss 21 out of the 100 antisemitic texts while maintaining a very low number of false alarms. This confirms the initial hypothesis that the larger model can be trained more effectively, albeit at substantially higher monetary cost.

To enhance the performance of the fine-tuned BERT model, we conducted several experiments targeting the strong class imbalance in the dataset. We reduced the number of examples from the 'not AS' class that are easily correctly classified. During model training, all data points contribute in the same way to the computation of the loss that guides the training process. Thus, reducing such examples, or penalising them in a different way, can potentially enhance the detection of the positive class. While these strategies led to a higher recall for the class 'AS', and thus an increased identification of antisemitic texts, it came at the cost of lower precision and a comparable F1 score. We additionally employed various strategies to augment the 'AS' class, including generating new texts by substituting some words with others having a similar meaning or by adding words that are assumed not to significantly alter the overall meaning of the sentence. Additionally, we translated texts labelled as antisemitic from the German and French corpora to English and performed forward-and-backward translation with English-language records. A random sample of translations was manually inspected. However, these strategies did not result in a noteworthy improvement of the F1 score for the class 'AS'. A significant challenge stems from the fact that standard pre-trained models as those we used to identify similar words for replacement may not effectively capture the nuanced context in corresponding messages. For instance, words like 'Israel' and 'Palestine' might be deemed similar from the perspective of a generic language model, but they are not interchangeable in the context of the Middle East conflict. Models that have undergone additional fine-tuning on a corpus reflecting such nuances would be more suitable, as well as other more sophisticated text augmentation strategies that we plan to explore in future research.

4.2. Domain generalisation: discourse and domain shift

Classifiers trained on a given corpus should ideally be able to generalise and, to a certain extent, transfer their 'knowledge' to other domains. In other words, they should be able to carry out the same task when made to encounter the same phenomenon but in a potentially different distribution of data. A difference in distribution is to be expected when a model is applied to data from a time range, platforms or discourses distinct from those represented in the training data. Phenomena such as antisemitism constitute a 'moving target' in the sense that codes, narratives and forms of expression evolve with time and differ from community to community. Against this background and considering the fact that our training corpus is rather small, especially with regards to class 'AS' it is rather to be expected that trained models will struggle with domain transfer.

We have evaluated the performance of the fine-tuned models (BERT-based and GPT-3.5-based) in two settings: (1) two new discourse events that were not represented in the training data and (2) a corpus from *Twitter* that was created and annotated using a different approach.

The two discourse events not represented in our training dataset, both from 2022, were the antisemitic incidents that occurred during the FIFA World Cup in Qatar and the discussion about Kanye West's radical antisemitic statements. These two resulted in a total of 2,612 text examples in English, only 107 of which were labelled as antisemitic by human annotators.

Jikeli et al. (2023) recently published a corpus containing tweets from 2019 to 2021. The corpus was obtained through a multi-step procedure that involved filtering a 10% *Twitter* sample from the Indiana University's Observatory on Social Media database using the keywords 'Jews' and 'Israel'. The texts were annotated by two individuals, using an annotation scheme based on the IHRA definition of antisemitism. The annotators were asked to apply one of five categories to each tweet according to whether it was antisemitic and their level of confidence in each case. They marked 6,941 texts overall. Two categories, 'probably antisemitic' and 'confident antisemitic', were merged into the overarching category 'antisemitic', while the other three ('confident', 'probably not antisemitic' and 'uncertain/neutral') were merged into 'not antisemitic'.

This process resulted in 1,250 (~18%) texts being included in the positive class.

Table 8.3 presents the evaluation of both fine-tuned models on each of the two datasets. As expected, the performance of both models declines when confronted with a data distribution shift, with the difference being more pronounced on the keyword-based *Twitter* dataset. The performance of GPT-3.5 is more robust on both of the datasets, especially with regard to class 'AS'. More precisely, both models manage to recognise texts in the class 'not AS' from the two new discourse events with an F1 score in the same range as before, while the F1 score for class 'AS' drops to 0.6 for the BERT model but remains high, at 0.76, for GPT-3.5. This suggests that, in contrast to GPT-3.5, the BERT model is strongly affected by the topics of the discourses it has seen during training and that it struggles more with recognising antisemitic speech related to a different topic.

Dataset	Class	Records	Precision	Recall	F1-score	Accuracy
(1) new discourse events	'AS'	107	0.63 / **0.73**	0.57 / **0.79**	0.6 / **0.76**	0.97 / **0.98**
	'not AS'	2,504	0.98 / **0.99**	0.99 / 0.99	0.98 / **0.99**	
(2) Twitter dataset by Jikeli et al.	'AS'	1,250	0.54 / **0.62**	0.52 / **0.8**	0.53 / **0.7**	0.83 / **0.88**
	'not AS'	5,691	0.9 / **0.95**	**0.9** / 0.89	0.9 / **0.92**	

Table 8.3: Evaluation of the fine-tuned BERT-like model and the fine-tuned GPT-3.5 model, separated by /, on (1) the dataset comprising two discourse events absent from training data, and (2) the *Twitter* dataset compiled by Jikeli et al. (2023). The best score is highlighted in bold.

The performance of the BERT model drops further on the second dataset, with an F1 score of 0.9 for class 'not AS' and an F1 score of 0.53 for class 'AS' (and an overall accuracy of 0.83). A similar tendency is visible for the GPT-3.5 model as well, however it still yields a solid F1 score of 0.7 for the class 'AS'. The performance drop between test data (Table 8.2) and this dataset, however, is not surprising, and it showcases well the effect of the corpus and annotation scheme used for training. The annotators of the *Twitter* dataset were allowed to use the surrounding context and references to external resources when labelling a tweet. One would therefore expect that, conceptually and empirically, the comments labelled as antisemitic have substantial intersection with the 'contextually antisemitic' comments in our corpus that were excluded from the training and test set.[11] Furthermore, the distribution of the two corpora is quite different: despite the fact that our training dataset also contains tweets,[12] the topic distributions differ significantly. Our corpus reflects certain discourses, while the *Twitter* corpus is a combination of random messages related to Jewishness and Israel and messages containing antisemitic slurs. In particular, the slur 'ZioNazi' was used as one of the filter keywords. This expression, however, occurs in 529, and thus almost 90%, of texts labelled as antisemitic in the *Twitter* corpus, but only about 20 times in our entire (and significantly larger) English-language corpus.

4.3 Concluding remarks on training custom models for the detection of antisemitic speech

We have fine-tuned different state-of-the-art large language models to distinguish antisemitic speech in an English-language corpus sourced from various online platforms spanning a time period of multiple years. In particular, the corpus was not created using keyword filters but instead reflects diverse topics and discourses likely to trigger antisemitism. Stemming from mainly mainstream platforms, the corpus contains a rather high amount of implicitly formulated antisemitic speech and displays a substantial class imbalance. These aspects contribute to an increased challenge when it comes to build effective classification models.

We have shown that openly available model architectures like BERT can be effectively leveraged to detect antisemitic speech in the described corpus. An F1 score for the class 'AS' of 0.7 can be considered satisfactory considering the complexity of the dataset. In practical-application scenarios, such as content moderation, it would be sufficient for a model to identify discussions with an alarming amount of antisemitic

---

11　This is supported by the fact that "lack of understanding of the context" is identified as one of the main reasons for annotator disagreement (Jikeli et al. 2023).

12　Note that our corpus also contains data from Twitter. We did not check for contamination of our dataset since, statistically, the chances are very low.

speech that need a closer look by human experts. At the same time, the performance of the model declines substantially when confronted with unseen discourses or a different dataset. This implies the necessity of a continuous effort in labelling a sufficient amount of data and further fine-tuning of the model.

At the same time, a fine-tuned GPT-3.5 model shows superior performance not only on the test data but also in discourse and domain transfer. As expected, the larger model is capable of providing better results, with F1 scores for class 'AS' above 0.7 and almost 1 for class 'not AS', using standard hyperparameters only and within 2 epochs of training. This model, however, incurs higher monetary costs for fine-tuning and application as it cannot be run without using OpenAI's API. Thus, the decision as to which approach might be more suitable depends on the specific application scenario and available resources.

To facilitate real-world application, we have established an inference service featuring our best BERT-based model within a web app. This service enables users to input text, receive predictions and view corresponding scores. A feedback loop has been implemented, allowing users to express agreement or disagreement, thereby enhancing our understanding of the model's performance and aiding in the collection of additional training data. The trained models can be provided upon request. Similarly, the code for the web service is available for sharing, facilitating the implementation of similar setups in other projects.

5. Future directions

5.1. Rethink the object of classification

Capturing the meaning of texts written by humans can be a challenging task. This is particularly the case for short messages, such as those commonly found in online and social media discussions. Authors may use subtle, coded, implicit expressions of their opinions, for instance, to attain a certain level of ambivalence and thereby avoid content-moderation measures. Examples of this can be found in fragmented expressions of beliefs in conspiracy theories (Steffen et al. 2022), implicit climate-change denials (Falkenberg and Baronchelli 2023) or the usage of codes in antisemitic narratives. Furthermore, references to world knowledge add to the difficulty of a model to 'comprehend' the content of a text. An extreme example of this is a statement by Nicholas J. Fuentes, a white supremacist political commentator and live streamer, who denied the Holocaust by 'jokingly' doubting the possibility of baking six million batches of cookies within five years.[13]

Moreover, comments are typically part of a longer thread, and this context is often needed to fully resolve the meaning of the individual post and its author's intention. Similarly, posts often make references to linked or embedded content that is increasingly multi-modal, as well as to current (political) events. The attempt to make such additional context available to the models is quite challenging, as, for example, relevant references can be made to any previous comment in a thread. This raises the question of whether it might be more appropriate to consider sub-threads or threads as entities instead of single comments. Because the dataset collected by Jikeli et al. (2023) took all this information into account when it was annotated, a model should have this context available as well in order to assess its comparative abilities fairly. The Decoding Antisemitism annotation scheme distinguishes between contextually antisemitic and antisemitic texts, but one might argue that annotators might not be able to fully exclude context when looking at an entire thread in sequential manner.

It is noteworthy that the Perspective API has announced plans to include conversation context—which may encompass additional text, URLs or even images—for comment evaluation.[14] When this feature becomes available, it would be intriguing to investigate whether the service's overall performance improves in scoring antisemitic speech as *toxic*.

In future research, we aim to explore various methods of providing context to individual comments within a classification model, as well

---

13   In one of his live streams, Fuentes reads the following text: "If I take one hour to cook a batch of cookies and the cookie monster has 15 ovens working 24 hours a day, every day for five years, how long does it take cookie monster to bake 6 million batches of cookies?" He then uses the cookie analogy in several subsequent statements of Holocaust denial. For the livestream, see https://mobile.twitter.com/CalebJHull/status/1189594371030695937 (last accessed on 23 February 2023). For more information, see e.g, https://www.adl.org/resources/blog/nicholas-j-fuentes-five-things-know (last accessed on 14 February 2023).

14   https://developers.perspectiveapi.com/s/about-the-api-key-concepts?language=en_US

as to develop models capable of classifying sub-threads instead of individual messages. The latter necessitates defining what should constitute an appropriate sub-thread.

5.2. Text classification with prompt-based generative models

Recently, OpenAI's further development of their Generative Pre-Trained Transformers, namely GPT-3.5 and the multi-modal advancement GPT-4, has received wide public attention because of their abilities to generate human-like responses to a given input. These models have been made publicly available through services such as ChatGPT, which allows users to easily interact with chatbots based on respective models via their web browser or API. While the introduction of these models has led to intense debates concerning the risks and potentials of so-called 'artificial general intelligence' (AGI), it also opens up new opportunities to approach the task of text classification.

In this chapter, we presented the results of fine-tuning a GPT-3.5 model for the detection of antisemitic texts. Because fine-tuning and applying OpenAI's models through their API incurs monetary cost, and the models remain with OpenAI, it would be of interest to explore the capabilities of comparable open models such as Meta's Llama-2 or Mistral AI's models Mistral and Mixtral.

Importantly, models such as GPT-3.5 and its competitors were built to facilitate few-shot learning or even zero-shot learning—scenarios in which the model is asked to classify texts into categories for which it has seen only few, or even no, in-context examples. This implies that the model is not fine-tuned, as in our experiments. Instead, it learns additional information from the task description and, perhaps, a few examples of antisemitic and not antisemitic texts provided as part of the textual instructions, the so-called prompt. In this context, design of the prompt has become a crucial task for engineers and researchers. Prompts influence the model's behaviour; they can restrict the form of its response, ask it to focus on certain aspects, or provide it with supplemental information to carry out the task, such as definitions or training examples (Liu et al. 2023; White et al. 2023).

Initial empirical evaluations indicate the huge potential of these models for increasing the efficiency of text classification. In a recent experiment, the zero-shot accuracy of ChatGPT exceeded that of crowdworkers in four out of five tasks related to content moderation, while being about twenty times cheaper (Gilardi, Alizadeh and Kubli 2023). Researchers are examining the potential of GPT-3 models for the classification of hateful content (Chiu, Collins and Alexander 2022; Wang and Chang 2022; Huang, Kwak and An 2023). Li et al. (2023) conduct extensive prompting experiments and compare the performance of ChatGPT to that of crowdworkers for the task of classifying texts as hateful, offensive or toxic (HOT). They find that ChatGPT achieves an accuracy of roughly 80% when compared to crowdworkers' annotations. While the abovementioned works address the more general phenomena of hateful speech or toxic language, the work of Mendelsohn et al. (2023) examines the performance of GPT-3 models for identifying and understanding the specific linguistic phenomenon of dog whistles, that is, "coded expressions that simultaneously convey one meaning to a broad audience and a second one, often hateful or provocative, to a narrow in-group" (Mendelsohn et al. 2023). Their experiments include antisemitic dog whistles and find that the performance of the model "varies widely across types of dog whistles and targeted groups" (Mendelsohn et al. 2023).

Our initial experiments with OpenAI's GPT-3.5 and GPT-4 and the open alternatives Llama-2 and Mistral suggest that prompting is not as effective as fine-tuning in detecting antisemitic speech. We are currently conducting experiments to explore the potential of prompting models for the detection of antisemitic comments in our corpus. These include investigating the impact of the different definitions of antisemitism, incorporating discourse event-related information and exploring various output constraints, such as allowing the model to differentiate the texts predicted to be antisemitic based on their antisemitic narratives. Additionally, we aim to further analyse the explanations generated by the model to justify its classification decisions. Moreover, we plan to investigate the potential benefits of including relevant context, such as preceding comments, in the prompt to enhance the detection accuracy.

It is important to acknowledge that perfection in automated classification is unattainable; even aiming for F1 scores substantially above those already achieved in our fine-tuning efforts might be unreasonable for corpora obtained without filtering by specific keywords. Antisemitism presents a particularly complex challenge compared to other hate ideologies. It is often conveyed using coded language that carries specific meanings for certain audiences while appearing innocuous to others. Antisemitic expressions may reference historical events, rendering them difficult to identify without contextual comprehension, and they are found in multiple political spheres or subcultures (Lauer and Potter 2023), each with distinct rhetorical nuances and argumentative strategies. Even for human experts, straightforward binary categorisation of texts as antisemitic or not antisemitic can prove challenging. Therefore, it is crucial to define realistic and appropriate application scenarios for such models and determine how they can best assist in this task.

References

Aluru, Sai Saketh, Binny Mathew, Punyajoy Saha, and Animesh Mukherjee, 2020. "Deep Learning Models for Multilingual Hate Speech Detection". Preprint, https://arxiv.org/abs/2004.06465

Basile, Valerio, Cristina Bosco, Elisabetta Fersini, Debora Nozza, Viviana Patti, Francisco Manuel Rangel Pardo, Paolo Rosso and Manuela Sanguinetti, 2019. "SemEval-2019 Task 5: Multilingual Detection of Hate Speech Against Immigrants and Women in Twitter". In: *Proceedings of the 13th International Workshop on Semantic Evaluation*. Minneapolis, MN, USA: Association for Computational Linguistics, 54–63, https://doi.org/10.18653/v1/S19-2007

Chandra, Mohit, Dheeraj Pailla, Himanshu Bhatia, Aadilmehdi Sanchawala, Manish Gupta, Manish Shrivastava and Ponnurangam Kumaraguru, 2021. "'Subverting the Jewtocracy': Online Antisemitism Detection Using Multimodal Deep Learning". In: *Proceedings of the 13th ACM Web Science Conference 2021* (WebSci '21), Virtual Event, United Kingdom, 148–157, https://doi.org/10.1145/3447535.3462502

Chiu, Ke-Li, Annie Collins and Rohan Alexander, 2022. "Detecting Hate Speech with GPT-3". Preprint, http://arxiv.org/abs/2103.12407

Dixon, Lucas, John Li, Jeffrey Sorensen, Nithum Thain and Lucy Vasserman, 2018. "Measuring and Mitigating Unintended Bias in Text Classification". In: *Proceedings of the 2018 AAAI/ACM Conference on AI, Ethics, and Society*. New Orleans LA USA: ACM, 67–73, https://doi.org/10.1145/3278721.3278729

Elroy, Or and Abraham Yosipof, 2022. "Analysis of COVID-19 5G Conspiracy Theory Tweets Using SentenceBERT Embedding". In: *Artificial Neural Networks and Machine Learning – ICANN 2022*: 31st International Conference on Artificial Neural Networks, Bristol, UK, September 6–9, 2022, Proceedings, Part II. Berlin: Springer-Verlag, 186–196, https://link.springer. com/chapter/10.1007/978-3-031-15931-2_16

Falkenberg, Mark and Andrea Baronchelli, 2023. "How Can We Better Understand the Role of Social Media in Spreading Climate Misinformation?" Grantham Research Institute on Climate Change and the Environment. January 2023, https://www.lse.ac.uk/granthaminstitute/ news/how-can-we-better-understand-the-role-of-social-media-in-spreading-climate-misinformation

Gilardi, Fabrizio, Meysam Alizadeh, and Maël Kubli, 2023. "ChatGPT Outperforms Crowd-Workers for Text-Annotation Tasks". In: *Proceedings of the National Academy of Sciences 120*, No. 30, e2305016120, https://doi. org/10.1073/pnas.2305016120

González-Pizarro, Felipe and Savvas Zannettou, 2022. "Understanding and Detecting Hateful Content Using Contrastive Learning". In: *Proceedings of the Seventeenth International AAAI Conference on Web and Social Media* (ICWSM 2023). June 5–8, 2023, Limassol, Cyprus. Palo Alto, CA: AAAI Press, 257-268, https://doi.org/10.1609/icwsm.v17i1.22143

Horta Ribeiro, Manoel, Shagun Jhaver, Savvas Zannettou, Jeremy Blackburn, Gianluca Stringhini, Emiliano De Cristofaro and Robert West, 2021. "Do Platform Migrations Compromise Content Moderation? Evidence from r/ The_Donald and r/Incels". In: *Proceedings of the ACM on Human-Computer Interaction 5* (CSCW2), 1–24, https://doi.org/10.1145/3476057

Hoseini, Mohamad, Philipe Melo, Fabricio Benevenuto, Anja Feldmann and Savvas Zannettou, 2023. "On the Globalization of the QAnon Conspiracy Theory Through Telegram". In: *Proceedings of the 15th ACM Web Science Conference 2023* (WebSci '23). Association for Computing Machinery, New York, USA, 75–85, https://doi.org/10.1145/3578503.3583603

Huang, Fan, Haewoon Kwak and Jisun An, 2023. "Is ChatGPT Better than Human Annotators? Potential and Limitations of ChatGPT in Explaining Implicit Hate Speech". In: *Companion Proceedings of the ACM Web Conference 2023*, 294–97. Austin, TX: ACM, https://doi.org/10.1145/3543873.3587368

Hutchinson, Ben, Vinodkumar Prabhakaran, Emily Denton, Kellie Webster, Yu Zhong and Stephen Denuyl, 2020. "Social Biases in NLP Models as Barriers for Persons with Disabilities". In: *Proceedings of the 58th Annual Meeting of the Association for Computational Linguistics*, 5491– 5501, https://doi. org/10.18653/v1/2020.acl-main.487

Jikeli, Günther, Sameer Karali, Daniel Miehling and Katharina Soemer, 2023. "Antisemitic Messages? A Guide to High-Quality Annotation and a Labeled Dataset of Tweets". Preprint, http://arxiv.org/abs/2304.14599

Jikeli, Günther, Damir Cavar, Weejeong Jeong, Daniel Miehling, Pauravi Wagh and Denizhan Pak, 2022. "Toward an AI Definition of Antisemitism?" In:

Monika Hübscher and Sabine von Mering (eds). *Antisemitism on Social Media.* Abingdon: Routledge, 193–212

Lauer, Stefan and Nicholas Potter (eds.), 2023. *Judenhass Underground. Antisemitismus in emanzipatorischen Subkulturen und Bewegungen.* Berlin / Leipzig: Hentrich & Hentrich Verlag

Lees, Alyssa, Vinh Q. Tran, Yi Tay, Jeffrey Sorensen, Jai Gupta, Donald Metzler and Lucy Vasserman,, 2022. "A New Generation of Perspective API: Efficient Multilingual Character-level Transformers". In: *KDD '22: Proceedings of the 28th ACM SIGKDD Conference on Knowledge Discovery and Data Mining 2022.* 3197–3207, https://doi.org/10.1145/3534678.3539147

Li, Lingyao, Lizhou Fan, Shubham Atreja and Libby Hemphill, 2023. "'HOT' ChatGPT: The Promise of ChatGPT in Detecting and Discriminating Hateful, Offensive, and Toxic Comments on Social Media". *ACM Transactions on the Web 18* (2), Article No. 30, 1–36, https://doi.org/10.1145/3643829

Liu, Pengfei, Weizhe Yuan, Jinlan Fu, Zhengbao Jiang, Hiroaki Hayashi and Neubig, Graham, 2023. "Pre-Train, Prompt, and Predict: A Systematic Survey of Prompting Methods in Natural Language Processing". *ACM Computing Surveys 55,* No. 9, Article No. 195, 1–35, https://doi.org/10.1145/3560815

Mandl, Thomas, Sandip Modha, Gautam Kishore Shahi, Hiren Madhu, Shrey Satapara, Prasenjit Majumder, Schaefer, Johannes, Tharindu Ranasinghe, Marcos Zampieri, Durgesh Nandini and Amit Kumar Jaiswal, 2021. "Overview of the HASOC Subtrack at FIRE 2021: Hate Speech and Offensive Content Identification in English and Indo-Aryan Languages", http://arxiv.org/abs/2112.09301

Mathew, Binny, Punyajoy Saha, Seid Muhie Yimam, Chris Biemann, Pawan Goyal and Animesh Mukherjee, 2022. "HateXplain: A Benchmark Dataset for Explainable Hate Speech Detection". In: *Proceedings of the AAAI Conference on Artificial Intelligence,* 35 (17), 14867–14875

Mendelsohn, Julia, Ronan Le Bras, Yejin Choi and Maarten Sap, 2023. "From Dogwhistles to Bullhorns: Unveiling Coded Rhetoric with Language Models". In: *Proceedings of the 61st Annual Meeting of the Association for Computational Linguistics (Volume 1: Long Papers),* Toronto, Canada, 15162–15180, https://doi.org/10.18653/v1/2023.acl-long.845

Meta, 2022. Community Standards Enforcement | Transparency Center, https://transparency.fb.com/data/community-standards-enforcement

Mihaljević, Helena and Elisabeth Steffen, 2022. "How Toxic Is Antisemitism? Potentials and Limitations of Automated Toxicity Scoring for Antisemitic Online Content". In: *Proceedings of the 2nd Workshop on Computational Linguistics for Political Text Analysis* (CPSS-2022), KONVENS 2022, 1–12. 01 January 2022. Potsdam, Germany

Moffitt, J. D., Catherine King and Kathleen M. Carley, 2021. "Hunting Conspiracy Theories During the COVID-19 Pandemic". *Social Media + Society*, 7 (3), https://doi.org/10.1177/20563051211043212

Phillips, Samantha C., Lynnette Hui Xian Ng, Kathleen M. Carley, 2022. "Hoaxes and Hidden Agendas: A Twitter Conspiracy Theory Dataset: Data Paper". In: *Companion Proceedings of the Web Conference 2022*. WWW '22. New York: Association for Computing Machinery, 876–880, https://doi.org/10.1145/3487553.3524665

Pogorelov, Konstantin, Daniel Thilo Schroder, Luk Burchard, Johannes Moe, Stefan Brenner, Petra Filkukova and Johannes Langguth, 2020. "FakeNews: Corona Virus and 5G Conspiracy Task at MediaEval 2020". In: *Working Notes Proceedings of the MediaEval 2020 Workshop*, http://ceur-ws.org/Vol-2882/paper64.pdf

Poletto, Fabio, Valerio Basile, Manuela Sanguinetti, Cristina Bosco and Viviana Patti, 2021. "Resources and Benchmark Corpora for Hate Speech Detection: A Systematic Review". *Language Resources and Evaluation*, 55 (2), 477–523, https://doi.org/10.1007/s10579-020-09502-8

Röttger, Paul, Bertram Vidgen, Dong Nguyen, Zeerak Waseem, Helen Margetts and Janet B. Pierrehumbert, 2021. "HateCheck: Functional Tests for Hate Speech Detection Models". In: *Proceedings of the 59th Annual Meeting of the Association for Computational Linguistics and the 11th International Joint Conference on Natural Language Processing (Volume 1: Long Papers)*, 41–58, https://doi.org/10.18653/v1/2021.acl-long.4

Steffen, Elisabeth, Helena Mihaljević, Milena Pustet, Nyco Bischoff, María do Mar Castro Varela, Yener Bayramoğlu and Bahar Oghalai, 2022. "Codes, Patterns and Shapes of Contemporary Online Antisemitism and Conspiracy Narratives — an Annotation Guide and Labeled German-Language Dataset in the Context of COVID-19". In: *Proceedings of the Seventeenth International AAAI Conference on Web and Social Media* (ICWSM 2023). June 5–8, 2023, Limassol, Cyprus. Palo Alto, CA: AAAI Press, https://doi.org/10.1609/icwsm.v17i1.22216

Wang, Yau-Shian and Yingshan Chang, 2022. "Toxicity Detection with Generative Prompt-Based Inference". Preprint, http://arxiv.org/abs/2205.12390

White, Jules, Quchen Fu, Sam Hays, Michael Sandborn, Carlos Olea, Henry Gilbert, Ashraf Elnashar, Jesse Spencer-Smith and Douglas C. Schmidt, 2023. "A Prompt Pattern Catalog to Enhance Prompt Engineering with ChatGPT". Preprint, http://arxiv.org/abs/2302.11382

Wiegand, Michael, Melanie Siegel and Josef Ruppenhofer, 2018. "Overview of the GermEval 2018 Shared Task on the Identification of Offensive Language". In: *Proceedings of GermEval 2018, 14th Conference on Natural Language Processing* (KONVENS 2018), https://epub.oeaw.ac.at/0xc1aa5576_0x003a10d2.pdf

Zampieri, Marcos, Shervin Malmasi, Preslav Nakov, Sara Rosenthal, Noura Farra and Ritesh Kumar, 2019. "SemEval-2019 Task 6: Identifying and Categorizing Offensive Language in Social Media (OffensEval)". In: *Proceedings of the 13th International Workshop on Semantic Evaluation.* Minneapolis, MN, USA: Association for Computational Linguistics, 75–86, https://doi.org/10.18653/v1/S19-2010

Zampieri, Marcos, Preslav Nakov, Sara Rosenthal, Pepa Atanasova, Georgi Karadzhov, Hamdy Mubarak, Leon Derczynski, Zeses Pitenis and Çağrı Çöltekin, 2020. "SemEval-2020 Task 12: Multilingual Offensive Language Identification in Social Media (OffensEval 2020)". In: *Proceedings of the Fourteenth Workshop on Semantic Evaluation,* 2020, https://doi.org/10.18653/v1/2020.semeval-1.188

About the Authors

Dr Laura Ascone's research focuses on computer-mediated communication, on the expression of emotions, as well as on hate speech. She defended her PhD in Linguistics at the Université Paris-Seine. Her thesis on "The Radicalisation through the Expression of Emotions on the Internet" dealt with the rhetorical strategies used in both jihadist propaganda and institutional counter-narrative. She then conducted postdoctoral research at the Université de Lorraine on online hate speech against migrants. She is currently a postdoctoral fellow at the Centre for Research on Antisemitism (ZfA) at the Technische Universität Berlin in the international project Decoding Antisemitism. She is also part of various research networks dealing with social issues such as Draine, a research group established as part of the Horizon 2020 European project *PRACTICIES* (*Partnership against violent radicalisation in the cities*). ORCID: https://orcid.org/0000-0002-7595-1156.

Dr Matthias J. Becker is a linguist, with a strong focus on pragmatics, cognitive linguistics, (critical) discourse and media studies, research on prejudice and nationalism, as well as on social media studies. At Freie Universität Berlin, he read linguistics, philosophy and literature, and has worked in several research projects on the use of language in political and media campaigns. His doctoral dissertation, published with Nomos in 2018, analyses the linguistic construction of national pride, antisemitic stereotypes and demonising historical analogies in British and German discourses on the Israeli-Palestinian conflict. An English version of the book (entitled *Antisemitism in Reader Comments: Analogies for Reckoning with the Past*) was published with Palgrave Macmillan in 2021. A consistent link between all his research activities is the question of how implicit hate speech—apparently accepted within various milieus of the political mainstream—is constructed and what conditions its production is subject to. Matthias is the creator and lead of the Decoding Antisemitism research project. ORCID: https://orcid.org/0000-0003-2847-4542.

Dr Matthew Bolton is a researcher, lecturer and writer focusing on conceptual history, critical theory, antisemitism and genocide studies. He received his PhD in Philosophy from the University of Roehampton, London in 2020, with a thesis exploring the relationship between the development of the concept of justice and the capitalist state form. Before joining the UK team of the Decoding Antisemitism project, he was an Associate Lecturer in Politics and Philosophy at the University of Chichester. In 2018, his co-authored monograph on the ideological underpinnings of the Corbyn movement, *Corbynism: A Critical Approach*, was published by Emerald Books. He has published articles in *British Politics*, *Political Quarterly*, the *Journal of Contemporary Antisemitism* and *Fathom*, and his work has received widespread media coverage in the UK. ORCID: https://orcid.org/0000-0001-8590-2211.

Alexis Chapelan is currently a PhD candidate, enrolled in a joint international PhD programme at the École des Hautes Études en Sciences Sociales (Paris, France) and the University of Bucharest (Romania). In 2019, he graduated with a Master of Political Science degree with a concentration in political theory from the École de Hautes Études en Sciences Sociales. He also holds a position as a teaching assistant at the University of Bucharest. He is mainly interested in exploring the intersection of intellectual history/history of ideas and sociolinguistics, applied to a broad array of research objects, such as political extremism, far-right ideologies, hate speech, conspiracy theories and populism. His doctoral thesis draws on the *Begriffsgeschichte* and semantic-history approaches, and undertakes a genealogical survey of the concept of "culture wars" in debates from the nineteenth century to the present day. His work has been published in peer-reviewed journals such as *The Journal of Transatlantic Studies* and *Studia Politica*, *The Romanian Review of Political Sciences and International Relations* as well as in collective-research volumes in Romania and Sweden. In addition, he is a member of the DiscourseNet network, of the International Political Science Association (IPSA) and of the International Society for the Sociology of Religion (ISSR). ORCID: https://orcid.org/0000-0002-8990-6188.

Prof. Helena Mihaljević holds a chair in Data Science at the Berlin University of Applied Sciences (HTW Berlin). Her expertise lies in analysing data and technology, utilising cutting-edge methods in data science, machine learning and natural language processing. She is an accomplished researcher with a passion for interdisciplinary projects. She has contributed to a variety of projects, including the algorithmic detection of conspiracy theories and antisemitic hate speech. In her current role as the principal investigator for the research project *Digital Hate*, she focuses on studying conspiracy narratives related to the COVID-19 pandemic. She is also a Co-Investigator on the international research project Decoding Antisemitism, coordinated by the Technische Universität Berlin. Prior to her role at HTW Berlin, Prof. Mihaljević served as a Senior Data Scientist and gained substantial experience in scientific information infrastructure. She earned her PhD in Mathematics with a focus on the topological dynamics of entire transcendental functions. ORCID: https://orcid.org/0000-0003-0782-5382.

Karolina Placzynta is a linguist and political scientist with a background in pragmatics, sociolinguistics and Critical Discourse Analysis. Her research is centred on the mainstreaming and marginalisation of discourses in the media, normalisation of bias, and intersections of discriminatory discourses. Before joining the UK team of the Decoding Antisemitism project, she researched the patterns of discursive representations of immigration in the British press, examining in the process online media debates within the political mainstream. As an experienced educator, she is interested in translating research findings into successful strategies for teaching and training. She is a member of the DiscourseNet association. ORCID: https://orcid.org/0000-0003-0323-2627.

Milena Pustet (BSc, University of Potsdam) is a research assistant at the Berlin University of Applied Sciences (HTW Berlin), specialising in data science, machine learning and natural language processing. As a member of the research projects *Digitaler Hass* and Decoding Antisemitism, which aim to better understand and combat online hate speech and antisemitism, her research focuses on understanding social phenomena online, particularly antisemitic and conspiracy-related discourses on social media. ORCID: https://orcid.org/0000-0003-3825-6530.

Marcus Scheiber is a linguist with research interests in social semiotics, corpus linguistics, Critical Discourse Analysis and multimodality research. He started his academic career at the Universities of Heidelberg and Bern and, as a visiting researcher and lecturer, at the University of Mumbai. He received his MA from the University of Heidelberg in 2018 with a thesis about internet memes. Since 2020, he has been pursuing a joint PhD project at the University of Vechta and University of Vienna entitled "The reality construction potential of multimodal communicative units in antisemitic communication", examining internet memes as communication formats in antisemitic communication strategies. In addition to his academic pursuits, he was employed as a data analyst at Amazon, where he was responsible for the further development and improvement of Alexa through qualitative annotation and transcription of speech data. ORCID: https://orcid.org/0009-0006-1714-2015.

Elisabeth Steffen is a researcher at the Berlin University of Applied Sciences (HTW Berlin). Her research interests include the intersections between natural language processing, supervised machine learning algorithms and cultural, social and political studies. This interdisciplinary focus is also reflected in her academic education as both a computer scientist (BA in Computer Science and Business Administration, HTW– University of Applied Sciences Berlin) and anthropologist of contemporary European societies (MA in European Ethnology, Humboldt University Berlin). Currently, she works as a research assistant in the project *Digitaler Hass* on conspiracy theories in the context of the COVID-19 pandemic. ORCID: https://orcid.org/0000-0003-0170-968X.

Chloé Vincent is currently preparing a PhD at Ghent University on how gender neutral pronouns in French affect text quality and mental gender representations. She previously worked on the French team of the Decoding Antisemitism project as a researcher and expert in quantitative analysis. She completed her MA in Linguistics at Queen Mary University of London in September 2020 where she specialised in sociolinguistics, learning both quantitative and qualitative methods. Her master's thesis consisted in analysing the attitudes of native French speakers towards French regional accents. In the previous years, she had completed her undergraduate degree in anthropology at Lumière

University Lyon 2, and a degree in French language teaching at Grenoble Alpes University, while working as a software developer. She also holds a Master of Engineering degree from Grenoble INP Graduate School of Engineering. ORCID: https://orcid.org/0009-0004-6622-4303.

List of Figures

List of Tables

Index

About the Team

Alessandra Tosi was the managing editor for this book.

Jennifer Moriarty proof-read this manuscript; Anja Pritchard indexed it.

Jeevanjot Kaur Nagpal designed the cover. The cover was produced in InDesign using the Fontin font.

Cameron Craig typeset the book in InDesign and produced the paperback and hardback editions. The main text font is Tex Gyre Pagella. The heading font is Californian FB.

Cameron also produced the PDF and HTML editions. The conversion was performed with open-source software and other tools freely available on our GitHub page at https://github.com/OpenBookPublishers.

Jeremy Bowman created the EPUB.

This book need not end here...

Share

All our books — including the one you have just read — are free to access online so that students, researchers and members of the public who can't afford a printed edition will have access to the same ideas. This title will be accessed online by hundreds of readers each month across the globe: why not share the link so that someone you know is one of them?

This book and additional content is available at:
https://doi.org/10.11647/OBP.0406

Donate

Open Book Publishers is an award-winning, scholar-led, not-for-profit press making knowledge freely available one book at a time. We don't charge authors to publish with us: instead, our work is supported by our library members and by donations from people who believe that research shouldn't be locked behind paywalls.

Why not join them in freeing knowledge by supporting us:
https://www.openbookpublishers.com/support-us

Follow @OpenBookPublish

Read more at the Open Book Publishers BLOG

You may also be interested in:

For Palestine
Essays from the Tom Hurndall Memorial Lecture Group
Ian Parker (Ed.)

https://doi.org/10.11647/obp.0345

Introducing Vigilant Audiences
Daniel Trottier, Rashid Gabdulhakov, and Qian Huang (Eds)

https://doi.org/10.11647/obp.0200

Peace and Democratic Society
Amartya Sen (Ed.)

https://doi.org/10.11647/obp.0014

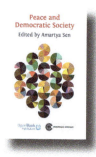